The Communist Party of Great Britain since 1920

Also by David Renton

RED SHIRTS AND BLACK: Fascism and Anti-Fascism in Oxford in the 'Thirties
FASCISM: Theory and Practice
FASCISM, ANTI-FASCISM AND BRITAIN IN THE 1940s
THE TWENTIETH CENTURY: A Century of Wars and Revolutions? (*with Keith Flett*)
SOCIALISM IN LIVERPOOL: Episodes in a History of Working-Class Struggle
THIS ROUGH GAME: Fascism and Anti-Fascism in European History
MARX ON GLOBALISATION
CLASSICAL MARXISM: Socialist Theory and the Second International

The Communist Party of Great Britain since 1920

James Eaden

and

David Renton

© James Eaden and David Renton 2002

All rights reserved. No reproduction, copy or transmission of this publication may be made without written permission.

No paragraph of this publication may be reproduced, copied or transmitted save with written permission or in accordance with the provisions of the Copyright, Designs and Patents Act 1988, or under the terms of any licence permitting limited copying issued by the Copyright Licensing Agency, 90 Tottenham Court Road, London W1T 4LP.

Any person who does any unauthorised act in relation to this publication may be liable to criminal prosecution and civil claims for damages.

The authors have asserted their rights to be identified as the authors of this work in accordance with the Copyright, Designs and Patents Act 1988.

First published 2002 by
PALGRAVE
Houndmills, Basingstoke, Hampshire RG21 6XS and
175 Fifth Avenue, New York, N. Y. 10010
Companies and representatives throughout the world

PALGRAVE is the new global academic imprint of
St. Martin's Press LLC Scholarly and Reference Division and
Palgrave Publishers Ltd (formerly Macmillan Press Ltd).

ISBN 0-333-94968-4

This book is printed on paper suitable for recycling and made from fully managed and sustained forest sources.

A catalogue record for this book is available from the British Library.

Library of Congress Cataloging-in-Publication Data
Eaden, James, 1957–
The Communist Party of Great Britain since 1920 / James Eaden and David Renton.
p. cm.
Includes bibliographical references and index.
ISBN 0-333-94968-4
1. Communist Party of Great Britain—History—20th century. I. Renton, David. II.Title.
JN1129.C62 E34 2002
324.241'0975'09—dc21   2001058053

10 9 8 7 6 5 4 3 2 1
11 10 09 08 07 06 05 04 03 02

Printed and bound in Great Britain by
Antony Rowe Ltd, Chippenham, Wiltshire

Contents

Acknowledgements	vii
Introduction: the Rise and Decline of British Bolshevism	ix
Primary sources	xii
Secondary sources	xii

1 High Hopes: 1920–28 — 1
- Before the Bolsheviks — 2
- Foundation — 7
- Bolshevisation — 15
- International — 19
- General Strike — 24
- Left turn — 31

2 The Zig-Zag Left: 1928–39 — 36
- Isolation and the new line — 37
- Challenges – right and left — 42
- The line changes (1) — 45
- The line changes (2) — 50
- Cable Street — 57
- Aid Spain — 60
- Moscow Trials — 65

3 The Party at War: its Finest Hour? — 69
- Imperialist war: 'what are we fighting for?' — 70
- 'Don't you know there's a war on?': putting the line into practice — 75
- What sort of party? — 81
- June 1941: all change — 84
- 'The issue is clear: victory over the fascist barbarians ...' — 85
- 'Everything for the Front must be the rallying call ...' — 87
- The electoral truce — 91
- Conclusion — 96

4 Past its Peak: 1945–56 — 98
- Revolutionaries and labour — 101
- The Cold War (1) — 104
- The party in crisis — 108
- The Cold War (2) — 113

5 The Monolith Cracks: 1956–68 — 118
The New Left — 122
The Campaign for Nuclear Disarmament — 124
Building in the unions — 127
Moscow or Peking? — 135
Party life in the 1960s — 136
The parliamentary road — 138
Conclusion — 142

6 Not Fade Away: from 1968 to Dissolution — 143
Street-fighting man: students and the anti-Vietnam War protests — 146
The British Disease: industrial militancy — 150
Up against the law: fighting the Industrial Relations Act — 155
White-collar workers — 158
Labour in office — 161
Anti-racism and anti-fascism: missing the boat — 165
Gramsci, Eurocommunism and *Marxism Today* — 168
The rise and fall of Bennism — 172
Death throes — 174
Dissolution and aftermath — 179

7 Conclusion — 184

Notes — 188

Bibliography — 212

Index — 215

Acknowledgements

We have both been thinking over the themes of this book for some years. Like so many young socialists of our generation both of us had early encounters with British Communists. Dave Renton was studying for his A-levels when he first met and was enthused by Raphael Samuel, the Communist historian and a co-founder of the New Left. James Eaden was taught as an undergraduate by Margaret Morris, a Communist Party member and labour historian.

In the process of writing this book, we have drawn on the encouragement and advice of many in the socialist and trade union movement, particularly from members of the Socialist Workers Party with whom we have both worked over the years and whose generous support and sharp criticism have helped us develop many of the insights and much of the analysis in the book. We would also thank the numerous British Communists who we have met over the years, both as activists within the socialist movement and in the research of this book. Despite our often sharp disagreements, they like us are motivated by a desire to rid the world of the poverty, war and crisis endemic to capitalism. Chris Bambery, Ian Birchall, Ralph Darlington, Shaun Doherty, Keith Flett, Gareth Jenkins, John McIlroy, Steve Silver and Sean Vernell have each read and commented on sections of the text. The help of all those listed above has been invaluable, but we remain responsible for any errors made along the way.

Alison Howson at Palgrave was extremely helpful, and provided us with an anonymous reviewer who made many valuable suggestions on an early draft of the text. David Orr of Edge Hill contributed to our practical research in the Public Records Office in London. We have also received valuable assistance from archivists and library staff working in the British Library, the British Newspaper Library in Colindale, the National Museum of Labour History and the Working-Class Movement Library in Salford.

We were given an opportunity to air the ideas behind the book in a public forum at a meeting held in spring 2000 at the Institute of Historical Research under the auspices of the London Socialist Historians' Group and would like to thank the organisers and participants of that event.

Dave Renton would like to thank his colleagues at work, including Roger Spalding who provided several useful leads, and Chris Parker. In a cash-strapped department within one of the worst-funded of all the colleges of Higher Education, Dave was encouraged to take up research leave, and facility time with the union. Chris was the kindest and most supportive head of department that anyone could hope for. Above all Dave would like to thank Anne Alexander for her advice, encouragement and much love.

James Eaden would like to thank teaching colleagues and students past and present for stimulus and encouragement, and especially Jeannie Robinson whose love, support and critical reading of the text has made it possible.

Introduction: the Rise and Decline of British Bolshevism

The history of the Communist Party of Great Britain followed the trajectory of the Russian Revolution and the Soviet Union. Its formation was influenced by the experience of October 1917. The degeneration of the Soviet state and the rise of Stalinism directly affected its political practice. And the final collapse of the party coincided with the break-up of the USSR. At its birth, in 1920, the party brought together members of the generation of working-class militants who had stood out against the First World War. One such figure was J. T. Murphy, a leader of the Shop Stewards' Movement in Sheffield; another was Arthur Horner, a former member of the South Wales Miners' Unofficial Reform Movement and a volunteer in James Connolly's Irish Citizens' Army. From 1929, the chairman of the party was Harry Pollitt, an activist in the Boilermakers' Union and an important figure in the 1919 strike which stopped the *Jolly George*, a ship bound for Poland with weapons to use against the Red Army. Rajani Palme Dutt, who was to become the intellectual mentor of many British Communists, had spent a year in jail as a conscientious objector during the war.[1] This generation of militants joined the Communist Party not only because they hated the war, but also because they were inspired by the example of the Bolshevik Revolution in Russia, and wanted workers to seize power in Britain.

The willingness of revolutionaries in Britain and elsewhere to follow the example of the Bolsheviks was matched by the eagerness of the early Soviet leadership to spread the revolution. For Lenin and Trotsky spreading the revolution was not some optional extra. The move to begin the October revolution in relatively backward Russia was predicated on the hope that revolution would spread to the more advanced capitalist west. To further this aim the leaders of the Russian Communist Party set up the Communist International (Comintern) in 1919 with the specific aim of establishing Communist parties across the world and encouraging workers' revolution. Despite revolutionary militancy and workers' uprisings in a number of European countries in the years following 1917, revolutions on the Russian model did not follow, and the Soviet State, exhausted by a destructive civil war, was to remain isolated. The working class which had been at the heart of the 1917 revolution in the cities was decimated, and the organs of democratic self-government, the soviets, were bureaucratised, even as the Bolshevik party found itself ruling Soviet Russia in the name of working-class revolution. Within the Russian party a major political conflict arose in 1923 over the direction of the state, an argument which was overlaid with the reverberations following Lenin's death in January 1924. Trotsky and the Left Opposition maintained a revolutionary internationalist position, while an emerging leadership group around Stalin and Bukharin argued that the construction of 'Socialism in One Country' was possible.[2] By late 1924 Trotsky and the Left Opposition had been marginalised and by 1927 Stalin had emerged as party leader and effective dictator.

As we shall discuss in the following chapter, the Comintern responded to the passing of the immediate postwar revolutionary crisis by adopting a set of United Front policies designed to enable Communist parties to build up a base of support in non-revolutionary circumstances. Where they were applied such tactics often worked. Yet the question of who formulated advice was also important. The early Comintern was inevitably dominated by the Russians. Foreign communists tended to adopt the role of pupils, 'being drilled into a theoretical understanding of Marxism as propounded by Lenin, Trotsky, Zinoviev, Bukharin and Radek.'[3] This dominance was re-enforced by the willingness of the Soviet State to provide material assistance to the newly-formed Communist parties.[4]

While Soviet leaders were focused on the task of helping overseas Communists to organise for revolution, this imbalance was not yet to have a decisive impact on the young, foreign groups. Many of the parties grew quickly and impressively in their early years under the tutelage of the Comintern. The adoption of the policy of 'Socialism in One Country' however had a direct impact on the International. Under the initial control of Zinoviev and then of Bukharin, the chief theoretician of Socialism in One Country, the Comintern transformed itself into an organisation whose primary purpose was to direct foreign Communist parties to operate in ways which would be of assistance to the Soviet State. In Eric Hobsbawm's phrase, 'the state interests of the Soviet Union prevailed over the world revolutionary interests of the Communist International'.[5] This shift in the relationship between the Comintern, the Soviet State that it came to serve and overseas communist parties, including the Communist Party of Great Britain, underpins the analysis put forward in this book. From the late 1920s onwards, the numerous shifts in line urged by Moscow onto the British Communist Party were not based on an assessment of what might be in the interests of British Communists or the working-class movement that they aspired to lead. Despite the material and financial support that continued to flow to the British party, and despite the extent that loyalty to the Soviet Union provided an ideological cement that kept the party intact, the influence of the Stalinised Comintern and of the USSR on the development of a Marxist party in Britain was overwhelmingly negative.

The Communist Party of Great Britain (CP or CPGB) was situated at the heart of the British Empire and therefore at the centre of world imperialism. It was to play a key role in the strategic thinking of Comintern officials throughout the 1920s and 1930s. However, the British Party did not build the mass base of working-class support that many continental Communist parties enjoyed. Unlike the European parties which had been set up after substantial splits within the existing Social Democratic parties, British Communists failed to break large numbers of activists from the Labour Party to join the CPGB. In contrast to Communists in Belgium or France, the British Party had just one elected MP at the outbreak of World War Two. The relative marginality of British Communists has led some historians to question the validity of focusing on the CPGB as an object of study. One historian, Stephen Fielding, has criticised the recent volume of academic works on the CP, dubbing the party 'interesting but irrelevent'.[6] However electoral support alone is a crude measure of influence, and there is substantial evidence of support for Communist activists both within workplaces and other sites of potential class conflict. Political identities are not like hats, we can wear more than one of them at the same times, and many workers who voted Labour, Liberal or even Conservative, came across Communists especially in the workplaces and had some relationship with them, being attracted or repelled by their organisational vigour and political edge.

As we shall argue, the Communist Party played a significant role in the history of the British left in the twentieth century. Its relatively small size masked an influence within the trade union movement which was to last through until the 1980s. The Communist Party also helped to shape the culture, assumptions and expectations of a broader left of trade union activists, anti-fascists, anti-nuclear campaigners, Labour Party members and others. The Communist Party as the representative, however distant, of 'actually existing socialism' was a crucial point of influence for the Labour left in Britain. It is no mere coincidence that the collapse of both the Soviet Union and of the Communist Party should coincide with the demise of the left within the Labour Party. Sometimes, especially in its earlier years, the party helped to give a sense of political clarity to left-wing campaigners and activists. At other times and increasingly so in the postwar period the impact of the party was often to act as a break on the development of protest.

Primary sources

There are three main sources for this study. Firstly, the authors have made use of primary material available in the Communist Party's own archives, in personal deposits, among government records held at the Public Records Office and elsewhere. Secondly, we draw on interview material with Communists and other activists. Thirdly, the book is anchored in a critical reading of the published secondary material.

Secondary sources

Perry Anderson has suggested a five-fold typology of Communist Party histories, which he divides into personal memories, official histories, independent left histories, works of liberal scholarship and Cold War monographs. Kevin Morgan adds to this list works from an avowedly Trotskyist perspective and histories of 'specific areas of Communist politics or particular industries and communities'.[7] To Anderson and Morgan's lists, we should also perhaps add the work of former Communist Party members or fellow-travellers, several of whom have been prepared since the collapse of the CPGB to take more critical positions on the party's history.[8]

Until the 1960s, published material on the Communist Party was meagre, beyond that published by the party itself or of a popular Cold War type. Henry Pelling's critical 1958 text was met by the highly detailed yet necessarily partisan official history from James Klugmann.[9] The most interesting independent study from this period was probably Kenneth Newton's academic description of branch life within the Communist Party. Comparing party membership to the structure of British society, he observed that the CP found its strongest support among teachers and miners and in engineering and shipbuilding. Its support was weakest among the self-employed, clerical and administrative workers. Communist cells were most often located in large factories. Party members enjoyed a deep love of reading. Only a minority of members were fully committed to the latest party line. Such cadres, Newton believed, were strikingly rare. Most members were more liberal, 'They are certainly deeply committed to a cause and an ideology, but they tend to be pragmatic, tentative, idealistic, humanitarian, and sometimes surprisingly cautious in their opinions.' Newton's survey was later supplemented by Denver and Bochel's sociological study of forty-three CP members in Dundee.[10] Not surprisingly, though, such sociological approaches went out of fashion in the 1960s and 1970s. In conditions of mass protest, CP studies focused on the earlier and more radical phases in the party's history, and increasingly through the 1970s and 1980s work of an independent or New Left orientation started to appear. Unsurprisingly, work published in this period tended to cover the pre-war history of the party, detailed scholarly research on the postwar period is far thinner on the ground.[11]

Much of this early work on the Communist Party of Great Britain did not explore the relationship between the decisions of the Comintern and the British party in any great detail, neither did it look critically at the complex relationships which existed between the national leadership of the party and often disparate groups or rank-and-file trade unionists in various industries and localities. One exception to this general absence of critical theory is the volume by Pearce and Woodhouse, *A History of Communism in Britain*. This book contains in the form of a critique of Macfarlane's work, a detailed and perceptive account of the role of the Comintern in the establishment and early years of the party. Pearce and Woodhouse were non-Communist socialists. Like the authors of this book, they did not assume that there was anything sinister or strange about Communists working together in a party, and in opposition to the British State. Kevin Morgan argues that Pearce and Woodhouse s initially sophisticated treatment of the party's early years 'gives way to a basically monocausal explanation of Communist politics', focusing almost exclusively on the 'incorrect' line of the party leadership, which is explained with reference to the bad advice from Stalinist Russia.[12] We shall return to this debate while discussing the General Strike, where the rival positions are examined in detail. All we will say here is that while there is some weight to Morgan's criticisms, we feel that Pearce and Woodhouse have the better of the argument. Indeed, one of the aims of this book is to extend Pearce and Woodhouse's approach to the whole period of the party's history including the post-1945 period which is not covered in their account. A total history is needed, which takes into account both the high politics of the party and the low. It is impossible to write a satisfying history of the Communist Party without offering Comintern pressure as one key factor which helps to explain the twists and turns of the party line.

One useful recent work is Nina Fishman's *The Communist Party and the Trade Unions 1933–1945* which examines Communist trade union activists at the height of the party's influence. Fishman describes herself as applying to CPBG history the revisionist approach which was developed by a range of scholars of Soviet Communism through the 1970s and 1980s. In the same way that these historians took questions of class seriously, and sought to understand Soviet society from below, so Fishman approaches party history from the perspective of the ordinary local activist:

> My approach to writing party history became revisionist because I soon found that party members did not conform to the stereotype of either official Communist heroics or ritual Labour witch-hunts. I have had the audacity to transcend the conventional polarities in the hope of contributing to a revisionist approach to British Communism.

However, in stressing the role of rank and file activists, we feel that Fishman underplays the importance of Comintern policy in helping to shape the world-view of Communist Party members. In this respect Fishman's work reflects some of the weaknesses of 'history from below', which in rescuing ordinary people from the condescension of posterity risks underplaying the broader historical and political framework. 'Men' as Marx argued 'make their own history, but not under circumstance chosen by themselves'.[13] In Fishman's eagerness to move away from a stereotypical assessment of British Communists as 'Moscow Dupes', she underestimates the continued influence of the foreign policy concerns of the Soviet State, the Comintern and the British party leadership on the political culture of Communist activists. She is correct to assert that Communist shop-floor activists compartmentalised their economic concerns away from their more general political philosophy. But we would see this defensiveness as a reduction of their politics. Fishman identifies Communist philosophy as 'life itself', a phrase taken rather out of context from Lenin's well-known pamphlet, *Left Wing Communism: an Infantile Disorder* (1920):

> Communism is emerging in positively every sphere of public life its beginnings are to be seen literally on all sides. The 'contagion' has

very thoroughly penetrated the organism and has completely permeated it. If special efforts are made to block one of the channels, the 'contagion' will find another one, sometimes very unexpectedly. Life will assert itself.[14]

This 'revolutionary pragmatism', Fishman identifies as a development from the home-grown Utopian traditions of pre-Communist British socialism. However, the aspect of 'life itself' which she downplays is the extent to which the perceived achievements of Soviet Socialism sustained the faith of Communist militants 'toiling away at their unremitting mass work.'[15]

There is also a problematic tendency in some of the recent scholarship towards a romanticised view of the party during the periods of the Popular Front. This view is prevalent in Noreen Branson's history of the party in the 1930s[16] Branson's book coincided with the apparent re-emergence of 'socialism with a human face', in the form of Mikhail Gorbachev's glasnost. It also helped to fuel a nostalgic Popular Front mood among mid-to-late 1980s British Communists, expressed in the rise of Eurocommunism and the success of the party's theoretical journal *Marxism Today*. This approach passes over the extent to which the new line of 1933–34 was driven by the Moscow-led Comintern's reaction to the strategic threat to the USSR posed by Hitler. The policy may have reflected pressures from national sections of the Comintern, but such demands were secondary in the minds of those who formulated it. The relative unimportance of the national Communist Parties is even clearer when you look at the sudden turn towards the second Popular Front, following the invasion of the Soviet Union in June 1941. To stress the unblemished virtues of the Popular Front is also to obscure the horrors which took place in Russia at the time of the International's lurch right. The comfortable alliances of the Popular Front, the willingness of sections of liberal and left-wing public opinion in Britain and elsewhere to go along with the anti-fascist credentials of Communism, coincided with the horrors of forced collectivisation, the Gulag and the Moscow Trials within the USSR. The Stalinist terror did not leave the Comintern untouched, affecting foreign Communists resident in Moscow. The terror within the Comintern apparatus took its toll especially on exiled Communists from fascist Europe. Yet, leading members of the British party were aware of the case of Rose Cohen, who had the misfortune of having struck up a relationship with Petrovsky, a purged Comintern official, and disappeared into the Gulags in 1937. In the CPGB, the relatively tame domestic counterpart of Stalinist terror entailed a struggle against the 'Trotsky-Fascists' of the Independent Labour Party and the Socialist League, as well as assaults on real Trotskyists.[17]

This is only the fourth book to offer a full history of the Communist Party of Great Britain, from its beginning to its end. The first was Willie Thompson's *The Good Old Cause* (1992). Thompson had been a member of the party for several decades, and wrote his book shortly after the dissolution of the Communist Party in 1990–91. Thompson's account reads in many ways like an apology for the CPGB in the last thirty years of its existence. Yet at other times it is brutally frank, as only an insider's account can be. While providing some useful insights and analysis into the broader questions of Communists and the left, Thompson's focus on the detailed inner-party conflicts of the 1970s and 1980s, while highly informative, can obscure the wider issues. The second book was Francis Beckett's *Enemy Within* (1995), an outsider's view of the Communist Party which is equally hostile to the CP and all other manifestations of radical left-wing politics. Beckett's journalistic account is remarkable chiefly for the interest it takes in the issue of 'Moscow Gold' and its pen-portraits of leading Communist activists. The third full history of the party, Keith Laybourn and Dylan Murphy's *Under the Red Flag* (1999) provides seemingly a more rounded account. Yet the end result is strangely lifeless, a text-book introduction to British Communism which conveys neither the highs nor the lows of the movement and which deals fairly abruptly with the postwar history of the party.[18] Thus we would argue that there is a gap in the literature, for a committed socialist history of the party, sympathetic to the views of the founders, critical of the husk that the Communist Party became. Furthermore, in this book we critically engage with the debates in the Communist Party and Comintern historiography; as such there is a critical spine running through the book. Inevitably in attempting to write a single volume history of the party we have had to trim and compromise. Significant areas of the party's life remain relatively untouched in our book and our choice of what to include may well infuriate specialists in the field or those with specific interests. Until later writers attempt a more definitive history of the party, those areas will have to be covered by monographs dedicated to particular aspects of party work.

In *The Good Old Cause*, Willie Thompson argued that there was little continuity between the Communist Party at its birth and at its end. The organisation whose delegates dissolved the party in December 1990 had 'virtually nothing in common with the one which was established in August 1920 except the name'. In this vein he continued, 'Political philosophy, objectives, strategy and style as they had developed over seventy years would all have been unrecognisable – where not abhorrent – to the founders and their immediate successors.'[19] We agree with Thompson's claim. The Communist Party of 1920 was a lively revolutionary party, while the organisation of 1990–91 was little more than a shell. The purpose of our book is to develop this insight. How had the party changed, and why?

One common approach is to argue that the formation of the Communist Party was premature. If only the founding members had waited – perhaps until Britain was in crisis, or the Labour Party transformed from below – then the establishment of the CPGB would have been more timely. L. J. Macfarlane argues that there was no hope of building a revolutionary party in the conservative climate of postwar Britain: 'The history of the Communist Party in the 1920s is the story of a struggle to form a revolutionary party in a non-revolutionary situation.'[20] J. T. Murphy helped to found the party in 1920 but left twelve years later, and then wrote *Preparing for Power*, an important study of the history of the British Labour movement, which contains Murphy's explanation of the isolation which the party faced in 1930. 'Had the Communists at this period not formed a separate party,' wrote Murphy, 'but organised themselves as an integral part of the Labour Party, seeking to transform it from within, such an isolation of their forces would not have been possible.' The failure of the party was due to sectarianism at its birth: 'Their isolation is the price the revolutionary movement has had to pay for making a formal challenge on fundamental principles abstracted from the immediate struggles of the workers and without regard to the relation of forces.'[21] In a similar vein, Willie Thompson explains the failures of the party in terms of its stunted beginnings: 'The essential character that the CP, regardless of changes in policy, purposes, strategy or social composition, was to maintain ever afterwards was set by the early 1920s. It did succeed in establishing itself as a permanent part of the British labour movement and wider political reality, but never as more than a marginal fragment.' Other historians have argued that the CP was the child of a number of small and sectarian ultra-left parties, incapable of working with trade unionists and Labour party socialists. It is no surprise, therefore, that the party failed to take root in the Labour movement.[22]

Yet the original Communist Party was a serious revolutionary organisation possessing a significant network of activists who had won respect for their anti-war agitation, and were known in their local areas. It was the first party which could speak for the majority of revolutionary socialists in Britain. The foundation membership of four thousand was not large, but respectable for a party of this type. Crucially, the CPGB did make a sustained attempt to go beyond the shrill ultra-radicalism of its parent bodies. As James Hinton and Richard Hyman have argued:

> The party began the decade with the heritage of three decades of revolutionary organisation, with a substantial cadre of industrial militants who had won widespread trust and respect as leaders of the wartime struggles; and with considerable advantages as British representatives of Lenin, whose revolution had been hailed far beyond the ranks of committed Marxists.[23]

Communist histories have recently begun their attempt to grapple with the legacy of their party's links to Soviet State. At the height of their success, Communists faced the accusation that they were merely Moscow's tools. Noreen Branson's recent history of the party touches on the dilemmas faced by ordinary members of the party in dealing with the impact of Moscow. Branson insists that rank and file Communists were never the heartless ogres of Cold War legend. 'In Britain those who joined the Communist Party were dedicated to the socialist cause and, in many cases, were prepared to make great personal sacrifices in working for it.' This is all true, yet begs more questions than it answers. If they were dedicated to democracy and workers' control, then why did these genuine socialists fall for the myth that Russia was a just society? Indeed how many Communists did swallow the myth? Few of the leading comrades who had been to Russia can seriously have believed that Russia was a workers' paradise. Branson explains the pro-Soviet attitude of ordinary Communists in terms of a collective failure of understanding. British Communists had joined a workers' party, but:

> What party members did not fully appreciate was that, in countries like the Soviet Union, and its post-war European neighbours, this was no longer the case. From the late 1920s onwards, the Communist Party of the Soviet Union had become the party which people joined if they wanted to further their careers. Here the party was closely intertwined with the state machine, a power structure which had become more and more centralised and bureaucratic. 'Soviets' were no longer a system of 'rule from below'.[24]

Branson dips her toes into the stream of critical analysis, but she does not go far enough. What her account misses is the centrality of the Russian experience to every aspect of life in the CP.

We argue here that the degeneration of the Russian Revolution shaped the history of the British Communist Party. This opinion has been criticised, most notably in Andrew Thorpe's recent book, *The British Communist Party and Moscow 1920–1943*.[25] Thorpe suggests that the British party was rarely controlled from Moscow, and 'that the relationship was more of a partnership – albeit an unequal one – than has often been alleged'. Thorpe claims that the weapons of coercion 'were not effective in themselves', nor were they 'sufficiently powerful to force the CPGB over sustained periods, to do what it itself did not wish to do.' Democratic centralism was weaker the further it was stretched, and political arguments still had to be won by the leadership in the local areas. Some of Thorpe's points are valid. Communication between London and Moscow was difficult. The journey between the two cities was arduous and took time. J. T. Murphy flew once, and never again. Other Comintern delegates relied on the lengthy crossing by boat. After 1929, there was no permanent official Comintern representative in Britain. Yet Thorpe's argument is ultimately unconvincing. If the British Communists changed their politics voluntarily, then what are we to make from the many instructions sent back from the Western European Bureau of the Communist International, in Berlin? Why did Communist Parties change their politics, in each country, at the same time? If the coercive power of the Comintern apparatus was limited, then historians' interest should be drawn to the powerful internal discipline that the British Communists developed in order to police themselves. Such Communists as Tom Bell seriously believed that Russia was 'the land of proletarian freedom'. They were not bought or coerced by a Moscow bureaucracy, they chose to obey.

In the chapters that follow we will record some of the achievements of the party particularly in the pre-war period. In the 1930s, the Communist Party of Great Britain provided the leaderships of the London busworkers' strikes, and the Pressed Steel strike. Communist Party members were central to the fight against fascism, and took a leading role in the Battle of Cable Street.[26] The CP's newspaper, the *Daily Worker*, was the only significant voice on the left that regularly supported strikes. In an account of growing up as a young socialist in the 1960s with parents who had themselves come from a Jewish Communist milieu Michael Rosen describes bringing home a young

Trotskyist, Adam Westoby, one day for tea. His mother listened politely as Westoby criticised the Communist Party, before responding, as many of her generation would have done,

> Who do you think was defending Jews in the East End of London in the 1930? It's all very well for you to sit here in the 1960s and talk about the betrayals of the CP over the years, but for us, as Jews and socialists in the 1930s, there was no choice. The CP were the only organisation that had the power and the organisation to oppose Mosley. As YCL-ers that was the only possible route to take.

Of course, there was a choice, activists did try to break away from Stalinism. But no sizeable counter-current was established before 1956, and Trotskyism or the New Left were the choice of a small minority of left activists. Ian Birchall wrote in the 1960s that the CPGB was still 'the only organisation that [bore] Marxist ideas – in however distorted a form – into significant sections of the British working class, and the only organisation that [was] able to offer some kind of national framework to industrial militants'.[27]

From its beginning to its demise, the Communist Party was an organisation which attracted the best and most tireless of militants. They dedicated themselves unselfishly to a fight against capitalism often to the detriment of their personal and family lives. Some of the tensions can be seen in Phil Cohen's interviews with party members' surviving children. Their relationships with their parents were often fond but distant, the tone of their memories combines admiration with regret. Party members sacrificed their time and personal lives for a cause in which they honestly believed.[28] In stressing the achievements of the Communist Party and its local activists, including the success of its foundation, the victory of strikes with Communist leadership, the formation of the National Unemployed Workers' Movement, and the party's positive role in opposing American imperialism during the Cold War, we suspect that our account will actually be *more* critical than the earlier accounts written by members of the non-Stalinist left. Indeed it is only if you see the heights to which the party rose, that you can understand the lows to which it fell.

The history of the Communist Party is the story of a flawed and ultimately failed attempt to build a Marxist tradition in Britain. The tragedy of the infant Communist Party was not in its failure, for every movement has its failures. Instead, as one commentator argues,

The tragedy is in the loss, from meaningful class politics, of a whole generation of working-class militants. The early CP contained thousands of workers dedicated to revolutionary socialism and with a wealth of rank-and-file trade union experience. That men like Pollitt, Mann, Murphy, Gallacher, Bell and hundred of others spent their talented lives in the sterile service of Stalinism, through all the betrayals, small and large, that were entailed, says a great deal for the conviction that originally brought them to the socialist movement.[29]

The party failed, but the hopes of the party's original founders should not be dismissed. The ending of the twentieth century which saw the rise and fall of the Communist parties also witnessed the re-emergence of radical campaigning, with a new generation of young anti-capitalist protestors taking to the streets to challenge the priorities of globalised free market capitalism. The traditional parties of the social democratic left such as New Labour have embraced neo-liberal economics and social authoritarianism. In the process, Labour has alienated itself from many of its natural supporters, to an extent that would have seemed inconceivable thirty or forty years ago. Yet radical and left-wing political ideas persist and have the potential to reach out to engage a new audience. An understanding of the history of Communism in Britain will help both a new generation of activists to learn from the past to avoid some pitfalls in the future and arm students of contemporary politics with an understanding of the dynamics of radical political organisation.

1
High Hopes: 1920–28

At its foundation, the Communist Party of Great Britain possessed a membership made up of trade union militants who had played a leading role in several years of industrial struggle. In Walter Kendall's words, 'The Communist Party absorbed within its framework practically the whole pre-existing revolutionary movement and leaders. This movement and its participants, whatever its other faults, was at least self-acting, autonomous, a genuine endeavour to come to grips with the problem of British reality.' The industrial leaders of the party, including such figures as Harry Pollitt, Arthur McManus, Tom Bell and Willie Gallacher, were known and respected across the working-class movement. The party also enjoyed considerable prestige for its position as the British sister party of the Russian Bolsheviks. Their successful revolution offered hope to the oppressed people of the whole world. The method of soviets or workers' councils connected with the authentic experience of militant workers in Britain, France, Italy and throughout Europe. Yet by the end of the decade, the Communist Party had taken up the suicidal politics of Class against Class, seeing its main enemy in the Labour Party which represented the mainstream of working-class opinion. So within ten years of its formation, the party's membership had halved and its support collapsed. As two historians of the party, James Hinton and Richard Hyman point out, 'By 1930 the CPGB was little more than an isolated sect; its membership below the level at its foundation, and its influence, though less easily recognisable, surely even more catastrophically dissipated.'[1] If the party was committed to revolutionary politics, flexible in its approach and sound in 1920, then it follows that its weak state at the end of the decade is evidence of a serious decline. The purpose of this chapter therefore is to explain why this degeneration took place.

The reversal in the fortunes of the Communist Party in the 1920s was a product of the combination of two specific factors. First, there were weaknesses hidden within the indigenous socialist tradition on which it drew. The CPGB was shaped by the limited socialist traditions inside which its members had been schooled. Although such weaknesses were not necessarily fatal, we shall argue that this was hardly a positive inheritance. Second, the British party was unduly dependent on the quality of the advice it received from seasoned revolutionaries in the Communist International. In 1920 and 1921, the role of the Comintern was generally positive. As the young Communist Party lurched from left to right, it was often the arguments of leading members of the International, including Lenin and Trotsky, which brought the British party back on track. By the middle of the decade, however, the Comintern itself had gone into decline. As the Russian Revolution degenerated from within, so the body which was set up to spread its gains across the world also declined. By 1928 or 1930, the Communist International was well on the way to becoming a fully Stalinised shell of its earlier self, and was no longer capable of leading any of its constituent parties toward a genuine revolutionary politics. The CPGB moved at its own speed and according to local conditions. Yet the direction in which it developed was clear. As the International declined, so the British party went down with it.

Before the Bolsheviks

Although the Communist Party was not decisively shaped by the nature of pre-1917 socialism, it was affected by the political traditions which it inherited from previous bodies. Thus the early history of the CPGB was shaped by the pre-existing traditions of the British left. At the turn of the century Britain was still the 'workshop of the world', the most powerful imperial power in the world. Precisely because the economy was so successful, a majority of workers naturally identified with the main political parties, the Liberals and the Conservatives. Even within the large minority who believed that there should be a separate workers' party, the majority supported reformism, which meant the tactics of the parliamentary Labour Party and the Independent Labour Party (ILP), which was associated with it. The big battalions of Labour and the trade unions were dominated by reformist ideas. As far as the Labour tradition was concerned, trade unionists could fight in the factories, but the law would be changed in parliament. In this way,

the excesses of capitalism could be reduced and the system transformed, without workers changing society themselves.
With regards to socialist politics, the main political opposition to the left of Labour came from the Social Democratic Federation, the SDF. This was a revolutionary party, but one without any living sense of how a workers' party could be built. It must be said that opinions on the SDF vary. Traditionally, most historians have been critical of the SDF, following arguments set down by William Morris and Frederick Engels at the time. More recently, Martin Crick has drawn attention to the role played by ordinary members of the SDF. According to Crick, the Federation 'was the pioneer organisation of the Socialist revival of the 1880s, the veteran campaigner of the free speech and unemployed agitation, a vital presence at the founding conference of the Labour Representation Committee.'[2] Of course, the rank and file contained many committed socialists. But the leadership of the SDF, personified in the dominant figure of the former Tory H. M. Hyndman, was middle class and remote. Like a religious sect possessed of a simple truth, the SDF ignored strikes, or described them as mere 'palliatives'. Indeed it had already been in existence for 16 years when the Federation first agreed that its members should be encouraged to join trade unions. Keith Laybourn suggests that the crucial weakness of the SDF was its 'failure to win substantial trade union support.'[3] This factor certainly explains the ability of the Labour Party to become the dominant force within the British left. Yet the SDF not only failed to displace Labour, it also failed to become a significant revolutionary party in its own right. The problem was an old one. The SDF – like the Labour Party and the ILP – saw politics and economics as separate categories. Like the Labour MPs, the members of the Federation gave no role to ordinary workers to change society themselves.

Although the pre-history of the British left is a story of inauspicious beginnings, the character of the socialist movement did begin to change. In successive waves of struggle after 1889, the working class itself was transformed by a gathering tide of struggle. Between 1905 and 1908 trade unions grew in size by 25 per cent, to a total of 2 500 000 members. In 1910 there were strikes in the mines and shipyards; in 1911, among dockers and rail workers. More and more workers were drawn into the movement. The number of trade unionists increased to four million. One militant union, the Workers' Union, with just 5000 members in 1910, grew until it was over 140 000 strong in the autumn of 1914. In such a radical atmosphere, the previously quiet organisations of the left blossomed. The mood among the rank and file in the unions was for syndicalism, namely the idea that trade unions themselves could take over the running of society. In every industry, workers should organise in a single bloc. Out of this organisation, a new way of running the world would emerge. While the reformists argued for political change through parliament, and the sectarians for political change from outside, syndicalism took the economic position of ordinary working people more seriously. The prophet of the movement was Daniel De Leon, who argued for revolutionary organisation at the point of production.

Syndicalism, with its emphasis on workers' self-activity, was an enormously positive development, a real threat to the dominance of capital over labour. But it could not fill the traditional gaps in left-wing practice. Emphasising economic change, there was no strategy for political progress. The solution to all political problems would be found in the workplace, where political differences were subordinated into the economic need for all-out struggle. In effect, the old fatal gap between politics and economics was left intact. It would be perfectly possible for a worker to be a strong fighting syndicalist in work, and a more timid supporter of Labour or even the Liberals in their home. The syndicalist groups also failed to build permanent organisations. George S. Yates founded the Socialist Labour Party (SLP) in 1903, to carry on De Leon's ideas, but it never recruited more than a few hundred members. The influence of syndicalism was felt instead through the success of individuals such as Tom Mann, or pamphlets, including Noah Ablett's rank and file bible, *The Miners' Next Step*. Syndicalism remained as an idea, a fighting mood pervasive in the class, but it was not a party.[4]

In the absence of a large party based on syndicalist ideas, it was the SDF which enjoyed a surprising new burst of life. Other socialist currents also flourished, and a movement grew for socialist unity. In 1907, Victor Grayson stood as a 'Labour and Socialist' candidate for Colne Valley, and was elected. In contrast to the many Labour MPs since, Grayson had a refreshing contempt for parliamentary conventions. Within a year of his election, he was expelled from the Commons for accusing MPs of conniving at murder by allowing poverty to continue. Grayson lost his seat in 1910, but the enthusiasm of his first victory continued. Grayson began to call for Socialist Unity, meaning in practice a radical socialist alliance between the SDF and the ILP. Receiving the strong support of Blatchford's Clarion Movement, Grayson called a Socialist Unity Conference, which was attended by Grayson himself, delegates from SDF and ILP branches, Clarion groups and some radical syndicalists. This conference resulted in the formation of the British Socialist Party, or BSP. Sadly the leadership of the SDF was unwilling to throw itself into the campaign. Hyndman offered, withdrew, and then offered his support again. This organisation originally claimed 35 000 members in 376 branches, but soon went into decline, having only 85 branches left by 1913. Grayson dropped out of all practical activity at about the same time.

There are different ways in which to judge this episode. On the one hand, the decline of the Socialist Unity project set back the hopes of creating a significant left block, with a different agenda to the parliamentary politics of the Labour Party. The British Socialist Party soon appeared to be no more than the old SDF with a new name. On the other hand, the very process of discussion associated with unification tended to break up some of the political lethargy of pre-1914 British socialism. After the formation of the BSP, Hyndman found himself more open to challenge from the rank and file of his own party. The anti-war left-wing within the BSP, organised around such individuals as John Maclean in Glasgow and Theodore Rothstein in London, was to provide some of the membership and a great deal of the leadership of the early CP.[5]

The outbreak of war in August 1914 temporarily quelled the fire of industrial unrest. Despite the previous ten years spent at peace conferences passing anti-war resolutions, the large majority of Labour MPs backed the war, as did most trade unions. Even the supposedly-revolutionary leadership of the BSP supported the war. With the jingo press pouring out stories of German atrocities, and only a tiny minority of socialist and pacifists offering any sort of opposition, it is no surprise that much of the working class was also drawn into the chauvinistic fervour. As Ian Birchall argues, the patriotic mood of 1914 has sometimes been exaggerated. A number of papers, including *The Times*, the *Economist* and the *Yorkshire Post* all bemoaned the lack of national spirit among British workers.[6] Much of the volunteering did not take place until late 1915, by which time it was effectively compulsory. Yet it remains true that most workers supported the declaration of war. Even those trade unionists who were more equivocal, still agreed to suspend their independent demands as they waited for the war to end. In this way, the war broke what had been a rising tide of class struggle, and the number of strike days fell by three-quarters, from twenty million per year in 1911–13 to five million per year, in 1914–18.

Although the original impact of the war was to impede the independent development of the workers' movement, the lull in the struggle did not last. As the war continued, unofficial movements sprang up, winning real support from workers in different industries. The shop stewards movement brought together radicalised workers from different industries. There were important rank and file movements among engineers in Glasgow and Sheffield, while miners' Reform Movements were set up in South Wales and in the Scottish coalfields. The ground was prepared for a new wave of struggle, which continued on from the pre-war upsurge. As early as February 1915, Glasgow engineers were the first group of workers to walk out against wartime pay restraint. In August, the Clyde Workers' Committee was set up following a strike against dilution, the practice of employing unskilled or semi-skilled workers on accepted, skilled work. The following year saw a first national conference of shop stewards, which was a revolutionary step given the conditions of war. In the summer of 1916, the BSP finally split, with a young anti-war majority expelling the jingo leadership of Hyndman. In March 1917, ten thousand workers from the shipyards in Barrow-in-Furness took strike action. May of that year witnessed the beginning of the largest strike movement of the war, as up to 200 000 workers walked out against the conscription of skilled engineers. By January 1918, the shop stewards movement was discussing a call for a general strike which could have brought an end to the war.[7]

The greatest blow against the war came with the Russian Revolution of October 1917. All over Europe, there was a an explosion of anger against the war and a real hope that something different could be constructed. Workers across the world hoped that Russia would be the harbinger of a new society. Millions saw Lenin and the Bolsheviks as leading the way forward to socialism. There were many things which workers could learn from the Bolsheviks. One was an absolute hostility to the war. The Russian Marxists had opposed the war from the beginning, in marked contrast to the moderate socialists of western Europe. Another inspiration was the demand for workers' power. While the German Social Democrats were only prepared to countenance a future in which workers' councils played a slightly greater role in the supervision of industry, Lenin promised a revolutionary change and the abolition of class inequality. This goal was summed up in the slogan, 'all power to the soviets'.

Britain was in no way isolated from this revolutionary wave. Soldiers refused to fight against the Russian Revolution. During 1918 and 1919 there were mutinies of British soldiers at Archangel, Kem, Kandalaksha, Murmansk, Onega and Seletskoi near the front line. At home, trade union membership doubled from four to eight million workers between 1914 and 1920. In 1919, coal heavers struck to prevent arms and supplies from being sent against the Russian Revolution. Two thousand soldiers in France mutinied and formed a soldiers' union. The anti-war mood crystallised in organisation. Councils of Action were set up in every area to organise protests and strikes against the possibility of a further war. Also in 1918, Labour's constitution was amended to include a new Clause Four, calling for the common ownership of industry. The Labour Party and the TUC established a National Council of Action, to organise 'the whole industrial strength of the workers against the war'. There were mass strikes in the mines, of Glasgow engineers, and even among the Metropolitan police. Between 1919 and 1921, British workers took nearly one hundred and fifty million days of strike action.[8]

In this ferment, large numbers of workers grew increasingly hostile towards the Labour leaders. The MPs and the trade union bureaucrats were seen to have voted and campaigned for the war and were regarded as traitors to the socialist cause. Tens of thousands of workers hoped for a revolutionary alternative which could challenge the old order, and Communist parties were set up across Europe. In Britain, at the height of the struggle, negotiations began to form a united revolutionary party. In June 1917, a United Socialist meeting was held between the Independent Labour Party and BSP. Both bodies called for the formation of soviets, on the soviet model. The first congress of the Communist International was held in revolutionary Petrograd in 1919. In Britain, Tom Bell and Arthur MacManus contacted the Russian Communist Party. Meanwhile, Sylvia Pankhurst ran a People's Russian Information Bureau from the same building as her paper, the *Workers' Dreadnought*. The Communist Party of Great Britain was finally established out of a Communist Unity Convention which was held at the Cannon Street hotel in London on 31 July and 1 August 1920.[9] This meeting was at once a sign of weakness and of strength. The largest Communist parties began as major factions within reformist parties – in Italy, the Socialist Party first sided with the Comintern, and only later split. In Britain, by contrast, unity was achieved by bringing together the fragments of an already-divided left.

Foundation

Franz Borkenau notes that 'In England, compared with the small sects out of which the Communist Party emerged, the latter was a mass party and its foundation a step away from sectarianism.'[10] Members from each of the Independent Labour Party, the British Socialist Party and the Socialist Labour Party all signed up to the new Communist Party. There were also other organisations which contributed, including Sylvia Pankhurst's Workers' Socialist Federation (WSF) which possessed a strong base in London's East End, the South Wales Socialist Society, the National Guild League and the Herald League, which grew out of the anti-war agitation of the trade union paper, the *Daily Herald*. The local branches of the Manchester Communist Party, for example, were based on the South Salford and Openshaw branches of the BSP, the Manchester Guild Communist Group, Gorton Socialist Society, and also activists from the local SLP, the Manchester Shop Stewards' and Workers Committee, Altrincham ILP and Manchester Labour College. Albert Inkpin moved directly from a position as national organiser of the BSP to the same post within the Communist Party. Otherwise, the leadership was dominated by former industrial militants from the Socialist Labour Party, including J. T. (Jack) Murphy, Tom Bell and Arthur McManus. The new party claimed at the outset to have 4000 members and also enjoyed a wide periphery of contacts within the Labour movement. By the mid-1920s, Communist Party sponsored publications enjoyed a circulation of between twenty and fifty thousand, which was impressive for a party of this size. By 1922 the Communist Party of Great Britain had established itself as *the* party of the revolutionary left.[11]

One of first challenges faced by the Communist Party was the question of how to relate to the Labour Party. If the CP enjoyed the support of only 4000 members, then it was clearly dwarfed by Labour, which enjoyed the support of the ILP, the socialist societies, and up to eight million members in affiliated trade unions. A number of leading Communists, including J. T. Murphy, Sylvia Pankhurst, Willie Gallacher and Harry Pollitt, believed from the start that the CP would be able to push the Labour Party quickly out of the way and establish itself as the major force within the British workers' movement. Gallacher wrote in Sylvia Pankhurst's paper *The Workers' Dreadnought* that 'the rank and file of the ILP in Scotland is becoming more and more disgusted with the thought of Parliament, and Soviets or workers' councils are being supported by almost every branch.' Pankhurst attended the second congress of the International. In her paper, she insisted that 'the Communist Party must keep its doctrine pure, and its independence of reformism inviolate; its mission is to lead the way, without stopping and turning by the direct road to the communist revolution.'[12] At the 1920 Unity Convention the motion calling for the new party to apply to affiliate to Labour was only passed by a narrow majority of 100 votes to 85.

The decisive voice, urging the new party to take the Labour Party more seriously, was Lenin, the Bolshevik leader. His pamphlet, *Left-Wing Communism: an Infantile Disorder* (1920) replied to Sylvia Pankhurst, arguing that 'revolution is impossible without a change in the views of the majority of the working class, and this change is brought about by the political experience of the masses, and never by propaganda alone.' From this stance, it followed that the party should support Labour in its contest with the Tories and Liberals. Only once Labour was elected, would the Communist Party be able to demonstrate to a majority of workers why Labour was not enough.[13] Although Lenin's advice did eventually win a majority within the Communist Party of Great Britain, it was not uniformly successful. John Maclean, who knew Willie Gallacher and distrusted the former members of Glasgow BSP, refused to believe that the new party would take Lenin's advice seriously, and declined to join.[14] Sylvia Pankhurst disagreed with Lenin and left the British party.

In August 1920, the executive of the Communist Party of Great Britain applied for affiliation to the Labour Party. Declaring against reformism and for the Soviet system, the initial approach was better designed for publication than to win the support of the Labour Party's leaders. The Labour executive responded by reminding the CPGB of Labour's own tradition, 'the basis of affiliation to the Labour Party is the acceptance of its constitution, principles and programme, with which the objects of the Communist Party do not appear to be in accord.' Yet this rejection was only implemented very unevenly. In some areas Communists were excluded from local Labour Parties. In other towns and cities, where Communists had some influence, the local parties were more sympathetic and did not take action against members of the CP.[15] The question then came up at Labour's 1922 Conference in Edinburgh, where the CP's application for affiliation was rejected by 3 086 000 votes to 261 000. Frank Hodges of the miners made the platform speech accusing the Communists of being 'the intellectual slaves of Moscow ... taking orders from the Asiatic mind.' Although affiliation was now dead as a tactic, the possibility remained that individual Communists could enter the Labour Party, and win recruits in this way. Indeed in 1922, there were Communists active in the Glasgow, Sheffield, Manchester and Birmingham Labour Parties, and the number of Communist delegates to the Labour Party conference rose from seven in 1922, to 38, one year later. As late as 1924, the view persisted within the Labour Party that individual members of the Communist Party should be allowed in, provided that their organisation was not. At that year's conference, the vote for Communist Party affiliation was defeated by 3 185 000 to 193 000, while the vote against individual CP membership was carried by just 1 804 000 to 1 540 000. Individual party members were not decisively excluded from Labour Party membership until the end of the decade.[16]

As well as the Labour Party, the CP also had to clarify its relations with other large forces on the left, including the ILP. The Independent Labour Party voted at its conference in 1920 to disaffiliate from the Second, Socialist International. However, the ILP leadership including Ramsay MacDonald spoke against uniting with the British Communist Party, and the conference did not vote to join the Communist, Third International. An internal opposition, the Left Wing Group, was formed to promote affiliation to the Comintern within the ILP. Then, having lost the same vote at the 1921 conference, the ILP lefts gave up their attempts to transform their party from within. Between one and two hundred members of the Independent Labour Party joined the British Communist Party in 1921, including the future Communist MP Saklatvala. More ILP members would follow at different times, over the next twenty years.

The Communist Party marked itself off from its parent bodies in the British socialist movement, by its emphasis on workplace politics, which it learned from the Russian Communists. This was a new approach for the British left. With its emphasis on the self-activity of workers, employed at the point of production, Bolshevism was a renewal of the revolutionary tradition of Marx and Engels. The SLP had possessed a similar emphasis on class struggle, but did not have the numbers or the organisation to leave a permanent mark. Other socialist parties in pre-war Britain, notably the BSP and ILP, had not given any sort of lead to industrial militants. The syndicalists had supported action, but without offering a coherent political strategy to the workers' movement. From its beginning, the CP placed a considerable emphasis on workshop organisation. In the summer of 1920, the Communist International argued that the way forward was through the construction of a parallel network of trade unions, and the Comintern established a Red International of Labour Unions (RILU) in 1921. By leading in the workshop committees, Communists would win support to build a revolutionary trade union International. Trade Union strategy was cast within an offensive framework, unemployed workers were to received full pay from their last employer, while workers' commissions should examine employers' books. This tactic of setting up fighting unions had greatest resonance in such countries as Spain where the union federations were already split, and where there were large syndicalist unions with a history of leading struggles. In 1920–21, leading British Communists tended to apply this line with some caution. They did not argue for splits in the unions, but rather for the consolidation of networks of socialist shop stewards, in opposition to the established trade union structures.

It is worth saying something here about the role played by the trade union bureaucracy, a theme recurring throughout the history of the Communist Party. The Bolshevik argument was that even the best professional trade union leaders become *representatives*, and thus have a tendency to become separated from the conditions of their members who continue to work at the point of production. As early as 1890, John Burns described the old guard of TUC delegates carrying 'good coats, large watch chains and high hats', in marked contrast to the poor clothes of their members The timidity of the bureaucracy was not only a British phenomenon. In 1908 Robert Michels described the conservatism of their counterparts in Germany.[17] The enormous growth of the unions in the postwar era had been a mixed blessing for the trade union leaders. On the one hand, more members meant more permanent officials and the position of full-timers became more secure. As Richard Hyman notes, 'At the turn of the century the largest union with centralised control, the Amalgamated Society of Engineers, had less than 100 000 members; by 1920 there were a dozen unions larger than this, many of them substantially so.'[18] On the other hand, the growth of the shop stewards movement meant that there was a potential alternative leadership, made up of workers themselves, and more closely linked to the needs of ordinary people. It was for all these reasons that the early CP insisted that revolutionaries had more in common with shop stewards in the trade unions than they did with the union full-timers. It would be an exaggeration to suggest that the British Communists had assimilated the full lessons of the Bolshevik theory of union bureaucracy, but there was a willingness to think, and this willingness would soon be lost.

From mid-1921, the industrial perspectives within the International changed. The original approach of the International had been based around the observation that capitalism was in crisis. By 1921, however, it seemed that the system had been briefly stabilised – at this stage, the Bolsheviks expected the lull to last more than two years. The Third World Congress of the Comintern opened with a speech by Leon

Trotsky, in which he argued that the postwar upturn in industrial protest had temporarily come to a halt, 'the open revolutionary struggle of the proletariat for power is at present passing through a stoppage'. One of the reasons for this change was the new period of high unemployment, which reduced the ability of workers to use strikes as a form of protest. Weaker at the point of production, trade unionists were less able to challenge the economic basis of society. At the Fourth Congress of the Communist International in 1921, J. T. Murphy described the industrial problems faced by revolutionaries in Britain, 'How can you build factory organisations when you have 1 750 000 walking the streets. You cannot build factory organisations in empty and depleted workshops.'[19] At the 1922 Plenum of the Executive Committee of the Comintern, Communists were encouraged to work together with non-revolutionary trade unionists, in a 'United Front' of all parties supported by the working class. Rather than simply exposing the failure of the trade union leadership, it was argued that revolutionaries should seek alliances with less militant workers and also sometimes with sections of the left-wing bureaucracy. Socialists should work for specific demands with friendly forces. Rather than setting up rival trade unions, socialists should work within the existing structures.

This new tactic was received with enthusiasm in Britain, where the economic downturn had proved especially sharp. The British economy had been built up in the early nineteenth century when it was the world's only manufacturing power, and was extended at the end of the nineteenth century, when Britain benefited from being the world's largest empire. The economy had thrived on guaranteed markets, for coal, shipbuilding, textiles, iron and steel. Yet the war had done untold damage to Britain's economic position. The country was now a debtor nation, while German reparations to France and Belgium meant that these goods were in competition with British products. In this new situation of over-production, British employers were forced to dismantle the war economy. Factories were closed, the number of strikes fell, and workers suffered.

As we have seen, the workers' struggle reached its height in 1918 and especially 1919. There were police strikes in Liverpool, troop mutinies, and Red Clydeside was subject to armed siege. Yet the slow-down in the economy from 1920 onwards reduced the scope for pure trade union struggle. Indeed having survived the wave of militancy, the employers felt confident to stage a major counter-offensive in 1921. Their first targets were the miners and the engineers. The defeat of the miners on Black Friday in 1921 gave the employers the chance to seek further attacks on transport, distribution and building in 1924. Then the miners union was attacked again in 1925 and 1926. The limits on the CP's support and influence within the working class were determined by the defensive nature of much trade union activity in this period. From 1921 through the 1922 engineering lock-out to the 1926 General Strike, the manual working-class base of the party suffered a series of sharp industrial defeats. At each turn, the precious band of experienced Communist industrial militants including J. T. Murphy and Wal Hannington with roots in the shop stewards movement built up in the last years of the world war, were victimised.

The first wave of cuts began in 1921. Unemployment rose from around 6 per cent in December 1920 to just under 18 per cent at the end of June 1921. The National Unemployed Workers' Movement was established that year, under the leadership of Wal Hannington, formerly an activist in the engineers' union. James Hinton and Richard Hyman record a wry joke of the time, 'that the shop steward leaders of 1918 had become the unemployed leaders of the 1920s'. Left-wing Boards of Guardians briefly refused to skimp on Poor Relief, and George Lansbury and 29 other Poplar Councillors were jailed in the autumn of 1921. The crucial engagement of the early 1920s took place however in the mines. The owners imposed unilateral wage cuts, and although the miners voted to strike, they were locked out on 1 April 1921. The Triple Alliance of Miners, Transport Workers and Railwaymen met and called a solidarity strike in support of the miners. This was called off on April 15, Black Friday. With its defeat the hopes collapsed of united working-class resistance to wage cuts. The miners fought on alone for 13 weeks, and were eventually forced to accept wage cuts of around 34 per cent. Communists blamed Jimmy Thomas, the leader of the National Union of Railwaymen. A superb cartoon by Will Hope in *The Communist* showed Thomas as Judas at the Last Supper. Yet the miner's defeat lasted. By the end of 1921, some six million workers across industry had suffered pay cuts of around 8 shillings per week. Trade union membership fell from 8.3 million in 1920, to 5.6 million by 1922 and eventually 4.4 million in 1933. Strike days fell from an annual average of 49 million in 1919–21 to under 12 million in 1922–25. In a period of cutbacks from 1921 to 1926, the space for independent action was reduced, and the position of the employers was strengthened.[20]

It was the combination of economic slowdown and advice from the International which led the British party to play down the RILU goal of establishing up rival unions, and accept instead the tactic of the United

Front. This approach was embodied in the National Minority Movement, which was launched in autumn 1923. The movement's first conference took place on 23–4 August 1924, and there were 270 delegates present, claiming to represent 200 000 workers. The Minority Movement was a militant force within the trade unions, it argued for an offensive policy of improving wages and conditions. Roderick Martin, the historian of the Minority Movement, describes it as 'an uneasy alliance between the Communist International and the extreme left wing of the British trade union movement'.[21] The hope was that strike action would win results, which would expose the failure of the bureaucracy. Impressed by the success of their action, workers would then join the Communist Party. Harry Pollitt explained the objectives as follows:

> We are not out to disrupt the unions, or to encourage any new unions. Our sole objective is to unite the workers in the factories by the formation of factory committees; to work for the formation of one union for each industry; to strengthen the local Trades Councils so that they shall be representative of every phase of the working-class movement, with its roots firmly embedded in the factories of each locality.

His emphasis was on strengthening the organisations of the Labour movement, the union branches and the trades councils, and even the TUC, 'We stand for the formation of a real General Council that shall have the power to direct, unite and co-ordinate all struggles and activities of the trade unions, and so make it possible to end the present chaos and go forward in a united attack in order to secure not only our immediate demands, but win workers' complete control of industry.' In Pollitt's speech, there were strong echoes of the old syndicalist demand for industrial trade unionism. Industrial unions would cover whole industries. At the top of the pyramid, a new body would represent the whole working class, regardless of trade or industry.[22]

The Minority Movement claimed 950 000 members in 1926. In order to reach this figure, any individual worker could have been counted several times. A leading steward in a large plant might attend a conference, as the delegate of a factory, a stewards' committee, or a trades council. With triple-counting, they might claim to represent several thousand workers – less than a hundred of whom may actually have taken part in any vote. Yet even if the claimed figure exaggerated Communist influence by a factor of ten, this would still suggest that this small party had considerable influence in the unions, a periphery much greater than its membership. The Minority Movement had support in the mining and engineering unions, on the railways and in many other workplaces. It was credited with helping to obtain the election of A. J. Cook, a prominent supporter of the Minority Movement, to the secretaryship of the Miners' Federation. Yet, there were serious problems with this new industrial policy. Few Communist militants in the factories seem to have understood how exactly such unity should be built. Could you have unity only with your fellow workers, or should agreement be allowed with members of the union machine? In such alliances, how could revolutionary politics come to dominate? What was the balance to be sought between working with rival forces, and raising an agenda of your own? In the absence of a serious discussion of these problems within the British party, the leadership for understandable reasons tended to follow the latest advice which it received from the Communist International. Yet the International itself was in a process of degeneration from within, and the quality of its advice was to decline dramatically in the space of just a few years.

Bolshevisation

Despite the excitement which followed the launch of the Communist Party in 1920, it took some time for the party to set up a sturdy network of local activists. The immediate revolutionary hopes of 1919 began to fade as the high-point of the upturn was passed. Party membership, which stood at 4000 in 1920, fell to 2500 one year later. For British Communists still struggling to establish themselves as a viable organisation, the application of the United Front – on Comintern advice – represented a potential way forward. Tactical alliances with members of the Labour Party and an orientation on trade unions, both represented means through which a larger revolutionary party could be built. For the British party as for many of the other young Communist Parties, the Comintern also prescribed a dose of Bolshevisation. Zinoviev argued that the failure of the workers' revolts of 1919–21 across Europe to result in the successful repeat of October 1917 lay not just in the objective conditions of capitalist stabilisation but also in the subjective failure of the new parties to put into practice the techniques learned by the Bolsheviks since 1903. Lenin argued that the national parties needed to think independently,[23] but this advice was lost, and the very opposite argument was put by Lenin's disciples.

The Comintern Third Congress had been keen to establish that party-building should not be a merely mechanistic, organisational process but should encompass a broad project of political education, yet as J. T. Murphy was to point out, organisational restructuring often took precedence over equally-important questions of political development, 'We had made our political adherence to its principles, but it is one thing to accept a principle and another to apply it to life. The Communist Party was supposed to be a Marxist party, but there were few within it who had more than a nodding acquaintance with the writings of Marx.'[24] More recently Stuart Macintyre's research has tended to confirm Murphy's account of the low level of political education within the British party. Before 1926, only a small number of Marx and Engels' works were available in English translation, and many of these only in expensive American editions. Other authors, including Lenin, Luxemburg or Trotsky were still harder to come by. Socialist ideas were assimilated through the writings of non-Marxist social scientists, atheists and evolutionists such as Ernst Haeckel, whose *Evolution of Man* was seen as a popular counterpart to Frederick Engels' *Origins of the Family, Private Property and the State*.[25] Yet if Murphy was right, and the party activists had little understanding of Marxism, then how could this situation be remedied?

In the winter of 1921–22, a Comintern commission charged with investigating the worrying lack of progress in the British Communist Party, invited Arthur MacManus the Party Secretary and the CPGB's rising star Harry Pollitt, back to Moscow. On his return to Britain, Pollitt established a commission to overhaul the Party's organisation. The other members of the troika included the national organiser Albert Inkpin and a young writer, Rajani Palme Dutt. The commission eventually produced a 40 000 word report into every aspect of the Communist Party's organisation. Some of its recommendations were accepted, while others received vociferous opposition. J. T. Murphy suggested that the report mistakenly prioritised organisational answers to political problems. 'If I were asked what are the principal defects of the Party today, I would answer unhesitatingly, formalism, organisational Fetishism, and lack of political training'.[26]

Despite his protests, Murphy's worries were misplaced. The real problem of the report was the broader issue of what constituted Bolshevisation? For the Bolshevik party was itself in ferment, with Lenin dying and Trotsky star's on the wane. The goals of greater clarity, discipline and centralisation could not be so positive once rival perspectives were banned both in Russia and within the British party.

Under Zinoviev's leadership, the International succumbed to faddism, leaning one way and then the next without any clear logic to the changed positions. The intention of Bolshevisation was to produce a party of leaders, where every member could build movements in their home area of workplace. The actual outcome of this process was to facilitate the shift towards Stalinisation, a process which was successful by the end of the decade.

Perhaps the most lasting significance of the report was that it established a clear link between the process of 'Bolshevisation' and the two young men who were to lead the Communist Party through the formative years of its existence, Harry Pollitt and Rajani Palme Dutt. Many writers have contrasted the personalities of these two leading Communists. In Kevin Morgan's words, Harry Pollitt 'was a product of the that open, generous socialist culture that produced the First World War ... Born in the heart of industrial Britain, his passionate sense of identity with his own working class would underpin and occasionally clash with his allegiance to international Communism.' Pollitt was the public face of the Communist Party. He was a skilled boilermarker, who had played a prominent role in the Openshaw Socialist Society, which affiliated to the BSP in 1911. Later Harry Pollitt was a leading activist in the movement against sending arms to the counter-revolutionaries in Russia. He was clearly a talented organiser. Following the 1922 report, Pollitt took charge of the CP paper *Workers Weekly*, and quickly built up a network of paper-sellers and factory-floor journalists. By 1923, *Workers Weekly* had a circulation of 50 000. This could not match the 200 000 plus circulation of the *Daily Herald*, but any socialist party would be content with a paper sale ten times the size of its membership.[27]

While Pollitt could appear open and sincere, Rajani Palme Dutt let himself be seen as quiet, close-minded and cold. The distinctive qualities of his Marxism were epitomised by a famous entry on the meaning of Communism that he wrote for the 1921 *Encyclopaedia Britannica*, which defined Marxism as the combination of the 'the strictest internal discipline' plus 'an external policy of revolutionary opportunism'. Such an approach was hardly designed to win converts! According to Willie Thompson, who saw Dutt at work late in his career, he 'possessed a brilliant intelligence ... but came to employ it ... in the composition of dishonest justifications for discreditable or criminal acts committed by the Soviet regime.'[28] Palme Dutt owed his rapid rise to prominence within the British party to the support of his later wife, Salme Pekkala, an early member of the Finnish left, and an acquaintance of Lenin. Dutt was used throughout the 1930s as the mouthpiece of the leadership of the Communist International within the British party, justifying each twist and turn in Comintern policy, as the International required.

Support for Harry Pollitt and Rajani Palme Dutt came in the mid-1920s from a layer of talented and largely middle-class Communists. They included Tom Wintringham the novelist, Robin Page Arnot, later the historian of the miners' union, Esmond Higgins, Rose Cohen and Salme Dutt. Robin Page Arnot and Rose Cohen had worked together in the Fabian Research Department, which became the Labour Research Department (LRD). This was also Palme Dutt's background, and even Harry Pollitt was given a post on the executive of the LRD between 1923 and 1935.[29] Although they are now less well-known than their counterparts in the 1930s, there was an early milieu of young bohemian Communists, who were radicalised by the pre-war labour unrest and took part in the fight against the First World War.

Some of the character of these rare middle-class Communists can be seen by looking at the three Communist MPs of the 1920s. The first was the curious figure of Lt-Col. C. J. Malone, a National Liberal MP who was won over by the experience of seeing Russia in revolt in 1919, and was afterwards a Communist MP for two years, and then sat with Labour. The second Communist in Parliament, Walter Newbold, did not last there even as long as Malone. Although an open member of the CP, Newbold was elected as a Labour candidate at Greenock in 1922, and remained in Parliament for less than a year. At this stage, individual CP membership of the Labour Party was still tolerated. Thomas Bell described Newbold as 'an eccentric individual with a Quaker upbringing–entirely unsuited for communist work. He went almost unkempt and unshaven, wearing a dirty collar and clothes, trying to look "proletarian"!' Beneath the aggressive contempt that was often hurled at renegade former members, there was may have been some truth in Bell's description. Newbold was a man of letters better suited to research than to sustained parliamentary agitation. The third Communist MP was Shapurji Saklatvala, the subject of a recent biography by Marc Wadsworth. 'Comrade Sak' was originally nominated by a Labour association and elected at Battersea in 1922. He was then expelled from the Labour Party, and stood again for Battersea as a Communist in 1924 and won, retaining the seat until 1929. Saklatvala had been born into a rich Bombay merchant family, and was a devout Parsee as well as a Communist. Indeed he drew criticism from members of the party for having had his children initiated into his family religion, at a public ceremony in Westminster.[30]

In the 1920s relatively few writers or intellectuals became Communists. Many of those who joined the party quickly left, while others (although tempted) never quite signed up. Harold Laski described the Russian Revolution as 'the greatest even in history since the Reformation', yet remained a prominent member of the Labour Party. The philosopher Bertrand Russell was another who sided with the Russian Communists, but not with British Bolshevism. 'The Russian Revolution is one of the great heroic events of world history ... Bolshevism deserves the gratitude and admiration of all the progressive part of mankind', he declared, but Russell also argued that there was no chance of a similar event taking place in Britain.[31]

International

From its inception, the Communist Party was proud to be a constituent member of the Communist International. National CPs agreed that the International should be based on democratic centralism, that decisions should be discussed and voted at the centre, and that the International Communist movement should act as one united force. The twenty-one Conditions of membership originally presented by Leon Trotsky and adopted at the Second Congress of the Comintern were intended to guard against the reformist dilution of the new Communist Parties. Communists could see the example of the Second International, where despite instances of collective discussion, individual parties had in practice been left to adopt policies free of central guidance. The result had been a continuous process of accommodation to the capitalist system, which culminated in 1914, when most of the socialist parties capitulated to nationalism and supported their own rulers in the First World War. By contrast, the relative centralisation within the International was originally a source of strength to the Communist Party of Great Britain. The revolutionaries gathered in Moscow had behind them the experiences of many years' revolutionary struggle. Lenin's insistence on serious parliamentary work, and the Comintern theory of the United Front, led the young CPGB both away from its early ultra-leftism and towards the mainstream of British workers. Stuart MacIntyre describes the tone of Lenin's meetings with Willie Gallacher and J. T. Murphy, at the Second Congress of the International in 1920:

In his dealing with the British delegates ... Lenin scrupulously avoided making use of his own authority and spent long hours in patient discussion – he thought it far more important to convince them of the efficacy of a style of Communist politics than to impose this or that decision upon them, for unless they shared an appreciation of the reasons for following a particular course of action, they would be incapable of implementing it properly.[32]

The easy and informal style of these early meetings stands in marked contrast with the subsequent formal and unequal relations between King Street and Moscow.

As Kevin McDermott has argued, the original problem with the democratic centralism of the Comintern lay in the unequal relationship between the teacher and the pupil. In Russia, the Bolsheviks had organised a successful workers' revolution, while in Britain, revolutionary forces were small and insignificant. It would have required real cheek for Murphy or Gallacher or any other British Communist to contradict revolutionaries of the standing of Zinoviev or Bukharin, let alone Lenin or Trotsky. Not surprisingly, the British party was noted from 1920 for its willingness to take orders. Indeed the German Communist, Teddy Thälmann, recorded in 1926 that the Communist Party of Great Britain was 'the only major party which had no difference with the Executive of the Comintern'.[33] Over time the inequality of political experience could have been solved, if only the British party had grown, and if the Russian Revolution had remained a real workers' democracy. But the pupil had no time to learn from the teacher, before the teacher itself had changed. By 1924 Lenin was dead, the hoped-for German October had failed, and in Russia the working class had been destroyed by foreign intervention and civil war. In this new situation, the function of the Russian party was transformed. The Soviet Communist Party with its cadres engaged in production, entrenched in their power and able to pass on their privileges, became a reactionary force, first holding back Russian workers, and then turning on them after 1928.

The degeneration of the British Communist Party is often described as a one-way process, in which British Communists meekly accepted the latest dictates of the International. Cold War historians have made great play of the sums received from Moscow, pointing out for example that the Communist International gave the British party £5,000 in 1924 and £16 000 in 1925. Such sums were considerably more than the party received in dues from its own members.[34] From this, it is argued that the CPGB was a mere plaything of Soviet policy. Although such impressions may be broadly correct, there was more unevenness than the simple model of CP subservience to Moscow would suggest. In truth, the International line often found local supporters in the branches, who would be motivated by local or personal concerns. Also, it should be recognised that there were elements of a two-way direction to the process. Members of the CPGB played a role within the middle-levels of the Communist International. Such figures as J. T. Murphy achieved positions within the International and their resistance was weaker when decisions which they had shaped later rebounded against them.

Many of the leading cadres of the British party were sent by the Communist International to assist in the building of Communist Parties throughout the world. Tom Mann and Peggy Garman were both in China in 1926 and 1927, at the time of the Shanghai uprising. Here, the International imposed on the Chinese Communist Party the notion that the Kuomintang was a 'bloc of four classes', including some workers as well as the native bourgeoisie, and hence that it must be supported uncorditionally in the struggle for national liberation. The Chinese Communist Party backed the Kuomintang, even as it butchered the Communist-led workers' movement. In effect, the Chinese Communists voted for their own destruction. Mann later expressed doubts about events in China, but both he and Gorman did play a role in legitimising a wretched Comintern policy.

Harry Pollitt was in Germany in July 1921, May 1923, July 1924 and December 1924. Although neither of his biographers mention it, his papers also include a letter which refers to his time at the Lenin School in Moscow. Indeed in 1956, Pollitt claimed to have visited Moscow 'fifty times' since 1921. J. T. Murphy was in Russia for most of the 1920s, and proposed the resolution expelling Trotsky from the Executive Committee of the International. Murphy was also on the directorate of the Lenin school which trained cadres to defend a very Stalinised version of Bolshevism. Harry Wicks was also sent to the Lenin school – although he drew the exact opposite lessons from his time in Russia and became an early British Trotskyist.[35] Perhaps more positively, the CPGB established a Colonial Committee in 1925 to coordinate the party's anti-imperialist work, and as John Callaghan has shown, its members were played an important part in setting up a significant Communist Party in India in 1927. Previous attempts had been to form an Indian party, but it was only after this initiative that a permanent organisation was established.[36]

The effects of the internal changes within the Communist International were catastrophic in Britain, and provide a major theme through this and the following chapters. As the International degenerated, so the first pressure on the British party was to the right. Rather than seeing the Minority Movement as a bridge towards a unity between Labour and Communist workers on the shop-floor, industrial militants in the CPGB were encouraged to see it as an alliance between ordinary workers and left-wing trade union bureaucrats. The whole emphasis of Communist Party industrial policy was changed. Independent organisation was limited and the importance of workers' self-activity was downplayed. Following the 1924 Trades Union Congress at Hull, an Anglo-Russian committee of TUC and Russian Trade Union leaders was set up. The slogan 'All Power to the General Council' acquired greater and greater prominence. The previous demand to reform the General Council, so that it would become the military command of the labour movement, was shelved. The argument was put instead that TUC lefts were already leading the British working class towards a new and revolutionary era of struggle.

The party's approach towards the Labour Party leadership changed in much the same way. A National Left-Wing Movement was set up to copy inside the Labour Party, the work of the Minority Movement within the trade unions. Criticisms of Ramsay MacDonald and the Labour leadership were downplayed. A minority of leading party members began to argue that the Left-Wing Movement could form the basis of a new party, a ginger group just slightly to the left of Labour. Their suggestion was that there was no need for the independent politics of the CP. Jack Murphy and Rajani Palme Dutt clashed over this question in 1925, with Murphy going so far as to recommend the dissolution of the British Communist Party.[37] The results of this rightward shift were to be felt during the General Strike 1926. Yet before the party could get there, it first went through the difficult experience of two years of sustained red scares.

Despite the efforts of Labour leaders to distance themselves from the Communist Party, the jingo press remained convinced that the party's Moscow connection was somehow Labour's weak link. There were three major occasions on which the press, the Tories and the establishment attempted to exploit red shock stories. The first came in the summer of 1924, when the party was accused of fomenting mutiny among British troops; the second came later in the same year, with the publication of the fraudulent 'Zinoviev Letter'. On 25 July 1924, the *Workers' Weekly* published an open letter to the armed forces, encouraging the 'workers in uniform' to 'form committees in every barracks, aerodrome or ship', and concluding with the words, 'Turn your weapons on your oppressors!' This appeal came quite out of the blue, there was no sustained agitation which preceded it, and the article may well have been intended to challenge prosecution. Rajani Palme Dutt, the editor of the *Workers' Weekly*, was absent at the time, and the acting editor was J. R. Campbell, a war veteran who had been wounded on active service. Whatever the party's intention, Campbell was arrested and charged under the Incitement to Mutiny Act of 1795. The party responded creatively to the charges. Threatening to question the Labour Prime Minister Ramsay MacDonald on a similar appeal he had issued in 1912, the CP received the support of a large minority of Labour MPs and the charges were dropped.[38]

The second important red scare came in the winter of the same year. The Conservative and Liberal MPs in the Commons responded to the dropping of the charges against the CP by blaming Labour, and the Opposition combined to bring down the government. In the election which followed, the Labour Party was described as the prisoner of the Communists. Winston Churchill claimed that Labour was ready to 'shake hands with murder'. In an atmosphere tinged with fear and no little paranoia, the Tory press published a letter, apparently written by Zinoviev for the Communist International, urging his British comrades to make ready for insurrection and civil war. The Zinoviev Letter was a clear forgery, probably manufactured by the British secret services, but it certainly fitted well with the Tory campaign which employed the obvious slogan, 'A vote for Labour is a vote for Bolshevism'. In response to the smears, the Labour vote rose, but many Liberals returned to the Tory fold, giving the Conservatives a large majority.[39] The third red scare came in October 1925 when around thirty detectives raided the London offices of the Communist Party. Twelve prominent Communists were arrested and accused of conspiracy, including Tom Bell, editor of *Communist Review*, Albert Inkpin, the party secretary, Harry Pollitt, general secretary of the National Minority Movement, and William Rust of the Young Communist League. All twelve were found guilty, and when they turned down the chance to be bound over, the judge sentenced each of these leading Communists to between six and twelve months in jail.[40]

Even if the Labour and the Liberal members of Parliament were hurt by these slanders, the Communist Party was not. The period from 1924 to 1926 represented the CP's most successful years to date. Membership rose from 5000 in June 1925 to 6000 ten months later, and 10 730 in October 1926. The number of factory branches was put at 316. A record 883 delegates attended the Minority Movement conference in March 1926, claiming to represent 957 000 workers. In terms of its size, the party was now at a first peak. The party also launched the National Left-Wing Movement, to campaign within the Labour Party. At the 1926 conference of this body, it was recorded that 65 groups had been established, the largest number being in London, Scotland and Yorkshire. Sixty Communists took part in the 1926 Conference of the Labour Party. The CPGB's strongest support was still restricted to a few marginal areas, the 'Little Moscows' of East Fife, the Vale of Leven and the Rhondda.[41] Yet, with the inception of the National Minority Movement, the party could develop its support within the unions. Standing as a loyal opposition, represented within the Labour movement, building the unions from below, party activists were well positioned to benefit from any large struggles to come.

General Strike

The years 1924–26 remained a time of industrial downturn. The number of strikes was falling, and the ones which did occur were typically defensive. Despite this, the employers' offensive did have the effect of radicalising workers to the left, as can be seen in the high Labour vote of 1924 and in the Communist Party's growth between 1924 and 1926. There was also a small increase in trade union membership between 1923 and 1925. This radicalisation reached its zenith with the 1926 General Strike in support of the miners. The role of the Communist Party before and during the heroic period of the General Strike has attracted criticism especially from Trotskyist historians, including Pearce and Woodhouse.[42] Their argument is that the Comintern, dominated by the rising Stalinist bureaucracy, pressurised the Communist Party into developing an all-too friendly relationship with left-wingers on the TUC General Council including Alonzo Swales of the Engineers, George Hicks of the Building Trade Workers and Alfred Purcell, leader of the Furniture Workers. This was sealed by the visit in 1924 of a Soviet delegation to the TUC conference which established the Anglo-Russian Trade Union Committee. Under pressure from the Comintern to maintain a good relationship with the Labour and Trade Union leadership in Britain, the Communist Party fell into the trap of supporting the leadership of the TUC uncritically in the General Strike. The slogan 'All Power to the General Council' thus disarmed the members of the unions, when after nine days the TUC

General Council called off the strike. Thus the hostility of the union leaders combined with the failure of the Communist Party to build as a rival pole of attraction, leaving the miners to go down to bitter defeat nine months later.

Much of the debate rests on the relationship between the Communist Party and the left-wing officials at the top of the trade union movement. The suggestion made is that in the run-up to the strike, the party's agitational literature did not take bureaucracy seriously. No distinction was made between such figures as A. J. Cook, a revolutionary trade unionist and a former member of the Communist Party, and Hicks or Purcell, left-wing bureaucrats on the TUC General Council with a temporary sympathy for the Russian state. Thus the sixth plenum of the Comintern Executive exaggerated the radical character of the Anglo-Russian committee, describing it as 'a new stage in the history of the international trade union movement ... it demonstrates the practical possibility of creating a unified International, and of a common struggle of workers of different political tendencies against reaction, fascism and the capitalist offensive.' Within the CPGB, Rajani Palme Dutt's editorials in *Labour Monthly* presented the TUC General Council as 'a leadership which is approaching more and more full recognition of the class struggle.'[43]

Despite Communist rhetoric, the TUC lefts were not a revolutionary force. Swales and the others first came to prominence as a group only in 1924, as the advent of the first Labour government shifted the balance of power within the General Council. Right-wing union leaders like Jimmy Thomas, Bondfield and Gosling were taken into MacDonald's government, and it was only in their absence that the TUC acquired a new verbal militancy. Alonzo Swales addressed the 1925 Trades Union Congress, calling for 'a militant and progressive policy, consistently and steadily pursued ... there cannot be any community of interest between the working class and the capitalist class.' Yet this Scarborough Congress barely contributed towards the organisation of a campaign. Apart from Swales and Cook, no other member of the General Council spoke in the debates. No attempt was made to arm the movement for the battles which were to come.[44]

Real preparations were desperately needed. The miners had already suffered deep wage cuts, with their average weekly wages falling from 90 shillings in 1921, to 48 shillings and sixpence, by 1925. So the miners' pay had already fallen by an average of 50 per cent, and now employers demanded further wage cuts of between 10 and 25 per cent. When miners were first locked-out to enforce this threat, the leaders of the road and rail unions responded by promising to support their fellow workers. On Red Friday, 31 July 1925, the Conservative government stepped into the breach, offering the coal-owners a nine-month subsidy if they withdrew their threat. Despite this important working-class victory, neither side believed the final contest had come. Arthur Cook the miners' leader, warned the readers of the Left-Wing Movement's paper, the *Sunday Worker*, that another fight would be needed to prevent the wage cuts, while the government and the mine owners responded by setting up an Organisation for the Maintenance of Supplies (OMS), to co-ordinate their response to any mass strike.

There is a mythic image of the General Strikes, which has been cultivated in the press and the popular memory. Stories abound of peaceful constitutional protest and policemen playing football with strikers. Somehow, these images are seen to reflect a national myth – that Britain has been a peaceful country, where conflict has always been resolved by compromise, and wars and domestic strife have been avoided. Keith Laybourn's history of the General Strike goes out of its way to insist that the conflict had no origins, and few consequences. Any struggle was a blip. In his words, 'Strike activity was declining during the early 1920s and there is ample evidence that the employers and trade unionists were actively involved in reducing the levels of industrial conflict from about 1916 onwards.'[45] It is quite true to say that some trade unionists were working to reduce the levels of conflict – but why was conciliation needed? In a situation of escalating conflict, it is more plausible to suggest that the leaders of the movement determined to restrain the activity of their members.

Despite the occasional sepia-coloured myths that have been passed down to us, the General Strike which finally broke out in May 1926 saw society divided overwhelmingly along class lines. The working-class response was solid. Two and a half million workers struck for the first eight days, and were then joined by a further million workers including engineers and ship builders on day nine. In each area Trades Councils were responsible for ensuring that local union branches kept to the General Council's instructions. A TUC communiqué reported the extent of working-class support, 'We have from all over the country reports that have surpassed all our expectations. Not only the railwaymen and transport men, but all other trades came out in a manner we did not expect immediately. The difficulty of the General Council has been to keep men in what we might call the second line of defence rather than call them out.'[46]

The support of workers for the General Strike was extraordinary. Less than 0.4 per cent of London firemen reported to work. Even with the assistance of OMS, no rail company managed to run more than 8 per cent of its freight or 20 per cent of its passenger trains. Four national unions, including the transport workers and the steel workers' unions, were bankrupted by their support for the strike. Meanwhile, the propertied classes also mobilised *en masse*. Four hundred thousand people volunteered to oppose the strike, and 200 000 special constables were sworn in. Cambridge students attempted to work the London docks, while car owners were sent to the Horse Guards Parade. Even members of the British Fascisti, led by Rotha Lintorn-Orman, were allowed to join OMS, in semi-militarised fascist brigades.

Although the large majority of workers remained solidly behind the strike, and indeed the numbers taking part grew daily, the Labour Party and the TUC General Council decided to end their support on the ninth day. Beatrice Webb described the strike as 'a proletarian distemper which had to run its course'. Ramsay MacDonald's ally Philip Snowden sneered at 'the futility and foolishness of such a trial of strength'. Within the leadership of the Trades Union Congress, Ernest Bevin claimed that 'there was uneasiness among the men who were entitled to pensions and superannuations'. More convincingly, Charles Dukes of the General and Municipal Workers Union told a 1926 special congress of the TUC that the real reason the strike was ended was to prevent the control of the movement being taken by the rank and file, 'Every day the authority was passing into the hands of men who had no authority and no control.'[47]

While the strike continued, the ordinary members of the Communist Party of Great Britain took part to the full. In Jeffrey Skelley phrase, the party's activists played a role 'out of all proportion to their numbers'. At a local level, they were the backbone of the movement, 'Wherever the Councils of Action were most effective, wherever the local strike was most solid, there a knot of CP members was usually to be found in the thick of it.' Members of the CPGB provided the activists and local leaders who held the movement together at a local level. The militant London busworkers remained out for two days after the official ending of the strike; here it was Communists who helped glue the strike together. In Battersea, Oxford, Edinburgh and elsewhere, members of the party were represented on the Councils of Action. The best evidence of the party's involvement is the attitude of the British police. Over 1200 Communists, or around one quarter of the party's pre-strike membership, were arrested for taking part in the events. Indeed an individual member of the Communist Party was more than 200 times more likely to be arrested in May 1926 than their contemporary within the Labour Party.[48]

Despite the activism of the party's members, the CP was caught off guard when the strike ended, and unable to provide any means of continuing support for the miners once the TUC had caved in. In the run-up to the strike, party literature refrained from even fraternal criticism of such TUC lefts as Purcell and Swales. The party's manifesto, *The Political Meeting of the General Strike*, emphasised only the demands of the Miners' Federation, including nationalisation and the replacement of the Tories with a Labour government. A March 1926 statement on the Royal Commission Report identified the danger of the TUC selling out, but warned only of the TUC right, 'a small number of Labour leaders who are so obsessed with the ideas of uniting all classes and speaking of the interests of the "community as a whole" that they fail to defend the workers they represent.'[49] The party saw no danger that the lefts too could sell out.

After the strike ended, the party quickly produced a leaflet, 'Stand by the Miners!'. It responded to the betrayal with anger, 'The General Council's decision to call off the General Strike is the greatest crime that has ever been permitted, not only against the miners, but against the working class of Britain and the whole world.' The leaflet assigned 'direct responsibility' to the Rights on the General Council, but noted that 'most of the so-called Left Wing have been no better than the Right.' Shortly afterwards, Willie Gallacher, Wal Hannington and other leading Communists issued a joint declaration, stating that 'the events of 1926 have shown that Purcell, Hicks and Bromley were only with the miners while it was a question of phrases and resolutions ... When the crisis came they ran away.' All these criticisms of the TUC lefts were justified – but the party had prepared nothing before the end of the strike to counter the betrayal. Important local activists such as Peter Kerrigan, one of the leaders of the Glasgow Committee, admit to having 'never thought' that the strike might be called off. For D. A. Wilson, a delegate on Bradford Trades Council, the news was also a 'surprise'. Even national figures, Jack Murphy, Tommy Jackson and George Hardy of the Minority Movement, record similar astonishment.[50]

How did the members of the British Communist Party respond to the suggestion that they had failed to prepare the movement for its betrayal by the TUC? Often, when historians raise such criticisms of a previous generation, they take the risk of lapsing into anachronism. It is far too easy to say 'we know better', without finding anyone at the time who thought the same. Not so in this case – the charge of failure was levelled at the time, by members of the Comintern. Tom Bell replied for the leadership of the British Communist Party at a meeting of the Executive Committee of the Communist International (ECCI) in June 1926.

> There is criticism from some quarters that our Party has not properly understood the left wing, that we have not criticised it and that we have been under illusions as to the role the left wing would play in times of crisis. As a matter of fact the Party discussed this question of the left last year and issued a manifesto explaining that the left wing and the leftists, are always to be found hesitant, timid, hysterical, weak and cowardly, when face to face with a real crisis. Our Party have clearly understood that in our campaign for promoting the Minority Movement, these left wing leaders would in all probability betray us in a crisis.[51]

If the party had been so well prepared, then why did so many leading Communists express their surprise at the news of the betrayal? If the Communists had successfully separated themselves from the left-wing of the General Council of the TUC, then why did they march under the slogan of 'All Power to the General Council'? If Tom Bell's explanation to the International appears evasive now, it can hardly have played much better at the time. The one genuine explanation Bell could have used to explain the debacle – that the tactics of 1926 came from Moscow, and they had failed – was the one explanation that he would not use then.

For Pearce and Woodhouse and other left critics of the Communist Party, it is the failure of the CP to differentiate itself from the TUC lefts which deserves greatest criticism. The leading members of the party were drawn from a milieu of trade union militants with many years' experience of working with such lefts at the top of the trade union machinery. At the start of the decade, the party's industrial propaganda made a serious attempt to educate new members in the experience which these older comrades had learned. A mistrust of the machinery is one of the oldest principles of militant trade unionism. Yet at the moment when such lessons needed to be remembered most clearly, and under advice from Stalin, Tomsky and Zinoviev in Moscow, the leaders of the Communist Party forgot the lessons of their own previous activity. The party's failure to offer an alternative pole of resistance was not inevitable. If the Communists had persuaded a layer of workers that such a betrayal was possible, if indeed the party had retained a stronger independent base within the trade union movement, then more pressure would have come from below, and a different final outcome might have been achieved by the movement.

Pearce and Woodhouse's case can certainly be criticised in parts. They almost suggest that a revolution was possible in Britain in 1926. Yet although the General Strike did challenge the institutions of British capital, the strike did not constitute a revolutionary situation. The control of the strike remained at the top of the labour movement, with each union calling out its own members. There was little co-ordination at the local level, the first meeting between different Councils of Action took place after the strike had been called off. Indeed one reason for the strike's premature end was precisely the General Council's fear that if the strike continued, the leaders would lose control of their members, and a more revolutionary situation could develop.[52] Despite this criticism, the important points of the Trotskyist argument remain otherwise vindicated. The CPGB was set up as a revolutionary party. Its aim was to convince workers that they had the power to change society. The Communists failed to distinguish themselves from the TUC lefts. The role played by the party was inadequate.

A number of historians, including Chris Wrigley and Keith Laybourn, have recently suggested that the consequences of trade union defeat in 1926 were limited. G. A. Philips writes that 'the reverses of this year simplified a previous ambivalence, without giving birth to new values.'[53] The common argument is that the number of strikes was already falling before the General Strike was declared. Therefore nothing changed. The point that these accounts miss is the enormous psychological blow that people suffered in 1926. Five years of small losses had already encouraged lethargy within the movement. This terrible, symbolic defeat made the demoralisation much worse. In the immediate aftermath of the strike, large numbers of militants were victimised, and many union branches were forced to call their members back out just to secure re-employment on the old terms. Over the next decade, trade union membership declined, and most important for Communists sensitive to working-class confidence, strikes fell in 1927 to the lowest figure since records began in 1891. Thanks also to the consequences of the Depression, strike figures were to remain at historically low levels until the mid-1930s. As important for the British party was the new situation within the Comintern after 1928. All the national sections of the International were presented with a new analysis which required a sharp turn to the left in the practice and rhetoric of the parties.

Left turn

Class against Class, or the 'Third Period' of 1929 –34 is widely accepted as a disaster for the international Communist movement. In describing Social Democratic parties as 'social fascists', the Communists separated themselves from the majority of ordinary workers. Through applying this formula to the German socialists in the SPD, the Comintern prevented united working-class resistance to fascism and thus effectively paved the way for the rise of Adolf Hitler. In most countries including Britain, Communist parties suffered from a haemorrhaging of support. Membership of the Communist Party of Great Britain fell from a high point of 10 730 members in autumn 1926 to 2724 in 1930. Yet the British party suffered less extreme disruption in terms of expulsion and vilification of 'rightist' leaders than many other parties. The survival of the leadership may well be due to the ability of figures including Harry Pollitt and Willie Gallacher to sense where Comintern functionaries would turn next. Franz Borkenau observes that the 'submission to Moscow' of Tom Bell, Albert Inkpin and other figures from the Communist Party's founding generation did at least avoid 'a complete break-up of the traditional leadership.'[54]

Mike Squires has argued that the Third Period was as much a product of British Communist desire as Comintern policy. Andrew Thorpe has made a similar claim, as part of his general argument that the changing politics of the British Communist Party were formulated by local leaders, according to local sentiment, as local conditions determined.[55] Clearly there were some activists who responded to the new turn with real enthusiasm. It seems that both Shapurji Saklatvala and Harry Pollitt were calling for a left turn some years before this became party policy between spring 1928 and autumn 1929. Saklatvala was motivated by his experience as a Member of Parliament, which convinced him that the Labour Party was now just another bosses' party. As early as 1925, he suggested that 'the real political crusade for Socialism has been abandoned by the Labour Party. Therefore only the Communist Party must now set itself up as the only anti-capitalist party.' By October 1927, Robin Page Arnot could describe the Labour Party Conference as 'a further stage in silent coalition with the bourgeoisie'. Allen Hutt was just one of several young London comrades who championed the new politics in 1928 and 1929. According to Hutt, the new line meant 'a new independence for the Communist Party both in political and economic struggles', and if it was delayed then this was due to the conservatism of his own party's leadership which had now been in place now for nearly ten years.[56]

Others were motivated by the changing mood within the Labour Party. As already mentioned, the National Left-Wing Movement held its foundation meeting in September 1926. The movement's paper, the *Sunday Worker*, was popular among Labour Party members looking for an alternative to MacDonald's leadership. The miners' leader A. J. Cook was a regular contributor. The paper soon achieved a circulation of 100 000 copies. Yet after the failure of the General Strike, the Labour leadership turned with new energy against Communist sympathisers within its own ranks. In 1927, eleven members of the Communist Party were banned from attending the Labour Party conference. The 1928 conference demanded that local associations should sign a 'loyalty clause'. In the same year, a national referendum within the Boilermakers' Society voted by three to one to deny Harry Pollitt and Aitken Ferguson the right to act as union delegates at TUC and Labour Party meetings. By 1929, twenty-six local Labour Parties had been expelled. The status of the National Left-Wing Movement naturally changed. Many Labour lefts chose to cut their ties. Meanwhile, Rajani Palme Dutt in Brussels fell victim to the strange illusion that the Left-Wing Movement was about to cut its ties to the CP. He described one editorial in the *Sunday Worker* as 'the definitive proclamation of the Leftwing as a new political party'.[57] The movement was chided for its decision to publish a separate manifesto alongside Labour and Communist brochures in Northampton. In 1929, the National Left-Wing Movement was finally closed down. In an atmosphere heavy with suspicion, it is not surprising that many ordinary Communists despaired of the Labour Party turning left, nor indeed that these young activists saw the new line as a genuine response to the experiences which they had lived through.

Although some younger comrades were enthusiastic, they did not initiate the new line. Thomas Bell's official history of the party insists that the decisive impetus came from the International, 'The tactical line of "Class against Class" was adopted not only for the British Communist Party, but was applied to a series of countries such as France and the Scandinavian countries, where social-democratic traditions were still strong in the Communist Parties.'[58] Indeed Bell is an important figure, as he was responsible for liaising with the Executive

Committee of the Communist International (ECCI). He told the February 1929 meeting of the ECCI how difficult it was to implement their advice. The following report was sent back to Moscow.

Our Party, like a number of other sections of the CI, is going through a testing time, our Party is trying to adjust itself to its new line in a very difficult period. Undoubtedly it is a far cry say, from Moscow to London, but it is not a far cry from WEB [the Comintern's Western European Bureau in Berlin] to London. I think it is necessary that the WEB should be instructed to insure [sic] that there is some daily contact with the Party.[59]

In Britain, the new line was introduced against the open resistance of such leading Communists as Wal Hannington of the National Unemployed Workers' Movement and Arthur Horner of the South Wales Miners' Federation. Horner was threatened with expulsion for his opposition to the new tactics. Robin Page Arnot sent the following message from Berlin: 'group to demand publicly his submission and repudiation [of] his opportunist mistaken opportunist line [–] can his expulsion be considered?' Wal Hannington showed real mettle in backing Horner against the threats of his critics. Eventually, Horner agreed to visit Moscow, to receive political education in the new line. He returned to admit that he had been wrong – and loyally intoned that Labour was the greatest enemy facing the trade union movement.[60] Other prominent Communists including Albert Inkpin were won round to the new policy, but only with deep reservations. In short, the Third Period was opposed by precisely those figures who had most experience of building mass campaigns.

So whatever the popularity of Class against Class among some younger Communists, the fact remains that the introduction of the policy was decided by external factors. Stalin's break with Bukharin and his 'Right' bloc in the Kremlin was justified in terms of a politics which claimed that global capitalism had now entered into a new period of deep crisis. This 'Third Period' line became policy across every Communist Party in the world. It was argued by members of the Comintern apparatus and their local supporters, always with vigour, and their speeches were often accompanied by expulsions of the critics. Those historians who find local factors to explain the shift are arguing – in effect – that every single Communist Party, just happened by coincidence to make exactly the same shift at the same time. This 'explanation' is profoundly implausible.

The politics of Class against Class had disastrous consequences in Britain. The Communist Party's election literature sneered at Labour, describing it as 'the third Capitalist party. It lays claim to the title of Socialist party, but has nothing to do with Socialism.' The tactics of the Third Period led to a complete reversal in the party's industrial policy. The CP leadership now demanded the formation of new unions in place of the old reformist shells. Losovsky outlined the new perspective in an article for the paper of the Red International of Labour Unions, 'It must always be kept in mind that the reformist organisations are tools in the hands of the bourgeois state and the employers' organisations to crush the revolutionary wing of the Labour movement and to enslave the broad proletarian movement.' Factory committees were to be created, while the Minority Movement was supposed to become a revolutionary alternative to the TUC.

The August 1929 Sixth Annual Conference of the Movement insisted that the best workers were outside the unions, and demanded 'unity between employed and unemployed workers, between organised and unorganised.' Workers inside the reformist unions were written off. 'Independent leadership' became the slogan, at a time when the rank and file was still reeling from the defeat of 1926. By 1930, the size of the Minority Movement had shrunk to just 700 subs-paying members. It was no longer anything more than a memory. In James's Hinton's words, 'the perspectives of "class against class" marked the demolition of the framework of organisation and activity carefully constructed in association with non-party militants. The isolation of the Communist Party from the bulk of the organised working-class movement reached its culmination.'[61] The first moment of opportunity had been lost.

It is appropriate to end this chapter by asking if the ultra-leftism of 1929 was an inevitable return to the habits of the pre-war British revolutionary left. Walter Newbold knew Pollitt and Gallacher before 1918 when they were both ultra-lefts. He suggested that the sectarianism of Class against Class was merely a return to the natural reflexes of this generation of militants, the revenge of the anti-parliamentary instincts of Sylvia Pankhurst and her old admirers like Gallacher:

> Men and women may be persuaded to abandon their rooted preconceptions ... . But they do not become able thereby to adapt their methods of thinking and acting from which they had deliberately swung away and to which they had sprung back without spontaneity.[62]

From this argument it would follow that the CP was always doomed to irrelevance by some British variant of original revolutionary sin. Workers will never fight, revolution is impossible. In Britain, workers simply don't do things that way.

The argument of this chapter has been different. We have suggested that the original leaders of the Communist Party made an impressive and sustained attempt to escape from the mistakes of the pre-war left. While the Russian Revolution was on the rise, such figures as Tom Bell, J. T. Murphy and Willie Gallacher benefited from the experience of a generation of successful revolutionaries in Russia. Old ideas about the self-activity of the working class were taken off the shelves, dusted down, and thought anew. Habits of isolation were lost. Lenin's advice, in particular, was crucial to winning the young British party to a policy of careful work with socialists inside the Labour Party. After 1924, however, Comintern instructions ceased to play such a positive role. Indeed by 1926, the assistance of the Comintern had become downright destructive. Turning from left to right and back, the British Communist Party was unable to offer any consistent alternative to Labour's reformist politics. Although at the decade's end, the CPGB remained a workers' party, the elements of its later degeneration were all in place.

2
The Zig-Zag Left: 1928–39

At the end of the 1920s, the Communist Party embarked on a destructive shift leftwards. In its policy, the party claimed that the main obstacle to revolution came from other forces within the workers' movement. The Labour Party and the trade unions constituted 'social fascism', an 'auxiliary apparatus of the bourgeoisie', which cheated the workers away from revolution. In 1929 it was announced that 'the Labour Government has already begun to show its Social–Fascist character', which was illustrated by Labour's policy of 'Fascism and violent suppression of the working class'. In its ultra-left practice, the Communist Party isolated itself from ordinary workers within the trade union and labour movement. The party attempted to implement its new politics in industry, through championing break-away red unions, although the unions formed in this way both failed. As Noreen Branson's official history of the party records, 'The trade union leaders had tried to destroy the party; ironically "Class against Class" made their job much easier.'[1] The fruits of its first ten years of successful political and industrial agitation were thrown away, and the party declined until it had just two and a half thousand members in November 1930. It was by no means obvious that the Communist Party would survive to see the decade's end.

Yet from the early 1930s onwards, the party's practice began to change. New forms of activity were thought up, so that the party could find new contacts, and a new milieu in which to grow. Slowly, some of the sectarianism was toned down. By 1932, the party's leadership was acting almost in the spirit of the United Front, and for the next two years, the British Communist Party was practically back to the habits of the party's founders. From 1935, there was another change in the party line. The Popular Front was a dramatic shift rightwards, which transformed the whole way in which the party operated. One positive consequence was a large influx of new members. It was in the late 1930s that Communists built the base for the much larger party of the postwar years. Another result was a change in the goals of the organisation. In the place of revolutionary Marxism, the politics of the Popular Front stressed slow change, alliances with the middle classes and sections of the ruling class. In itself this new line took the Communist Party away from its original revolutionary politics, but the Popular Front also contained the additional distortion of loyalty to the Soviet state. It was the cumulative effect of these lurches, left and right, which established the character of British Communism, placing its leadership in the hands of a cadre incapable of seeing beyond the party line, and separating the Communist Party decisively from the creative possibilities of the party's early years.

Isolation and the new line

The new party line of the late 1920s distinguished itself from the earlier politics of the Communist Party in several ways. One of the most striking features of this period was the attempt to establish left unions in hostility to the existing structures of the workers' movement. The Communist Party encouraged a first breakaway from the Tailors' and Garment Workers' Union in March 1929. A second breakaway, the Scottish Mine Workers' Union, took place one year later. The story of the rival textile union which the Communist Party formed is especially instructive. First, a group of tailors went on strike at Rego Clothiers in Edmonton, London. The union executive refused to support the strike and sacked a leading London organiser, Sam Elsbury, who had supported the action, and who was also a member of the Central Committee of the British Communist Party. The United Clothing Workers Union then recruited in Edmonton and elsewhere. But the union had no money to support strikes, and so the CP attempted to fill the gap, recruiting directly with the promise that it would fund the dispute. Yet the Communists were a small party, they had their own cash crisis and were in uncertain receipt of Russian funds. Sam Elsbury was forced to criticise his own party for failing to deliver the promised support. By December he had been expelled from the Communist Party, and the new union was no more.[2]

By contrast, the Scottish Mine Workers' Union could claim to be the legitimate successor to the Fife Union, which collapsed when the existing secretary – a man called Adamson – refused to recognise his defeat in branch elections. The SMWU commanded minority support in Stirling and Ayr, and majority support in Fife. As a result, this union was more durable than the UCWU. Yet even the Scottish Mine Workers' Union only existed until 1935. It was isolated from the county unions and the miners' national federation. In an industry which prided itself on solidarity, the notion of separate organisation failed to impress non-CP activists. In textiles and mining, and in other industries, party members were seen by many workers as a divisive nuisance. The failure of these breakaways convinced some militants to hold back, and the new line was afterwards applied with more caution. But the damage was done, and the party's audience diminished.

The members of the Communist Party responded to their isolation by establishing themselves in a world-within-a-world, a total community cut off from the mainstream Labour movement which Communists saw as hopelessly corrupted by the degenerate politics of reformism. This safe Communist sub-world encompassed cafés and restaurants, such as the pro-Soviet Scala cinema in London's Charlotte Street, Henderson's 'Bomb Shop' which became Colletts bookstore, Communist Books in King Street, the Workers' bookshop in London's Farringdon Road, and the Clarion Café which survived in Manchester's Market Street until 1936. Communist Party socials and other events flourished. In the first week of January 1934 alone, there were party-run dances or Whist Drives organised by the League of Socialist Freethinkers, the Rebel Players, London Friends' of the Soviet Union, and the Federation of Student Societies. These were also the years which saw the first real growth in the Workers' Theatre Movement and the British Workers' Sports Federation. Secured in this way from the hostility of their audience, individual Communists could sustain themselves without needing to test their politics in the outside world.[3]

At the same time, the party also undertook to publish the *Daily Worker*, which began in 1930. The idea of a Communist daily had been suggested to the British comrades by Lenin as early as August 1921. With sense, Lenin insisted that 'if 2/3 workers do not pay special contributions for their paper – it will be no workers' paper'. Yet innumerable problems, the small size of the organisation and a lack of resources, had prevented the paper from being set up for 1926, when it would have been of real use. Instead, the daily paper was launched on New Year's Day 1930 on an unreal perspective of imminent revolutionary crisis. The Communist internal publication, *Party Life*, argued that events in the outside world were moving too fast, and weekly publications could not keep pace, 'Our party is too slow to mobilise itself in this situation let alone masses of workers ... The Daily is therefore a matter of life or death for the new era of revolutionary struggle ... It can and will knit the party into a quickly moving, highly politicised organisation which can, overnight, get together and punch 100% on the central question of each day.'[4] Despite the urgency of this perspective, the party was now at the nadir of its fortunes, while outside the Communist Party branches, strikes were at the lowest level since records began.

Lacking funds and experience, the journalists of the *Daily Worker* fought just to get their paper off the ground. One source describes the conditions which they worked under, 'Its first editor recalled producing an edition without electricity, typing articles by candlelight in an unheated office.' The party explicitly rejected the offer of assistance from journalists in its Fleet Street branch, with Palme Dutt writing in the *Communist Review* that 'Capitalist journalists – consciously or unconsciously – are *spiritual, ideological* agents of capitalism, in the same sense as clergymen. The trade and technique of capitalist journalists, as of capitalist politicians, is to lie.' The *Daily Worker* just about survived, largely thanks to a fund-raising campaign, which raised over nine thousand pounds in the first two years of the paper's existence.

Less optimistically, you could say that *Daily Worker* wasted party resources. There was an enormous difference between sustaining one (even two) weekly newspapers, and a single daily paper. The routine of the party journalists changed, the nature of their sources, even the practicalities of distribution. Unlike its Fleet Street competitors, the *Worker* could not take advertising, or not in sufficient quantities to cover the costs of publication. Harry Pollitt and Rajani Palme Dutt complained of the money that went into the paper. Perhaps half of all the finance then flowing into Britain from Moscow was spent on the new daily. Keith Laybourn and Dylan Murphy put the loss at £500 per week – a crippling debt.[5]

The paper's strength was its politics. Compared to the *Daily Herald*, the *Worker* contained a good number of serious feature articles and also took a strong interest in 'minority' issues, including women's politics. The first issue had on its women's page an article by Clara Robbins about a textile strike in Lancashire. In the conspiracy trials of the 1930s, the *Daily Worker* was a chief target for the authorities. In the paper's first year, one Communist was sentenced to 18 months hard labour for calling on troops to oppose British colonialism in India. When the *Daily Worker* took his side, its publishers were jailed for five, six and nine months each. The paper also played a key role in organising the unemployed. By 1939, the *Daily Worker* was selling an impressive 40 000 to 50 000 copies a day.[6] Compared to the sales with which the paper had begun, this was an extraordinary growth.

Despite the ultra-left politics of Third Period Stalinism, the Communist Party of Great Britain was not yet a lost cause. Local activists were desperate to build socialist organisation, and as we have seen, it was often the keenest and most active of party members who argued for the new Moscow line. One way in which these Communists squared the circle between their desire to fight and their isolation from the mass of trade unionists was by taking part in what you might call community campaigns. These were activities which could be built away from the world of work, and in environments where the party's ultra-leftism did not prove as catastrophic as it did in the trade unions.

One of these community campaigns was the trespass movement which began on April 24 1932. On that day, around six hundred ramblers and Young Communists walked from Hayfield, in Derbyshire, to Kinder Scout, a high plateau in the Peak district, roughly halfway between Manchester and Sheffield. On the way down, several of the marchers were arrested, and accused of assaulting a group of gamekeepers. The trial which resulted was a joke. Held in Derby, so that only the prosecution could afford to bring witnesses, the jury included two brigadier generals, three colonels, two majors and three captains, altogether eleven members of the land-owning class. One of the accused was said to possess a book by Lenin. Another was identified as having sold the *Daily Worker*. Eventually five defendants were found guilty, and sentenced to between two and six months in jail. After such a set-up, official walking groups were compelled to take sides, with the Ramblers' Federation protesting against the sentence. During the weeks of the trial, thousands of walkers illegally visited the route of the march. The British Workers' Sports Federation organised further mass demonstrations, at Abbey Brook in the Peaks, and Leith Hill in Surrey.[7]

Assessed critically, such community campaigns fitted with the politics of the Third Period. Relying on young workers and the unemployed, the party was insulated from the effects of its ultra-leftism. More positively, the party's ability to organise could also be seen as a sign of its continuing vitality. If the CP had already been the Stalinist puppet of Cold War mythology, then its members could not have intervened in these campaigns with the creativity which they did.

The best-known of these campaigns was the National Unemployed Workers' Movement (NUWM), set up by former engineer Wal Hannington, from an earlier series of campaigns of the unemployed.

Among these early movements was John Maclean's 'Tramp Trust Unlimited', five propagandists who toured Scotland in 1920–1, distributing up to 150 000 leaflets a time. Maclean refused to join the Communist Party, but Harry McShane did join in 1922, and led the Glasgow contingent on their 1932 hunger march to London. The centre of the agitation was in London, where an April 1921 meeting led to the formation of a national organisation, which became the NUWM.[8]

The unemployed workers' movement went into decline with the CP in the mid-1920s, but grew again in importance as unemployment rose from 1929 onwards. By November 1930, one third of the party's membership was unemployed. In the same year, the National Insurance Umpire agreed that the Movement was an association of the unemployed, with the same rights to represent its members as a trade union. From then on, officials would insist that NUWM members showed their identity cards, if they wanted representation. The movement gained an official place in the system. Many of the Communists who did this work were successful advocates on behalf of their members. They had a considerable knowledge of the system, and were confident to engage in the arguments. Unemployed workers with their representation were roughly twice as likely to win their appeals. The success of Movement full-timers was a powerful incentive to recruitment. The NUWM also grew after the introduction of the Family Means Test in November 1931. Under this humiliating measures, workers had to prove that their entire families were genuinely in need of assistance. If they could not, benefit would not be paid. Wal Hannington, the dominant personality within NUWM, suggested that the Means Test was an even worse attack on the unemployed than the 10 per cent cut in benefit which accompanied it.[9]

The NUWM was the greatest success of the CP in the years between the General Strike and the Popular Front. The National Unemployed Workers' Movement was a large, popular movement, which established a presence in people's lives. Its success kept the CP afloat through some difficult years, and made it easier for the party later to take on the forces of British fascism, a political movement which elsewhere depended on the support of the unemployed. Typically, however, the leaders of the British Communist Party came close to throwing away their own success. In October 1931, the Comintern Secretariat instructed the London comrades to 'Strengthen party faction in NUWM eliminating [its] separation and deviation from party line especially conciliatory attitude to the ILP.'[10] In 1932–33, the Central

Committee made a series of objections to the way in which Wal Hannington ran the NUWM. The suggestion was that the comrades in the NUWM were too willing to criticise the National Government – when they should turn their real fire on the class traitors among the Labour opposition. Hannington was eventually forced off the party's CC in 1933.[11] There was no permanent rift, but some pointless souring of the relationship.

The National Unemployed Workers' Movement grew to a peak of 50 000 subs-paying members in 1932, organised in 386 branches. The dues were necessary, if a real movement was to be established, and if the unemployed were to become part of an organised class force. A campaign was built up against the Unemployed Insurance Bill of 1934, the hated 'Slave Act', which recommended compulsory labour camps for the unemployed. Through the NUWM, the British Communist Party also organised a number of hunger marches, to raise the plight of the workless. There were five such national marches between 1929 and 1936. The 1934 march involved at least 700 people who marched from Glasgow sparking large regional demonstrations as they went. In January 1935, the government attempted to impose centralised means-testing. After 40 000 people marched in Sheffield, 20 000 in Glasgow, 12 000 in Coatbridge and 300 000 across South Wales, the government backed down. One consequence of the NUWM's work was the formation of the National Council of Civil Liberties, which was originally set up as a legal body campaigning on behalf of the many unemployed workers arrested by the police.

Ironically, of all the unemployed protests of the 1930s the best known today is the Jarrow Crusade, largely organised by 'Red' Ellen Wilkinson, the local Labour MP. This was one of the few protests which was not led by the CP. Communists and NUWM members gave active support to the Crusade, but did not take a prominent role on the platforms. That task were left to members of the Labour Party – although the national Labour leadership opposed Jarrow, and few local Labour Parties supported the Crusade. Indeed, when the march came to Chesterfield, even the trades council refused to back it. Otherwise, the National Unemployed Workers' Movement largely had the field to itself. The NUWM was the most successful body campaigning for the unemployed.[12]

Challenges – right and left

While the Communist Party of Great Britain underwent its left turn, events in broader society were working in a favourable direction. The

Wall Street Crash of 1929 and the subsequent Depression seem to bear out the Comintern's predictions that capitalism would soon enter a decisive period of crisis. The collapse of the second Labour government in 1931, with Prime Minister Ramsay MacDonald defecting to form a National Government, also seemed to fit Communist predictions. The party had warned that Labour and trade union leaders could not be trusted, and events seemed to prove the Communist Party correct. These were years in which the party should have grown rapidly. Yet the dismal record of Ramsay MacDonald's Labour government did not work in the Communists' favour. The sectarianism of Class against Class prevented the CP from reaping the rewards.

The total history of the General Strike, which saw first a rise in working-class consciousness, and then a defeat for the radical aspirations of the movement, had the effect of solidifying Labour's working-class support between 1926 and 1929. Labour's 1929 election manifesto promised wholesale nationalisation of the utilities and significant public works to combat unemployment, and the Labour vote rose to 8 400 000. Labour was thus able to form a second government with 287 MPs. Whatever hopes Labour voters had held were quickly dashed. Following the Wall Street crash, unemployment rose dramatically, from 1 433 000 at the time of the 1929 election, to 2 725 000 by December 1930. The recession threw millions of people out of work, and the state was obliged to borrow to pay for benefits. The government spent £2 million a day just on keeping sterling afloat. The crisis came to a head in August 1931. With Montagu Norman (the Governor of the Bank of England) demanding cuts, MacDonald came to the conclusion that the real cause of the crisis was neither the greed of the bankers, nor the chaos of their system, but the unwillingness of unemployed workers to pay for the crisis. He was prepared to cave into the banks but not the trade unions. MacDonald told the cabinet, 'If we yield now to the TUC, we shall never be able to call our bodies or souls or intelligences our own.' On 23 August, the cabinet voted 11–9 in favour of a 10 per cent cut in unemployment benefit. But the bankers had demanded a unanimous vote. When Ramsay MacDonald failed to obtain this, the government resigned. Within two days MacDonald and four other members of the cabinet switched sides, forming a National Government with the Conservatives and Liberals. For four years, Ramsay MacDonald remained as the prime minister of an effectively Tory government.[13]

Ramsay MacDonald's betrayal drew an immediate working-class response. Sixty thousand unemployed workers rioted in Glasgow and a further 30 000 in Manchester. The Independent Labour Party disaffiliated from the Labour Party in disgust, its 17 000 members forming their own party to the left of Labour. Elsewhere, in the single month of December 1931, 20 000 marched in Newcastle against the means test, while seamen and dockers prepared for a strike against wage cuts, and huge marches in the Potteries. Protests in Bootle and Keighley won concessions for the unemployed. Twelve thousand unpaid sailors in Cromarty Firth protested, leading to the Invergordon mutiny. The *Daily Worker* was blamed for the protests, although as the official historian of British Communism Noreen Branson records, 'the staff were as much surprised by the Invergordon "strike" as anyone else.' One of the leaders was Fred Copeman. Copeman was not a member of the party in 1931, but he respected the CP for supporting Invergordon, and became a fellow-traveller of the Communists, active in the unemployed movement and in Spain.[14]

Despite the presence of the Communists within the protests of the sailors and the unemployed, the party did not give an adequate lead to the mood of anger against MacDonald's betrayal. There was no longer a CP cadre in the factories, where its influence would have been most keenly felt. Noreen Branson and Bill Moore's history of Labour–Communist relations records the irrelevance of the party's industrial work by 1931, 'All was not well. The New Line [had] played havoc with the party's industrial work – the members [had] ceased to work seriously in the unions.'[15] Many of the best members of the party tried to shape the events unfolding around them, but they remained isolated as a result of Class against Class, and the party was unable to lead the anger within the labour movement.

Meanwhile, the struggles between the Bolsheviks in Russia were beginning to be reported in the non-party press. Although the form of the Opposition developed over time, Trotsky's supporters consistently argued that the Russian Revolution was being choked by bureaucracy. By the late 1920s, sections of the major European parties, including French, Polish and German Communists, had declared for Trotsky. By contrast, the leaders of the CPGB never attempted to understand the matter at stake. In the *Communist Review* of February 1924, Tom Bell described the divisions as a sign of the healthy democracy within the Russian party. Discussing bureaucratisation, Bell wrote that 'it was especially Trotsky who brought this discussion to the front, which is proof enough ... that this crisis did not represent any danger for the unity of the Party.' In 1925, a collection by J. T. Murphy included the sentence 'Let us remind friend and foe alike that Comrade Trotsky belongs to our party and not theirs'. In February 1926, the British party published Leon Trotsky's *Where is Britain Going?*, which was also favourably reviewed by Rajani Palme Dutt in the CP's theoretical magazine, *Labour Monthly* Yet from the defeat of the General Strike onwards, the British party snapped in line, and it was Murphy who moved the removal of Trotsky from the Executive Committee of the Comintern in September 1927. These contradictory arguments coming from leading British Communists reflect both the widening gulf between the regime and Trotsky, and also the low level of political debate within the British party. By the moment of Palme Dutt's review, Leon Trotsky was on the way out of the leadership in Russia. But even the high priest of British Stalinism was behind the times.[16]

One consequence of the failure of the British party in 1931 was to encourage a small group of dissidents, who came into contact with Trotsky's criticisms of the International. The arguments of this Balham Group, whose leaders included Harry Wicks and Reg Groves, were hardly noticed at the time, and grew in importance only later as the Trotskyist parties came to eclipse the Communist Party as the dominant force on the British left. Yet what is significant is that Trotskyism was born in response to the failure of mainstream Communism in Britain. These were originally Communist militants who criticised the CP from within. 'Without clearly communicated aims and a related strategy of progressively extending struggle, the militants in the workshop, union branch and at labour exchange had nothing in the way of political ideas and purposes around which to rally and unite the movement – except resistance to the cuts.' The Balham Group blamed the revival of Labour after 1931 on the sectarianism of Third Period Stalinism. 'Only our failure as communists to create – under fire – a revolutionary party allowed the Labour Party subsequently to restore its influence over the workers.'[17] Over time, the Trotskyists would develop a theory of Russia, they would also campaign against the Russian show trials, and the failure of Stalinism to prevent the rise of Hitler in Germany. Yet it was because they had a different notion of how to build a revolutionary party that the British Trotskyists first emerged.

The line changes (1)

With the collapse of the 1929–31 government, Labour went into opposition. Ramsay MacDonald became prime minister of a National Government, presiding over a solid majority of Tory MPs. The run on the pound was stayed, the budget left unbalanced. Labour's vote fell by some two million, the Liberals were almost annihilated, and the

National Government Conservatives were left with a majority which would last them until 1945. Among Labour supporters, there was a definite shift leftwards. As we have seen, the ILP left the Labour Party, while a successor organisation, the Socialist League, was established for socialists who wanted to remain within Labour. Smaller and less working-class than the ILP, the League was also radicalised by the experience of MacDonald's 1931 betrayal. Stafford Cripps' 1932 pamphlet asked *Can Socialism Come by Constitutional Means?* He concluded that it could, provided Labour armed itself with Emergency Power legislation to combat the hostility of banks and industry. Several prominent members of the Socialist League including the lawyer D. N. Pritt as well as Stafford Cripps, were strongly influenced by the party, and tended to defend CP co-operation with Labour. In this way, around the time of the 1931 election, the British Communists were given some space for a shift away from the constant ultra-leftism of Class against Class.

The exact origins of the change are obscure and contested, but two broad descriptions of the process have emerged. The first is Nina Fishman's claim that 'pragmatists' in the party, primarily Pollitt and Gallacher, were able to take advantage of the growing ambiguity in the Comintern line to wrest control of the party back from the Young Turks who had championed Class against Class, while continuing to mouth Third Period rhetoric themselves. In her explanation, a key moment is the 11th Plenum of the Executive Committee of the Communist International in February 1931, where a new emphasis is said to have emerged, giving local parties more freedom to interpret the tactical implications of the Third Period line. Alongside the ritual denunciations of Right Deviation and Social Fascism, the statements of leading Comintern officials such as Manuilsky increasingly contained warning of the dangers of left sectarianism.

Did the Comintern allow the British party the freedom to create a new climate of tolerance? To understand the CPGB, you must say something about its leadership. Harry Pollitt, Johnny Campbell and Willie Gallacher were the public face of the party through much of the 1930s. These three were highly experienced revolutionary activists, acutely sensitive to the milieu of the British Labour movement within which they worked. There is little doubt that they were horrified by the damage that the Third Period ultra-leftism had brought to the party. But the argument that Harry Pollitt and the others had pulled the wool over the eyes of Comintern officials is implausible. We should take the ultra-revolutionary rhetoric of the Third Period with a dose of scepticism. It may have been taken seriously by the Young Turks of the British Communist Party, and even by some Comintern officials, but within the highest echelons of the Soviet apparatus, the diplomatic *raison d'état* of the USSR took precedence.[18] For Pollitt and the leadership of the party, the move away from Class against Class did not mark a move away from adherence to a Comintern line. Instead, as Communists were threatened with slump, fascism and war, so the Soviet Union was to become an increasingly important authority.

The second explanation appears in Keith Laybourn and Dylan Murphy's *Under the Red Flag*. Their suggestion is that the change of emphasis emerged out of the experience of failure, crucially the failure of the party to organise in the trade unions. In July 1930, the Communist Party attempted to recover lost ground through a major initiative, the Workers' Charter, which was designed to draw together employed and unemployed workers in a common struggle against redundancies. This action had initially been proposed at the Fifth World Congress of the Red International of Labour Union (RILU). The Charter demanded the introduction of the seven-hour day, opposition to speed-up, increased unemployment benefits, and a minimum wage. The *Workers Charter* pamphlet was said to have sold 120 000 copies, but when the party attempted to organise a national demonstration in support of its demands, only a few hundred demonstrators showed up. Laybourn and Murphy suggest that the overlapping of responsibilities with the Minority Movement, which continued to exist, may have caused additional confusion For a tiny party, the CP was remarkably good at sustaining several layers of bureaucracy.[19]

The failure of the Workers' Charter movement encouraged the Comintern to establish a special commission into the state of the British party. Although the creation of this panel was a clear criticism of the British party, the British leadership did not hesitate to speak up for their own condemnation. So it was Harry Pollitt who addressed a December 1931 meeting of the ECCI to explain the reasons for the Commission. 'In view of the very favourable objective situation in England, there was felt in the International a serious alarm at the failure of the Party to play a decisive role in the economic struggles and its failure to develop the mass movement, and this alarm was accentuated into great apprehension on the very weak results which the Party obtained in the most recent general election.'[20] From the minutes of the meetings – all filed, and sent to Moscow – it appears that few new practical suggestions were made beyond self-abasement. Pollitt told a meeting of the party's Political Bureau in January 1932,

'We have to face up to the fact that the resolutions passed by the party have remained paper resolutions ... not only is the party isolated from the masses, but the leadership is isolated from the party.' Two days later, he castigated the Central Committee, saying that they had 'assist[ed] in the development of the "lesser evil" idea ... the main danger to the working-class is the Labour Party.'[21] But appearances are deceptive. By January 1932, Pollitt had secured agreement from Moscow that 'Class Against Class' could be modified in respect of the need to win trade union support.

For whatever reason, the perspectives of the party did change. Between the leftism of the Third Period and the rightism of the Popular Front, there was a brief window in which the party returned to something like the United Front position of the early 1920s. In the factories, on the railways and in the mines, the party re-adopted the practice of building rank and file movements. In 1933 and 1934, there was a serious and extended discussion of how a national movement could be built, linking together the different rank and file campaigns. The party's discussion magazine, *International Press Correspondence*, reported strikes among aircraft workers, engineers and miners. In early 1935, leading CP trade unionist Reg Bishop claimed, 'some 800 000 building workers are straining at the leash for action to compel the granting of their demand for wage increases.'[22]

The best known rank and file campaign was the one organised by the London busmen. In January 1932, the party still had no more than a dozen members working on the buses. Yet, when the London General Omnibus Company imposed a one shilling per week wage cut, these activists persuaded their union branch to pass a resolution against the cuts and circulate it around the fleet. A mass meeting was called, the party recruited in five or six garages, and its rank-and-file paper. *The Busman's Punch* increased its sale rapidly from 1500 to 8000 copies. The busworkers forced a strike vote, and the London General backed down. But the legacy of successful walkouts again in 1933 and 1935 was undermined by the defeat of the Coronation Strike in May 1937.[23]

From the middle years of the decade onwards, the Communist Party devoted increasing energy and resources to anti-fascist work. The first significant British fascist party was the British Union of Fascists (BUF), which was formed by Sir Oswald Mosley in October 1932. Oswald Mosley was a well-known politician, with a certain profile in the press, he had been a minister in MacDonald's second Labour government. By 1934, his party claimed around forty to fifty thousand members. With the support of Lord Rothermere's *Daily Mail*, the fascists were able to recruit from a large pool of disgruntled Tories. Fascist groups were set up in the Universities of London and Birmingham, Stowe School, and Winchester, Beaumont and Worksop Colleges. According to Mosley's son Nicholas, 'The mood in the Black House was that the BUF would probably be in power within 12 months.'[24] As a sign of its growing confidence, the British Union called a major rally, to take place at Olympia on 7 June 1934. This was the moment at which the BUF was expected to enter the mainstream; MPs, peers, diplomats, big businessmen and leading journalists were invited to hear Mosley speak, and 12 000 people showed up on that day.

At this stage, with the British Union of Fascists at its peak, anti-fascists began to co-ordinate their opposition. There were anti-fascist groups in Britain going back at least to the National Union For Combating Fascism organised by Ethel Carnie Holdsworth, in the early 1920s. In 1924, the Plebs League published an important pamphlet, influenced by Klara Zetkin, warning that 'fascism has special characteristics which give it an international importance greater even than that derived from its success in Italy.'[25] However, there was not yet any national organisation which played a co-ordinating role. The Labour Party was the largest force on the left and could have filled the gap. To this end, Labour conducted surveys to examine the extent of the fascist danger, published anti-fascist pamphlets, and even supported two large demonstrations against Mosley, in 1933 and 1936. But the leadership of the party argued that fascism should be opposed in parliament, not in the streets, and Labour was determined not to associate itself too closely with the forces of radical anti-fascism. The next group which could have filled the vacuum was the Communist Party itself. Yet during the Third Period, the party tended to argue that the most dangerous fascists were not the BUF but the 'social fascists' of the Labour Party and the ILP. Through 1934, therefore, the lead was taken by a series of small ad hoc anti-fascist groups, which were set up in different areas, including the Anti Fascist League in Tyneside and the Red Shirts in Oxford. In the days leading to Olympia, these independent anti-fascists did everything they could to prepare an adequate response to fascism.[26]

Having dallied in the run up to Olympia, the Communist Party now changed tack and took full part in the campaign. The *Daily Worker* published route maps and arranged transport. Altogether around 10 000 anti-fascists demonstrated outside Olympia, where they were attacked by 760 mounted police. Several hundred anti-fascists forged tickets, or sent letters and got in. There, they heckled Mosley and disrupted his speech. Mosley paused, and the organisers of the meeting shone spotlights on the hecklers so that they could be identified and removed. The hecklers were then attacked by stewards and several dozen were beaten up. The middle- and ruling-class elements watching Mosley were now forced to consider whether they really wanted to support such a brutal movement. The Tory Party did not face the crisis of legitimacy that its sister parties had experienced in Italy or Germany. The establishment had no need for the BUF. Geoffrey Lloyd, the Parliamentary Private Secretary to Prime Minister Stanley Baldwin, observed the Olympia rally. Afterwards, he wrote: 'I can only say that it was a deeply shocking scene for an Englishman to see in London ... I came to the conclusion that Mosley was a political maniac and that all decent English people must combine to kill this movement.'

Thus, the result of the events at Olympia was that the fascist violence proved counter-productive. Many middle-class supporters of fascism were disgusted and left, and the British Union of Fascists quickly went into decline. Lord Rothermere withdrew his support for Mosley. Dr. Robert Forgan, a prominent supporter who had followed Mosley from the 1920s, also left. Within a year, BUF membership fell from 40 000 to 5000. Vernon Kell of MI5 went so far as to argue that 'Mosley has suffered a check which is likely to prove decisive'.[27] As it happened, Kell's hope was premature. The BUF did recover, but it was two years before the fascist party was able to regain the initiative. In the meantime, the Communist Party could congratulate itself on a successful intervention.

The line changes (2)

As we have argued, the political line of the British Communist Party was already in transition by the end of 1931. The party gave up on its attempts to form left unions in rivalry to the existing movement, and the edge of its sectarianism was blunted. Yet the Communist Party's politics remained ultra-left, and its rhetoric continue to follow the Class against Class line. So John Strachey, a CP fellow-traveller, described the trade union leaders in 1932 as 'the trusted and petted servants of all capitalist Governments'. The following year, Communists in Chelsea suggested that the party should return to a policy of critical support for the Labour Party. They were denounced in the *Communist Review* as Trotskyists. Also in 1933, Harry Pollitt stood against the Labour Party's Arthur Henderson on a 'Class Against Class' platform. In 1934, Rajani Palme Dutt's *Fascism and Social Revolution* still defended the categorisation of reformist parties as social fascist.[28] Yet the same year also saw firm signs of a change of emphasis, for example the Communist Party now finally recognised that the Independent Labour Party was not a fascist party. Even then, another twelve months was needed before the change of emphasis became an entire new line.

Once again, it was international events which sparked the transformation in the Communist Party's politics. In Germany, Hitler's seizure of power discredited the rival positions of the two major parties, the German Socialists (SPD) and Communists (KPD). Both had refused to unite against the fascist threat, but the failure of the KPD was more shocking. They were supposed to be the most committed anti-fascists, and their failure was more telling because more was expected of them. Here much of the blame should be placed on the sectarianism of the Third Period. Stalin argued in 1929 that 'Fascism is the bourgeoisie's fighting organisation that relies on the active support of social democracy ... Fascism and social democracy are not antipodes but twins.' Just ten weeks before Hitler came to power, German communists still argued that the Socialists were 'the main social buttress of the bourgeoisie'. It was the disastrous politics of the Communist International which made united action impossible and paved the way for the German left's defeat.[29]

Adolf Hilter's victory, and the news of the rapid destruction of German Social Democracy which followed over the subsequent weeks, shocked Communists around the world. When activists warned of the imminent fascist threat, they were thinking of events in their own town, their own country. There was a genuine fear that capitalism was transforming itself into fascism. Harry Pollitt addressed a Central Committee meeting in suitably apocalyptic terms. 'Important task; preparation for illegality. Thirty-eight illegal sections in Communist International, in a year or 18 months there will hardly be a legal section left ... It must be clear that the Government have got their [spies] in our party and there is too light-hearted an attitude being taken to that question.'[30]

Eventually, this catastrophe would discredit the ultra-left politics of the Communist International during the Third Period. In the meantime, the Soviet government was keen for a counter-weight to the threat of Nazi Germany, and turned towards a strategy of peaceful coexistence with the Western powers. This time, rank-and-file dissent from within the European Communist Parties worked in conjunction with the changing needs of Soviet foreign policy. On 5 March 1933, the Comintern announced a new line. Its member-parties were now encouraged to work in united fronts with reformist parties. In October 1934, a Popular Front alliance between Radicals, Socialists and Communists was signed in France. Yet as late as January 1934, the British *Daily Worker* still argued that 'Social Democracy continues to play the role of the main social prop of the bourgeoisie.' Such a line might have been applied – with difficulty – to characterise the parliamentary democracies, but the CP went further, and continued to apply the theory of social fascism 'in the countries of open fascist dictatorship'. In other words, Social Democracy was still the main enemy even where its militants were murdered and its organisation crushed![31]

The full change of line finally came at the seventh congress of the Comintern in July and August 1935. Here, Georgi Dimitrov (fresh from his defence in Germany, where he had been tried, but not convicted, for starting the Reichstag fire) argued that Fascism represented a distinctive form of capitalist rule. Fascism was not 'an ordinary succession of one bourgeois government by another, but a substitution of one state form of class domination of the bourgeoisie, bourgeois democracy, by another form, open terroristic dictatorship.' Hitler and Mussolini brought 'unbridled chauvinism and annexationist war ... rabid reaction and counter-revolution.' Fascism as a regime would introduce an extreme form of anti-proletarian rule, 'a most ferocious attack by capital on the toiling masses ... the most vicious enemy of the working class and of all the toilers.'[32] This new formula was to entail an entire change of line. The Western Communist Parties moved to embrace sections of the so-called 'progressive bourgeoisie' under the heading of the Popular Front.

The Popular Front policy was not simply a new way of understanding fascism. At a time when the rise of the far right was the most urgent challenge facing socialists, a new way of understanding fascism meant a whole new approach to every other aspect of party life. The Popular Front therefore was both a short-term tactic, and the beginning of a long-term reformist and parliamentary strategy. Even if Noreen Branson's interpretation of the Popular Front can be questioned, she does capture the significance of the new line. It was a transformation in the way that Communists thought:

> Extra-parliamentary action ceased to be seen as an alternative to parliamentary action; on the contrary, it was realised that the way forward must involve a combination of the two. The object must be to transform and democratise the state machine, and to change the

parliamentary system, not to 'replace' it. So began work on a different concept: that of the British road to socialism.

Although Branson describes the shift in the CP's politics as a necessary step, when an obvious truth was finally 'realised', the party's critics were less supportive of the new line. Fenner Brockway of the Independent Labour Party characterised the Popular Front as a reformist charade. The rival social classes were supposed to come together in a movement of national unity, while the capitalist profit system would be left intact. 'The class struggle against Capitalism is to retire in favour of an all-class coalition for "democracy".'[33]

The impact of the Popular Front line can be seen most clearly in the Communists' changing attitude towards the Labour Party. Between 1929 and 1935, the CPGB tended to argue that the Labour leaders were 'social fascists', quite as bad as real fascism. As late as November 1934, Pollitt could still tell the Political Bureau, 'The united front against fascism and war is the supreme task facing our party ... our criticisms of the programme of the Labour Party not only remains but must be strengthened.'[34] After the seventh congress of the International, there was an immediate somersault. In November 1935, the British party wrote to Labour, suggesting an electoral pact in the coming elections. This was rejected outright by Labour's National Executive, 'The National Executive Committee is as firmly convinced as were their predecessors that any weakening in the Labour Party's defence of political democracy, such as the affiliation of the Communist Party would imply, would inevitably assist the forces of reaction, would endanger our existing liberties, and would retard the achievement of socialism in this country.'[35]

In the 1935 election, the National Government retained a majority of 250 plus. The Communist Party stood just two candidates in the election and one of them, Willie Gallacher, was elected in West Fife. One of his first actions was to assure the Labour whips that he would vote with them and not with Maxton's Independent Labour Party. He would not become 'an added source of irritation' to Labour's serious parliamentary work. Gallacher told *Labour Monthly* of his admiration for Clement Attlee, chided the Socialist League for their opposition to the League of Nations, and shook an admonitory finger at the left-wing ILP. It became hard to remember that Gallacher had once been John Maclean's fiery disciple![36]

When its proposed electoral pact with Labour was turned down, the Communist Party applied for affiliation. By June 1936, over nine hundred trade unions, activist groups and other left-wing bodies had passed resolutions supporting the party's campaign. Some of these were mere front bodies, others were organisations with real influence. Among the larger groups, the Independent Labour Party and the Miners' Federation were early recruits to the affiliation cause. Despite the idiocies of Class against Class, the patient work of long-term activists within the local Miners' Federations was starting to pay off.

The Communist Party also received support from the Socialist League's Unity campaign, launched in January 1937, although the politics of that campaign was rather different. The CP wanted to affiliate to Labour, presumably dissolving itself in the process. The Socialist League was already a group inside Labour, and was therefore less bothered by the question of affiliation. Instead, their argument was that Socialists should generate some sort of deep alliance, co-operating among themselves to win left-wing positions within the movement. The Unity campaign was not conceived as a Popular Front, but as a militant United Front. Such Labour lefts as Barbara Betts (later Barbara Castle) stood out against the CP's Popular Front as a 'travesty of Lenin'. Indeed with Labour, the Socialist League and the Independent Labour Party all rejecting the Popular Front approach, this Unity Campaign was the broadest organised unity that the Communist Party could achieve. The Socialist League actively backed the Unity Campaign, with Cripps and Nye Bevan speaking on platforms at Communist Party events. Indeed, so firm was its support for Unity, that the League was itself expelled from the Labour Party in January 1937.[37]

Even if the Labour Party's ranks were divided, most of the Labour leadership still stood out against affiliation. At Labour's 1936 conference, Walter Citrine of the TUC taunted Communists with the contradictions between the new Popular Front and their old Class against Class line, 'After years of derision of the principles of the Labour Movement, after pouring out gallons of ink in denunciation of its leaders, after abuse of its unions as pillars of capitalism and reformist organisations ... after all the attacks we have experienced since 1925, we have now the curiously incongruous spectacle of the Communist organisations wanting to come into our midst and be part of the movement they have so derided.' The fact that Citrine could criticise the Communists from the left, shows just how exposed the party was by the shifts in its tactics. At the 1937 Labour Party Conference, it was Herbert Morrison's turn. After telling delegates that he disagreed with the Russian revolutionary Leon Trotsky, Morrison admitted that Trotsky was a socialist. To laugher, Herbert Morrison then asked,

'Would Mr Pollitt appear on a platform with socialist, working-class Trotsky? He would not. If some of the leaders of the POUM in Spain, a working-class party, came to London, and the ILP wanted another United Front platforms with them and Mr. Pollitt, Mr. Pollitt would not appear. But Mr. Pollitt will appear with the Duchess of Atholl.'[38] The affiliation motions were defeated by majorities of three to one.

The four years of the Popular Front were to witness a long succession of conferences and similar gatherings at which the CP could present the fruits of its Popular Front campaign. One such was a Congress of Peace and Friendship with the USSR, held in London in December 1935, and attended by 773 delegates claiming to represent more than a million and a half people. It is worth describing in some length, to convey the tenor of CP agitation at this time. The speakers included Fabians, peers, Tory and Liberal MPs. Such figures as Lord Listowel, the MPs Robert Boothby, Vyvyan Adams, and F. Seymour Cocks, Sidney Webb, Viscount Hastings, Lord Marley, Dr. Maude Royden and Professor Blackett were hardly chosen for their proletarian credentials. Alongside them, the top table also included Dave Springhall, Saklatvala, Andrew Rothstein, and other Communists. One speaker, Mr. Marshall, introduced as a 'capitalist', begged for more trade with Russia. Sidney Webb described how in the USSR, 'All the people are eager for greater production. This never happens in any other country ... There is no unemployment among actors in the USSR.' Dr. Maude Royden, a lay Christian preacher, expressed her surprise at being invited to speak, then went on to give the support of the Anglican church for the Russian experiment, 'We Christians see realised in actual fact in Russia, several of the most important teachings of our Master, in whose realisation in this country we have almost ceased to believe.'[39]

The Popular Front witnessed a series of such gatherings, in which the great and the good would be invited to announce their support for a Communism from which the residual working-class politics had been cut out. It was the need to appease such right-wing individuals, which dominated the politics of the Popular Front. Having returned from Spain, George Orwell attacked the CP's new line, condemning 'the nauseous spectacle of bishops, Communists, cocoa-magnates, publishers, duchesses and Labour MPs marching arm in arm to the tune of *Rule Britannia*'.[40] Boothby and Adams, mentioned above, were both Conservatives. The Duchess of Atholl, involved in the Popular Front campaign to Aid Spain, was a Scottish landowner and anti-Bolshevik from the Tory right. The United Front of the 1920s had been an alliance with working-class forces, in which some form of shared socialist politics dominated. The Popular Front of the 1930s was something else indeed.

We have argued that there was a great difference between the open Marxism of the Communist Party's founders, and the left sectarianism of Class against Class. There is the same gulf between the party's revolutionary beginnings and the right-wing populism of the Popular Front strategy. From 1935 onwards, the British Communist Party presented its politics as a mere left-wing extension of Labour's reformism. The Popular Front also saw a change in the party's attitude towards the trade unions. The party remained committed to building the trade union movement. 'Over one hundred members of our party have been presented with the Tolpuddle medal for recruiting and scores of others are entitled to it if they would only apply', reported the Central Committee to the Fourteenth Congress in May 1937. Yet there was no longer any demand in the party's publications for fighting unions, nor for any self-activity on the part of ordinary workers. Instead, the Communist Party's internal magazine, *Discussion*, featured an article on 'Why we don't want Rank and File Movements'. In this piece one activist 'PJ' argued that such movements were a diversion of energy from the more important task of winning over the trade union machine. The trade unions were described as battalions, to be captured from the top down, 'A union is like an army which must go into battle as a single force.' The fact that this article could be published in a Communist magazine marks the direction in which the party was now moving.

The years after 1935 were a time of economic recovery. Increased armament expenditure combined with a sense of union revival after the great defeat of 1926. Yet as conditions improved, the party's sympathy for industrial work waned. October 1935 saw a wave of struggles in the South Wales coalfields against company unions. Workers occupied Nine Mile Point to remove scab labourers still working from a previous dispute. One result of these protests was a shift to the left in the union, symbolised by the election of Arthur Horner as President of the South Wales Miners Federation in 1936. Yet the level of strikes in the Welsh mines was falling, a trend welcomed in the July 1937 issue of *Labour Monthly*. There was no need for workers to fight, because 'the union machine is used to express the workers' demands'. The rank and file paper, *Busman's Punch*, was closed down in November 1937, following the busworkers' defeat in the Coronation Strike. Meanwhile, the discussions on building a national rank and file movement, which had taken up much of the party's attention in 1933 and 1934, were shelved. At the 1938 Congress of the Communist Party, no report was given on industrial and trade union work. By the end of the 1930s, the party had more members than ever before, yet the Popular Front compares in one sense with the dark years around 1930. There were less Communist-led strikes than at any time since the party's formation. 'The Communist Party', writes labour historian Brian Pearce, 'lost all interest in promoting workers' revolution'.[41]

Cable Street

Having described the Popular Front as a degeneration of the part's politics, it is important to stress that the party remained a workers' party, if of a rather deformed sort. There were tensions inside the politics of the Popular Front, between the Communists' genuine desire to fight fascism and the paucity of their alternative strategy. There were also contradictions between the politics of the leadership, and the demands of the working class rank and file. Some of these tensions could be seen in the party's continuing agitation against fascism. At the Seventh Congress, Georgi Dimitrov had warned the CP not to devote too much energy to the small fry of Mosley's BUF, 'at the present stage, fighting the fascist danger in Britain means primarily fighting the National Government and its reactionary measures.' Yet anti-fascist work remained a priority for the Communist Party even after 1935.

Despite the anti-fascist victory at Olympia, fascism did not vanish. The BUF was rebuilt on military lines by Major-General J. F. C. Fuller, while the fascist party dropped the middle-class disaffected Conservatives who had joined in 1933–34 in favour of a new layer of working-class racists from East London. The fascists aimed to recruit workers ground down by the experience of poverty, isolated from the labour movement and attracted to the BUF's anti-semitism. Leslie Paul, a churchman living in the area described how the fascists recruited 'bitter, hopeless and even degenerating individuals whose unwantedness had become the very core of their lives.' Soon the BUF was on the rise again. The fascists established new branches in Stepney, Limehouse and Bethnal Green. They claimed to have 4000 members in Shoreditch alone, 'The BUF won recruits, particularly from the younger elements in Shoreditch, Bethnal Green and Stepney. Jews were attacked every time they were outnumbered or in no position to defend themselves.'[42] Then Mosley announced a march from the Royal Mint to Limehouse, to be held on 4 October 1936.

Quickly, anti-fascists determined to oppose this demonstration. Central to the anti-fascist movement was a generation of London Jews who aligned themselves with the Communist Party. Many belonged to the Jewish People's Council, a Communist front-organisation which collected 100 000 signtures for a protest in just 48 hours. Individual members of the Labour Party, the ILP and trade unionists called for the march to be banned. The role of the Communist Party in the campaign was equivocal. Originally, the party supported a rival Popular Front demonstration in Trafalgar Square. If you were to be forgiving, you might say that the Communists were more concerned with the people dying in Spain, than they were with the facist threat in London. With just two days to go, and under intense pressure from its supporters, the London Committee of the CP changed tack, and agreed to back the anti-Mosley demonstration.

Although the CP joined the movement, other groups remained hostile. The leaders of the Jewish Board of Deputies insisted that Jews should avoid the protest. The *Daily Herald* said the same. On the day itself, at least 100 000 people showed up to blockade Gardiner's Corner, the nub of any route from the City into East London. There they were attacked by large numbers of police, many on horseback, who tried to force a way through for around two thousand members of the British Union of Fascists. When the police charges failed to make headway, they turned their attention instead on Cable Street. When the police failed there, too, Sir Philip Game ordered the fascists to turn round. They then marched westwards to the Embankment and dispersed.[43]

The chief effect of the Battle of Cable Street was to encourage Jews, socialists, and anti-fascists living in the East End. Phil Piratin, then active in Stepney Communist Party describes how the talk went round the barber shops and the bookies, 'nothing had changed physically ... but the people were changed ... Each one was a hero.' A lesson was learned for the future; the state would not protect Jews from fascists, instead the community would have to defend itself. It was the left which claimed the credit for the successful confrontation. According to Gisela Lebzelter, 'Compared to the defence activities of Anglo-Jewry, the motley anti-fascist left, embracing not only Communists but civil liberty champions of various shades, mounted a far more successful defence against fascist anti-semitism.' One further result of 4 October 1936 was the passing of the Public Order Act, which banned paramilitary uniforms and gave the police powers to prevent demonstrations. Communists pointed out that the bill was used more often against the left than it ever was against the right, 'the people of Stepney learnt that if law and order were to be maintained they would have to do it themselves, for the police were acting as their enemies.'[44]

In the aftermath of Cable Street, the BUF remained upbeat, and even won new recruits in the East End. According to the fascist press, 650 new members joined after one meeting at Bethnal Green. Then in the 1937 London City Council elections, the British Union of fascists obtained 23 per cent of the vote where they stood, failing to win the three or four outright victories predicted by Mosley. After the 1937 election, the BUF went into crisis. The layer of Cable Street fascists had melted away. Meanwhile, the Communist Party took a more prominent role in local campaigns, opposing evictions, and winning support in areas where the BUF had enjoyed a monopoly. The CP campaign weakened the BUF in its East End strongholds. Perhaps because the organisation was no longer recruiting on the expected scale, the British Union of Fascists went into financial crisis. The Northern Command HQ had to be closed down and the number of paid staff was reduced by three-quarters. The BUF then suffered a debilitating split when William Joyce and John Beckett and their allies left to form a rival party, the National Socialist League.[45]

At the heart of Cable Street was a layer of East End Jews who aligned themselves with the party. Some were members of the CP, others anarchists or Zionists who accepted the leadership of the party in the fight against fascism. Given that these Jewish left-wingers were a visible minority within the party, it is worth examining their politics in more detail. How far did the Jewish Communists identify themselves by race, and to what extent did they identify themselves as workers? Henry Srebrnik argues that many Jewish Communists were 'left-wing Diaspora nationalists', aware of racism, and enticed towards Communism only in so far as it assisted communal self-defence, 'one important factor for the Jewish attraction to the Communist Party in Britain was the CP's self-appointed role as a steadfast opponent to all manifestations of domestic fascism'. Bob Darke made a similar point in 1951, 'East End Jews never turn down requests to buy party literature or support party activity. This is not because they are Communists or even potential Communists. It is a recognition of the work the party puts in against anti-semitism.'[46]

There must be some truth to Srebrnik's argument. Looking beyond the Jewish Communists, it is clear that racism was a reality for all Jews then living in East London. The novelist Emmanuel Litvinoff, who grew up in Bethnal Green around this time, has one of his characters say that, 'Night after night I suffered with Mosley's fascists', while

Ralph Finn, another writer, targeted his anger against the polite racism of official British society, 'As long as you bring credit to the flag they will stand up and salute you and forget your background and hail you as one of their own. But overstep the mark ever so slightly, even to the extent of growing old, and they will put you back where you belong.'[47] The Jewish Left adopted its values and its communal identity from the wider Jewish East End. Yet to accept that race was also an important part of the Jewish East End and of Jewish Communist identity, does not mean that class should be ignored. For the Jewish Communists, class was the most important factor in political self-definition. Alte Bloomfield was a member of this milieu, and his daughter Jude's description is close to how he would have seen himself:

> My father was in the London East End Communist Party in the 1930s and he was part of the Jewish East End culture and anti-fascist movement. He was self-educated, very typical of a certain kind of working-class culture in the East End. He was a shop steward and a television tester and he was also a steward on the famous Cable Street march.[48]

Both Jewish *and* working class; for Alte Bloomfield, there was no contradiction between the two.

Aid Spain

The best instincts of the CP were evident at Cable Street. If the party's intervention was shaped by the Popular Front, then this distinction was not yet decisive. The contradictions in the party's anti-fascist politics were much more evident in the campaign on behalf of Republican Spain. There, a Popular Front composed of two bourgeois parties, the Socialists, Communists and the independent Marxist POUM, came together to win the elections of February 1936. Five months later, in July, Franco began his military uprising against the elected government. Immediately, however, Franco's troops were pushed back by successful workers' uprisings, most famously in Barcelona. The question of tactics then came to the fore, and revolutionary Spain divided into two camps. On the one side were the Communists and the bourgeois parties, who followed the logic of the Popular Front in arguing that the victory of the war required that the left should end the revolution, disarming the workers' militia and seeking an alliance with Britain and France. On the other side were the POUM and the anarchists, who insisted that the revolution was the very life-blood of the government. They argued that the Republic should offer Morocco its independence, which would separate Franco's colonial troops from their leaders. The left insisted that to disarm the workers' militias would be to undermine the revolution, and would cause the war to be lost. In Spain, the argument was won by the Communist Party, which disarmed the workers, and imposed a terror on its former allies in the revolutionary camp. The government of anti-fascist unity saw its enemies among the most resolute anti-fascists and, having imprisoned them, was itself destroyed by Franco.[49]

The Communist Party campaigned on behalf of the Communists in Spain, and its agitation reflected the politics of the Popular Front. Beneath such headlines as 'Neutrality is Treason', the *Daily Worker* rightly exposed the perils of non-intervention. At the 1936 Trades Union Congress, Bill Zak of the Furnishing Trades Association, warned that appeasing Spanish fascism would only 'increase the audacity of the fascist powers'. An Aid for Spain campaign sent medical facilities and food to the embattled Republican North. The British Communist Party also contributed to the formation of a British Battalion of the International Brigade. As George Matthews records, 'About half of the 1500 members of the British Battalion [were] members of the Communist Party or the Young Communist League.' Half again of the 533 who were killed were Communists. Prominent Communists among the Brigadiers included Bill Alexander, Bob Cooney, Peter Kerrigan, Will Paynter, William Rust and SamWild. Later generations of socialists can only admire the generosity of spirit and heroism of the volunteers who died. The Central Committee of the CPGB was not far off the mark when it declared that the party's campaign had constituted 'the proudest pages in our party history; it had saved the honour of the British Labour Movement'.[50]

Yet for all the spirit of the volunteers, there's was a tarnished cause. The only way that the suppression of the POUM and the anarchists could be justified was with a series of lies. In January 1937, even before the suppression of the Spanish left, the *International Press Correspondence* printed an article by Michael Kolzov, 'The Trotskyist Criminals in Spain',

> The adherents of this organisation [the POUM] were a handful of persons who had been expelled from other parties for disruption, swindling and theft. They collected troops of their own, and at first all went well. Then a remarkable thing became apparent. Three

commanders, leading the three POUM columns, made a practice of leaving the front with their troops at the moment when fighting began ...

In May, after the POUM had been banned, Claud Cockburn ('Frank Pitcairn') of the *Daily Worker* defended the action of the Republican government, 'In the past, the leaders of the POUM have frequently sought to deny their complicity as agents of a fascist cause against the People's Front. This time they are convicted out of their own mouths as clearly as their allies, operating in the Soviet Union, who confessed to the crimes of espionage, sabotage, and attempted murder against the government of the Soviet Union.' His criticisms of the so-called 'Catalonian rising' were also picked up by British left weeklies, *Tribune* and the *New Statesman*. The journalists who praised the International Brigadiers, used the genuine courage of these volunteers to justify the imprisonment and murder of the Spanish left.[51]

From the first unveiling of the Popular Front in 1935, the size of the Communist Party trebled in four years. Party membership rose from 6500 in February 1935, to 12 250 in May 1937, and 17 750 in July 1939. The CP built up an impressive periphery of fellow-travellers and other supporters. 'In the year 1937–8, the Party's Central Propaganda Department issued 17 penny pamphlets of which 300 000 were sold; this was in addition to others sold by the districts.' By 1939, the sales of the *Daily Worker*, had risen to between 40 000 and 50 000, a number which was exceeded at times of crisis. As with so many other aspects of party life in Popular Front, the changing composition of the party's membership has been a subject of some debate. Greater membership accompanied lower levels of activity. Writing in 1938, Trotsky was contemptuous of the middle-class recruits to Communism, 'A whole generation of the left intelligentsia has ... turned its eyes eastwards and has tied ... its fate not so much to the revolutionary working class as to a victorious revolution, which is not the same.' In a similar vein, Hugo Dewar suggests that there was a connection between the dilution of the CPGB's politics in the Popular Front and the character of the members who joined. Noreen Branson replies that professional support was needed if the British Communist Party was to respond to the urgent threat of fascism.[52]

The strong pressure on authors was reflected in a famous pamphlet, *Authors Take Sides on the Spanish War*, published by *Left Review* in 1937. Instigated by Nancy Cunard, a letter was sent to several hundred British writers, 'Are you for, or against, the legal Government and the people of Republican Spain? Are you for, or against, Franco and Fascism?'. One hundred and forty-nine replies were published in the phamplet, 127 'FOR the Government', and only five 'AGAINST'. The division between these two figures may be misleading. Among those counted 'NEUTRAL?' included several writers with a sympathy for the fascist right.[53] There was no place for George Orwell, who returned from witnessing the defeat of the Spanish Revolution at first hand, to find that left-wing publishers would not take his *Homage to Catalonia*.

The most important achievement of the Popular Front in Britain was the formation of the Left Book Club. Victor Gollancz took up this idea following the meeting which established the left unity paper, *Tribune*. In his founding statement, Gollancz emphasised the connection between the Left Book Club and methods of organising copied from the French Popular Front, 'France has, indeed, for a long time now been an example and an inspiration ... what the Left Book Club is intending to do is to provide the indispensable basis of *knowledge* without which a really effective United Front of all men and women of good will cannot be built.' In its first ten years, the Club sold six millions books – an extraordinary number. Over 100 Left Book Club titles were published in their distinctive salmon-pink covers. They included scientific and historical titles, as well as socialist classics and CP pamphlets. Around one third were written by party members, and all full-time Left Book Club workers were in the party. Local reading groups were also set up. By April 1939, there were 1200 local groups with 57 000 members. Communist Party members dominated the local Book Clubs, yet a movement was built with a real periphery. In September 1938, over two million Left Book Club leaflets were distributed on the 'Hitler Menace'. With the onset of war, the Club's activities were wound down and Gollancz left the party.[54]

Although Virginia Woolf was invited to write for the *Daily Worker*, the two best-known literary figures associated with the Popular Front were W. H. Auden and Stephen Spender. Auden was influenced at different times by Freud (like Strachey) and Christianity as well as the ideas of Karl Marx. On his departure for Spain in December 1936, he wrote to an old teacher, extolling the need for individual acts of conscience in the face of a powerful enemy, but also admitting some confusion as to what he should expect on his journey of self-discovery, 'I feel I ought to go; but O I do hope there are not too many surrealists there'. Auden's subsequent poem, 'Spain 1937', expressed a shallow existentialism, 'I am your choice, your decision: yes I am Spain.' Auden's utopia displayed a depressing similarity to pre-war Edwardian

Britain. At the same time, Stephen Spender was travelling on his own route towards Marxism. His *Forward From Liberalism* (1937), defended Communism as the means to achieve the supremacy of aesthetics. 'The final aim of the civilised man must be an unpolitical age, where conditions of peace and security are conducive to a classical art, rooted not in small oligarchy but in the lives of the whole people'. Hugh MacDiarmid's 'Third Hymn to Lenin' disparaged these fair-weather comrades, 'Michael Roberts and All Angels! Auden, Spender, these bhoyos / All yellow twicers; not one of them / With a tithe of Carlisle's courage and integrity / Unlike these pseudos I am of, not for, the working class.'[55] MacDiarmid's politics had its own flaws. But in this case his criticisms were convincing.

The CPGB's celebration of literary celebrity during the late 1930s marked a sharp turn from the earlier habits of the British party. The early Communist Party can of course be criticised. In the 1920s, the party was not just working class, but 'workerist' as well, promoting a limited vision of working-class politics. The CP deliberately rejected the backing of middle-class socialists, including several of its first MPs. Claiming to uphold a proletarian common sense, the leadership was hostile towards anything that smacked of 'theory', and in the process disarmed the membership, preventing it from achieving a serious understanding of Marxist politics. Yet if the early CP bent the stick too far, this was still an honest error, in marked contrast to the middle-class faddism of the Popular Front.

In the previous chapter, we quoted a party statement from March 1926, criticising the right wing on the TUC General Council. The Communist Party warned the miners of the two threats which they faced, 'In the first place there is the direct offensive of the capitalist class'. On the other hazard to avoid, it is worth quoting the 1926 declaration at length:

> The second danger comes from the existence of a small number of Labour leaders who are so obsessed with the ideas of uniting all classes and speaking of the interests of the 'community as a whole' that they fail to defend the workers they represent. Around them will be gathered all the doctrinaire intellectuals, with their utopian theories, who have been attracted to the labour movement. With them, too, will be all the weak vacillating elements on the fringes of the working class movement. All these will make their appeals and address their little questions and notes of censure to the capitalist class and bid the workers be reasonable.[56]

Doctrinaire intellectuals looking only for national unity, pacifists at a time of class war, what better description could there be of the politics of the Popular Front?

Moscow Trials

While thousands of ordinary people were disgusted by the prospect of fascism and war, and pledged themselves to resist authoritarianism of all sorts, the Communist Party which they chose to join was tainted by its role as the British advocate of Stalin's regime. Between 1936 and 1938, four major trials were held in Russia, in which such prominent Bolsheviks as Trotsky, Zinoviev, Kamenev and Bukharin were condemned of espionage and plotting to undermine the regime. Beneath this grisly facade of judicial murder, millions of Soviet citizens were imprisoned, killed or committed to internal exile. Ordinary Russians died, in unimaginable number. Yet for Marxists, tyranny and injustice were things which could only take place in a class society. Rather than revising their opinion of the first socialist society, British Communists turned a blind eye towards the murderous character of Soviet society. They persuaded themselves that the stories appearing in the capitalist press were lies and distortions like those of the 1920s. Convinced opponents of all tyranny and deceit, members of the party taught themselves to accept the lies that they heard from Moscow.

On 24 August 1935, just five weeks before the Battle of Cable Street, the *Daily Worker* defended the first of the Moscow trials, 'The extent and organisation of the plot, with its cold-blooded killings of the leaders of the international working class, has shocked the Labour and socialist movement of the world.' The Anglo-Russian Parliamentary Committee published a pamphlet, *The Moscow Trial* (1936), which included D. N. Pritt's verdict, 'the charge was true, the confession correct, and the prosecution fairly conducted.' Elsewhere Pritt wrote that 'it is alas beyond question' that Zinovievite and Trotskyite 'centres' were to blame for the murder of Kirov. British Communists and fellow-travellers would not question the court, nor would they debate the most obvious of discrepancies which appeared between the statements of consecutive witnesses. Jack Cohen told the CP monthly *Discussion* that Trotsky had called for terrorist acts since 1933. No evidence was given, except for the verdicts at the trials. Pat Sloan in the *New Statesman,* Walter Holmes in the *Daily Worker,* Reg Bishop in *Inprecorr,* Ivor Montagu in *Left Book News,* Robin Page Arnot in *Labour Monthly,* one after another these honest Communists parroted Stalin's line. After the second trial, the barrage that lies grew worse, and after the third, worse still. The more dishonest they were, the more unreal the Communists' language became. Trotskyists, ILPers and other socialists who questioned the verdicts were dismissed as 'degenerates' or 'fascists'. Harry Pollitt acclaimed the third public trial as 'a new triumph in the history of progress.' John Strachey welcomed 'the greatest anti-fascist victory which we have yet recorded.'[57]

Historians have attempted to make sense of the role played by British Communists in defending Stalinism. According to the Communist author Noreen Branson, 'Communists were reluctant to believe that the government of the first socialist country could be responsible for such atrocities ... the notion that Trotskyists could be allied with fascists or used as tools of the latter seemed plausible after the experience of the POUM in Spain.'[58] It is a matter of regret that historians still find a need to defend the worst aspects of CP history. For British Communists, their debt to Russia could no longer be separated from fidelity to socialism. Yet the effect of such loyalty was to tie the party to the defence of tyranny. Rather than impressing by their obedience to the International, the socialism of the British Communists was and is still tarnished by its association with the crimes of Stalin.

From the moment that Hitler came to power in January 1933, the world was set on a course to war. The Nazi party had raised itself up on the back of countless promises, to restore German national honour and to undo the hated Versailles treaty. Hitler's means to deliver on these pledges was through military expansion. With the largest industrial power in Europe committed to aggression, European war became inevitable. War could only have been averted if the democracies had determined from the outset to oppose fascism. Yet the rulers of Britain and France saw Russia as a greater threat to their interests, and took no action as Nazi Germany prepared for the conflict. When Italy and Germany sent troops and planes to France, during the Spanish Civil War, the democracies retaliated with non-intervention. In March 1938, German troops annexed Austria. Hitler's eyes then turned on Czechoslovakia. The 'peace' deal signed between Chamberlain and Hitler at Munich in September 1938 granted the Sudetenland to Germany, and convinced Hitler that there would be no obstacle to his continuing march east. It was only when Germany invaded Poland on 1 September 1939, that Britain and France made their first act of resistance, declaring war on Germany, and beginning the Second World War.

As the world moved closer to war, the CP was torn between conflicting loyalties. For some time, Communists had taken part in the international fight against fascism, through their fight against the BUF and their support of the Spanish Republicans. Party members regarded fascism as a particular threat to workers' organisations, which could only be resisted by the action of the whole working class. The logic of these struggles pointed towards a revolutionary fight against capitalism and war. Meanwhile, the Soviet Union was pushing for collective security, a set of alliances binding Russia to France and Britain. It was hard to square this line with the party's hostility towards the National Government. The logic of international alliances pointed instead towards a Communist truce with the British establishment. Class hostilities should be called off, while the war against fascism was fought. In the spring of 1939, the confusion between rival principles emerged in the CP's position on the conscription proposals put forward by the Chamberlain government. Was conscription to be seen as an example of the growing compulsion of labour associated with the Tory National Government? Or should it be supported as showing Britain's belated determination to oppose Hitler's fascism? Rajani Palme Dutt and Harry Pollitt clashed over this issue, with Dutt complaining that Pollitt was abandoning domestic class considerations and turning the Communists into a 'foreign policy party'.[59]

In the shadow of the war, the traditional link between socialism and opposition to militarism was broken. Under the impact of the Popular Front, many of the values of the left were reversed. The Communist argument was now in favour of strengthening the military power of the state. In 1938, armament was supported as the means to prevent war. One year later, the main demand was to ensure that when there was a war, fascism would lose it. In Oxford, A. D. Lindsay stood as a Popular Front candidate against the Munich agreement. Communist students leafleted in working-class areas, for a lapsed member of the Labour Party, supported by the Liberals, and Conservatives including Macmillan and Churchill. The Communist Party also devoted time and energy to exposing the appeasers within the British ruling class. A prominent role was played by Claud Cockburn, not a member of the party, but a journalist on the *Daily Worker*. Cockburn's duplicated broadsheet, *The Week*, exposed the machinations of Lord Halifax, the Home Secretary, Geoffrey Dawson of *The Times*, Nancy Astor MP and other members of the Cliveden Set.[60]

The tensions within the CP's anti-war line came out at the time of the Hitler–Stalin pact. All the party had done to oppose fascism seemed to be undermined by its support for a deal which left Hitler in place. The Communists' proud record of speaking up for the victims of imperialist aggression was compromised by their support for the subsequent Russian invasion of Finland. After he left the Communist Party in the 1940s, and became a Catholic, Douglas Hyde tried to explain the reasoning of those Communists who could switch their politics on order and support the Hitler–Stalin pact. His account is jaundiced, but conveys something of the logic of a Communist who made the required leap of faith:

> In fighting for a Communist Britain I am fighting for a better Britain and for the destruction of all that is rotten and decadent. In that fight I have the assistance of all who are operating on the same world front against capitalism. My desire to make my country Communist therefore makes me an internationalist. But at one point in that world front there is on my side, a great State, the USSR, where a strong-point has been established, around which all future battles will tend to turn and without which any other, local victories must fail. At all costs, therefore, Russia, bastion of Communism, must be defended. The defeat of the USSR would mean the end of any chance of world Communism for generations.

The Soviet–German Pact in August 1939, Hyde argued, did not trouble the trained Communist at all, 'The Soviet leaders had a responsibility to the working class of the world and could, if necessary, for this reason make an alliance with the devil himself.' David Goldfinger, a prominent Jewish Communist, defended the deal in his memoirs. Stalin's actions had saved the people of Poland, 'The pact had for the time being saved a population of some 11 000 000, and possibly the world from destruction'.[61]

When war was finally declared on 3 September 1939, the *Daily Worker* outlined its alternative, namely a 'War on Two Fronts', In a war between democracy and fascism, the left should side with the Western governments against fascism. Yet Communists would continue to criticise the politics which had brought the people of Europe to this low point, 'We are in support of all necessary measures to secure the victory of democracy over fascism. But fascism will not be defeated by the Chamberlain government.'[62] This was a line which allowed the Communists to support the war and also to retain their criticism of the class which was running it. Yet the merits of this policy were never properly tested. It was only a matter of weeks before the party's leadership would be overthrown, on orders from Moscow, and a whole new line was launched.

3
The Party at War: its Finest Hour?

By the time Neville Chamberlain spoke to the nation over the BBC on the morning of 3 September 1939, announcing the official declaration of war between Britain and Germany, the Central Committee of the Communist Party had already publicly declared their position in support of the war, but against the Chamberlain government. In a two page, tabloid newsprint 'special', entitled *'War Communist Policy: to the Men and Women of Great Britain'*, 250 000 of which were printed overnight on 2 September, the party explained their view:

> You are now being called upon to take part in the most cruel war in the history of the world. One that need never have taken place. One that could have been avoided even in the very last days of the crisis, had we had a People's Government in Britain. Now that the war has come, we have no hesitation in stating the policy of the Communist Party. We are in support of all necessary measures to secure the victory of democracy over fascism. But fascism will not be defeated by the Chamberlain Government.[1]

Thus was born the short lived War on Two Fronts policy, pronounced by the Communist Party's General Secretary Harry Pollitt, which had been gestating within the Communist Party leadership through 1938 and 1939. The War on Two Fronts grew out of an uneasy attempt to combine an appeal to the British Government to form an anti-fascist alliance with the characterisation of the Chamberlain government as being open to fascist influence. Numbers of party members immediately volunteered for active service. Bernard McKenna from Manchester, a Spanish Civil War veteran recalls:

> On my return to Britain I was fixed up with a job in a clothing factory, but when war broke out I left my job and joined the RAF ... I saw joining up and fighting in the Second World War as a continuation of the fight against fascism. As soon as the war broke out the CP said that it was an anti-fascist war and we should all join up and fight. I'd have joined anyway.[2]

Other party members claim that they immediately recognised the difficulties with the War on Two Fronts line. Bill Moore, who had been central to the Communist Party backed the Peace Council in Sheffield which had argued for collective security and campaigned for Britain to ally itself to the Soviet Union, remembers:

> There were divisions within the party at this stage as far as I could tell. I was very much surprised at the party line to support the war. I'd been in the Peace Movement for four years and had been reading deeply on the question of war ... It seemed to me that to support the war was to support the people who were running the war ... We were playing into their hands.[3]

Yet others were initially prepared to go along with the line despite reservations. Fred Westacott, then an engineering worker in the Southampton aircraft industry, remembers that:

> The general position in the party branch in Southampton was to go along with Pollitt's line. I began to have doubts, however, very quickly, within a couple of weeks, and it became apparent through what we were hearing that there was discussion and disagreement about the line. By the time that the party line officially changed, I was already firmly of the opinion that it was an imperialist war.[4]

Imperialist war: 'what are we fighting for?'[5]

The unceremonious ditching of the War on Two Fronts line came in dramatic fashion after a series of meetings of the Central Committee and Political Bureau,[6] which lasted from 24 September to 3 October. The War on Two Fronts policy had already come in for criticism from Rajani Palme Dutt, the party's theoretician in chief who had close links to the Comintern apparatus in Moscow, and his protégé Bill Rust.[7] Statements emerging from the Comintern suggested that the war was to be characterised as Imperialist. On the evening of 24 October David

The Party at War: its Finest Hour? 71

Springhall, the party's representative on the Comintern, arrived at the party's King Street headquarters straight from Moscow, bringing with him confirmation of the Comintern's position. Initially Pollitt and the majority of the Central Committee seemed unconvinced, however a few days later written confirmation of Springhall's assertions arrived in the shape of a Comintern 'Short Thesis'. Faced with such a clear and unambiguous policy directive from the Comintern, any attempt by Pollitt and the his supporters on the Central Committee somehow to fudge the position on the war was now untenable. After the party Central Committee meeting on 2 and 3 October which voted 21–3 in support of the Comintern's thesis, Harry Pollitt and Johnny Campbell were removed from their positions as General Secretary and *Daily Worker* Editor respectively. Willie Gallacher had voted with Pollitt and Campbell, and at the Central Committee meeting had spoken out in very harsh terms against the 'three ruthless revolutionaries', Dutt, Rust and Springhall, but as the party's only serving MP his resignation was unthinkable, and he asked that his vote be recorded in favour of the resolution.[8]

Reaction from party activists to Pollitt's resignation and the new line varied widely. Fred Westacott recalls his response:

> Pollitt was a popular figure in the party. When he and Johnny Campbell resigned, they didn't fight for their position, they took the line that they supported the new line. There was a feeling that, why should he resign, even though he had come out with the wrong line? ... There was great affection for Pollitt, never any anti-Pollitt feeling, the view was that he had erred at the beginning the war.

Bill Moore, himself an early opponent of Pollitt's political line on the war, remembers his own reactions thus:

> I can't remember the reaction of anybody else, but for myself I was a little bit disappointed, but he (Pollitt) was such an open, honest man, that you felt ... well ... he's got it wrong this time. But I don't recall losing any confidence in him, it was a one-off. I don't think that he ever lost sympathy, however much people disagreed with him.

Pollitt and Campbell did not fight publicly for their positions after they had been defeated in the Central Committee and there is no evidence of an open anti-Pollitt campaign in the party press at this time. A statement on Pollitt's position was issued over his name in the *Daily Worker* on 13 October, headlined 'Harry Pollitt Answers Press Slanders' in response to wide-ranging press coverage of his resignation.[9] This was followed by a full recantation in the *Daily Worker* by Pollitt and Campbell on 23 November under the headline 'Two Declarations',[10] Pollitt later produced a document entitled *1939-41*, written 'for the information of my family, so that they may be aware in case of any press misrepresentation, where I stood in relation to these historical events'.[11] In the document Pollitt reasserted his belief in the correctness of his original War on Two Fronts position and sharply critised those in the party leadership who opposed him.

Party members, friends and political acquaintances had an opportunity to express their sympathies to Pollitt due to the death of his mother soon after his dismissal. Many of the letters which Pollitt received on his mother's death act both as letters of condolence but also as letters of sympathy for his own political loss. Leading figures in and around the party such as Rajani Palme Dutt and John Strachey, took the opportunity of condolence letters to stretch out a hand to Pollitt; Dutt signing off with '... Let me know if there is anything we can do from here'.[12] The occasion of Pollitt's fiftieth birthday in November 1940, allowed the party publicly to declare his re-integration into the fold, among the greetings he received was a message signed by all the staff at the *Daily Worker* headed by Bill Rust, who along with Rajani Palme Dutt, had been most responsible for his removal from office in October 1939.[13]

Reactions to the change in line from War on Two Fronts to Imperialist War among party members are difficult to gauge. Individual party members were torn between loyalty to the Soviet Union and the party line, personal loyalty and affection for Pollitt, loyalty to their erstwhile Popular Front allies, the reactions of their work mates and families, a genuine class hostility to Chamberlain and the Men of Munich, a vivid self-identity as the best anti-fascists, memories of the horrors of the Great War and of anti-war activism and, in a handful of cases, a theorised Leninist conception of imperialism and the notion of revolutionary defeatism.

District meetings were held around the country to endorse the new line. These meetings recorded high votes in support of the new line which were duly reported in the *Daily Worker*.[14] It appears that in very few cases was a position put at District meetings in support of the old line. Monty Johnstone argues that this willingness of the party to 'about turn' so sharply 'brings to mind pre-perestroika Soviet elections'.[15] Indeed Harry Pollitt's mother, Mary Louisa Pollitt, a veteran socialist and foundation member of the Communist Party wrote in bitter terms in her last letter to her son: 'If they had made a statement and put your policy and theirs, I know which one would have carried, instead of which I don't suppose many knew anything about it'. She signed off with what can only be interpreted as a barbed reference to Palme Dutt: 'I bet I know who your successor will be'.[16]

The long-term party loyalist Fred Westacott however claims that in the Southampton branch the old line had quickly become unpopular: 'There had been doubts already, the arguments and discussions tended to go on before the change of line not afterwards. When the CC came down and said this was the line we accepted it'. Bill Moore recalls asking the North Midlands District Secretary Finlay Hart about reactions to the new line:

> Because I'd been a bit out of touch with the branch at the time, I asked Finlay what the reaction to the change in party line had been amongst the party in Sheffield. He said that there had been very little disagreement. The Sheffield working class have always been a tough lot, and the party had always been hard-line.

For another Sheffield party member at the time, Charlie Darville, the reaction to the party's opposition to the war was very different:

> I thought it was crazy, everything I had been arguing until then had been based on anti-fascism. I couldn't really understand what was going on. I didn't go to many party meetings at the time, but people told me about it and of course I read about it in the *Daily Worker*.[17]

The Manchester Spanish Civil War veteran Bernard McKenna who had enlisted straight away in September 1939:

> After a few months the CP decided it wasn't an anti-fascist war but an imperialist war. Myself and several other party members took no notice of the party line. We thought they were round the bend, so we just carried on. Then in 1941 when Hitler attacked Russia it became an anti-fascist war again.

McKenna, who was to break with the CP after the war over the party's denunciations of Tito, recalls that when as a serving soldier he returned to Manchester on leave:

> I was dumbfounded to hear many party people telling me I was wrong. I had many rows, failing to convince them that Hitler was still a baddy and I got the feeling that I was being shunned as a political innocent.

Jack Beal, a railway clerical worker, Communist and member of the Co-operative Movement writes in his unpublished memoirs:

> I could not for myself accept that this war was other than a just war, although the Communist Party and its press at that moment believed otherwise, saying that it was an imperialist struggle between rival imperialist powers, calling on the working class to put an end to the war in its own interests. My loyalties were to my country ... I could not but feel that if they were to invade and conquer our island Britain, that they would show no mercy or clemency to us.[18]

Kevin Morgan cites further evidence from Ipswich and Oxford to suggest opposition or resistance to the new line. The case of Oxford raises in particular the issue of the Popular Frontism of the CP in the late 1930s. Recruits who came to the party during both the large scale anti-Mosley mobilisations in Oxford in 1936 and the Popular Front by-election campaign in Oxford in 1938, were particularly hostile to the imperialist war line.

There is little evidence of a mass exodus from the party, certainly nothing on the scale of the defections seen in the wake of the Soviet intervention in Hungary in November 1956. One interesting but probably untypical example concerned a Manchester party member, who arrived late at the branch meeting which had been called to endorse the new line. Having missed the debate and vote he was informed by the chair that his vote had been recorded in the minutes as 'agreeing with Comrade Stalin' so that the branch could report a unanimous vote of support to King Street. He walked out of the meeting, more in protest at the procedure than the policy, and although he never rejoined the party remained within its orbit until 1956.[19] National figures for Communist Party membership are difficult to evaluate since the official figures show no record of membership between the 1939 figure of 17 756 and December 1941 when 22 738 members were recorded. Large sections of the membership, the functioning of branches and whole districts of the party were severely affected by military call up and the extensive relocation of population that took place in the first year of the war.[20] There is also some evidence that the party, anticipating a greater degree of state repression than it eventually faced, instructed some members to go underground to maintain a shadow organisation in the event of wide-scale internment. Party members who were called up were often advised by their district secretaries not to take their party cards with them, and party members in the forces were subject to the attentions of military intelligence throughout the war.[21]

'Don't you know there's a war on?': putting the line into practice

The effect of the change of line lost the Communist Party much of its softer Popular Front support, and peeled away some of the looser outer layers of members. For those members who either were able to continue their mainly workplace-based party activity, or who had been more thoroughly integrated into the culture of the party, the effect seems to have been marginal. As we shall see there was a sizeable anti-war current for the Communists to swim in. The Communist Party claimed to have continued to recruit strongly through the period of the change in line. Some of the claims for membership can be explained by Communist Party members who had worked as 'entrists' within the Labour Party and the Labour League of Youth following instructions to publicly join the Communist Party. The *Daily Worker's* claim of '500 new recruits for the Young Communist League in London alone since start of the War'[22] needs to be seen in this context. Evidence that other anti-war organisations grew significantly in this period suggests that the CP, despite the political difficulties suffered from the loss of Popular Front allies, and the organisational disruption caused by the war, continued to attract recruits. Accurate circulation figures for the *Daily Worker* are not available, but circulation of *Labour Monthly* grew sharply doubling to 21 000 by December 1940,[23] confirming an audience for radical anti-war ideas.

The Churchillian account of the early phase of the Second World War as 'our finest hour' when Britons rallied round the flag has been widely challenged. Writers such as Angus Calder and Clive Ponting[24] have used Mass Observation records to suggest that popular reactions to the war did not in any way represent a shelving of pre-war class tensions, diminished feelings of 'them and us', but in many ways sharpened them. Wartime introduced an added air of crisis and volatility into popular consciousness, surges of popular patriotism and foreigner baiting were quickly overtaken by moods of cynicism and class-based militancy. Popular attitudes to pacifists and conscientious objectors during the early phase of the war appear softer in tone than in the early phases of the 1914–18 war.[25] The Peace Pledge Union, which claimed 140 000 members at the outbreak of war, saw the circulation of its weekly paper *Peace News* rise from 19 300 to 35 000 in the first six months of the war.[26] Fred Westacott recalls the atmosphere:

> Generally there was not the animosity that would have existed in World War 1 when pacifists were attacked. I never felt my position against the war put me in any danger. Blokes at work used to talk about the war in quite open terms, a lot of the middle aged men had had experience in the First War and were quite cynical about patriotic talk. At the factory where I was working at near Southampton, we working overtime on the Sunday that war was declared, they had played Chamberlain's speech in the morning over the loudspeaker system and in the afternoon there was a walkout. It was over a tiny incident, one of the blokes had drilled a hole in the bottom of a tin mug as a joke, so management stopped the tea break ... 'didn't we know there was a war on?' ... so we walked out.

Within this mood there were significant fluctuations. In same month, April 1940, we can find two very different examples of strikes over the issue of conscientious objectors. At the Platting Chair Company in Manchester, workers walked out to demand the reinstatement of a worker who had been sacked because he had refused to register for military service, while at a glassworks in Yeovil workers struck, refusing to work with a conscientious objector.[27]

The Communist Party was not alone in 1939–40 in opposing the war. The Independent Labour Party, which had undergone a period of stagnation during the mid to late 1930s, was able to capitalise on the potential anti-war feeling, claiming to have put on 1000 new members from September 1939 to April 1940 and appointing six new full time regional organisers. Within the Labour Party there is also evidence of opposition to the war and to the political truce called by Labour. Over 90 Constituency Labour Parties put forward anti-war resolutions for the Bournemouth conference in June 1940.[28]

Amongst industrial workers the pressures of the developing war economy stimulated wage militancy. The introduction of the Cost Plus system, whereby employers engaged on war production charged the government production costs plus a ten per cent profit margin, fuelled shop floor resentment of war profiteering and stimulated demands for higher pay. Croucher argues that by 1940, over 60 per cent engineering workers were operating under piece rate systems, in a situation where national wage rates were depressed. Piece rates created a situation whereby local shop floor bargaining backed up with the threat of militancy, could create substantial upward movement in local wage rates without necessarily resorting to strike action. Localised militancy fitted into a perception amongst workers that they were low paid and that rising prices and the costs of wartime dislocation were hitting family budgets. The official Cost of Living Index suggests that prices rose 20 per cent between September 1939 and August 1940, followed by a 13 per cent rise in the following year.[29] The shop floor was to provide an arena in which Communists could continue to operate with some success.

The party carried its anti-war message onto the electoral field by standing candidates in by-elections in 1939 and 1940 with very mixed results. However we need to put their performance and that of other anti-war candidates, into a wider context. In the 1914–18, anti-war by-election candidates had received low votes, for example in March 1917 anti-war candidates standing in Stockton and South Aberdeen received 596 and 333 votes respectively. This was three years into the war when most accounts suggest that war weariness was well developed and any jingoism of 1914 had faded. At the Stretford by-election in November 1939, two anti-war candidates stood, Gowrie for the Communist Party and Edwards for the Independent Labour Party. On a low turnout they received a total of 5943 votes. 20 per cent of the votes cast, against a Labour-supported Conservative candidate. At subsequent by-elections candidates who opposed the war received a range of results. Pollitt, standing as an open Communist Party candidate in Silvertown in London's dockland in February 1940, received a disappointing 6 per cent of the vote, whereas in the same month a Communist-backed Independent Labour candidate received 19 per cent of the vote in Southwark. In March 1940 a 'Workers and Pensioners Anti-War Candidate' standing in Kettering won 27 per cent of the vote in the most impressive anti-war vote of this period. Yet the following month only 7 per cent of the voters of Battersea voted for a similar CP-backed candidate, and in June Isobel Brown, standing on a Communist Party ticket received an even more disappointing 4 per cent. The wide fluctuations in the votes received by these candidates reflects a variety of factors, the strength of the candidate, the particular phase of the Phoney War, and specific aspects of the CP's line. Pollitt's election, for example, coincided with the height of the Finnish War, which placed the CP on the defensive as the Soviet Union was widely perceived as attacking a defenceless 'small nation'.

Anti-war feelings were not consistent and did not reflect the majority view at any one time. Particular events such as the Finnish War and the Fall of France created surges of sentiment which made it temporarily difficult to hold an anti-war line. Nevertheless being anti-war or at least highly critical of the Chamberlain government did not consign Communists or other opponents of the war to the political wilderness. Neither is it the case that the ending of the Phoney War created a situation where Communists could not operate. Specifically war-related issues, such as the inadequate provision of air raid protection, or the compulsory mobilisation of industrial workers for night-time fire watching duties, continued to create issues around which Communists could mobilise with some success.

Nina Fishman, in her study focusing on the activities of Communists in the engineering industry where the party had built up a substantial base from the mid 1930s, argues that continuity with the pre-war work-place policies of the party predominate. Whereas the Comintern was calling on British workers to launch strikes against the war, Communist militants, although willing to exploit local factory based grievances and continuing to push for an extension of effective shop floor organisation, avoided bitter all-out strikes and attempted to operate in the flexible constitutional manner which had informed their tactics in the pre-war period. Thus when a lengthy strike broke out at the British Auxiliaries factory in Glasgow in September 1940 over the dismissal of a union convenor: '... Party activists and full time party officials closed ranks with AEU full time officials to defuse the combustible situation' although 'there was strong pressure for a Glasgow wide general strike in solidarity and the high morale of union activists made this possibility real enough to all concerned.' In April 1941 a similar dispute at Swifts Scales in West London was defused by the intervention of party AEU officials. Displaying great ingenuity, party shop stewards at Armstrong's in Coventry, convened as a 'holiday committee', and called the strike they had organised a 'holiday' thus avoiding possible victimisation.[30]

This pragmatic approach to industrial disputes by party activists in the period reflects the de facto autonomy which had grown up during the 1930s for leading party trade unionists. There is little evidence of the party leadership attempting with any conviction to impose a new and more revolutionary 'party line' on industrial militants.[31] However this does not mean that more leftist and combative expressions of working-class anger were not developed by sections of the party. In February 1941 a large scale strike movement among apprentices broke out in the West of Scotland, under the leadership of a hastily convened Clyde Apprentice Committee, dominated by the Young Communist League (YCL). The strike quickly spread to other engineering centres in the North of England in a display of the sort of rank and file-ism which some party AEU stalwarts deplored. The YCL-led committee initially resisted attempts by leading AEU officials, including party members, to bring the strike to a hasty and constitutional settlement. The authorities eventually moved to threaten six 'ringleaders' under the terms of Order 1305 of the Emergency Powers Act which had been introduced in September 1939 and embraced a wide range of industrial relations measures. Order 1305 gave the government the power to impose binding arbitration in disputes with powers of arrest if flouted. Faced with the threat of detention, the apprentices' strike folded.[32]

In the period of the Popular Front in the run up to the Second World War, the Communist Party had been very active in developing alliances with other political forces. In the Sheffield Peace Council, a CP-led organisation, local clergy and members of the Liberal Party were represented. Bill Moore recalls:

> The Soviet–Nazi pact had the effect of breaking up the alliances we had in Sheffield. A lot of people were horrified. The alliances we had build up around disarmament were developed by Aid to Spain, which was massive, strengthened by the campaigns around Munich and Czechoslovakia. Up to August 1939 the alliances we had built not only held but were strengthened. Then suddenly the Nazi–Soviet pact ... instead of being allied to us, those people became hostile.

Popular Front alliances had generally been with groups clearly identified as being to the right of the party. Groups independent of the Communist Party on the left had been in scorned due to the taint of either real or imagined Trotskyism, despite pre-war criticism from Comintern officials of the British party's softness towards Trotskyists.[33] Bereft of their erstwhile Popular Front allies, there is evidence that some party members temporarily shelved their antipathy to the 'Trotsky fascists'. Unsuccessful overtures were made to the ILP in the run-up to the Stretford by-election in December 1939 with the aim of avoiding a split in the anti-war vote. Within some trade union organisations, especially those where unlike engineering the CP did not have a dominant position, there is evidence of Communists collaborating with Trotskyists. The one trade union to pass a resolution which formally adhered to the CP's characterisation of the war as imperialist was the Shop Assistants Union (now known as USDAW) at their Easter 1940 National Conference. The resolution was proposed by a member of the Trotskyist Workers International League and seconded by a Communist. Yet the same conference also defeated a resolution put forward by a CP dominated branch of the union supporting the foreign policy of the Soviet Union.[34] When, in the wake of the London Blitz in the autumn of 1940, a mass movement developed demanding deep shelters and access to the sanctuary of London Underground stations, the London Underground Station and Shelterers Committee elected Harry Ratner, a Trotskyist, as Chairman and Alfie Bass (later to make his name as a TV comic actor), a Communist, as Secretary.

Although there is evidence of the party moving towards some more militant forms of direct action to fit in with the radical rhetoric of the Imperialist War phase, we can begin to see through 1940 a rowing back from openly anti-war positions and a re-emphasis on the centrality of anti-fascism. The ending of the Phoney War with the Norwegian Campaign of April 1940 and the fall of France created a sharper political mood around the question of the war. At the top of British politics this brought into the open the sharp divide within the Conservative Party demonstrated in the famous Norway debate in the House of Commons in May and the subsequent fall of the Chamberlain government. Although the reaction of the party's chief ideologue, Palme Dutt, to Labour's entry into a Coalition government was to claim in inimitable Third Period style that this was further evidence of Labour's fascisisation, the position of the party was gradually shifting.

The new orientation was focused on the notion of the need for a People's Peace which could be brought about by a People's Government, all the time stressing that the war remained fundamentally imperialist. Although still a substantial distance from the War on Two Fronts of September 1939, the insistence on a directly negotiated peace with Germany was shelved. The shifting terminology used at different stages to describe the German Government in the *Daily Worker* merits close study. In the run up to the announcement of the Nazi–Soviet pact in August 1939, the German government are routinely described as 'Nazi'. In a lead article on the pact on 23 August the term is never used to describe the German Government, later in the month and in early September it has been fully restored. However after the change of line in October the term once again disappears, only to make a gradual comeback.

The practical outcome of the new orientation was the People's Convention, an attempt to rebuild a form of Popular Frontism, based this time round on the need for peace and a defence of living standards and democratic freedoms. The culmination of this approach was the National Convention held in January 1941 which, although a CP-run operation, brought together a respectable sample of left-wing opinion. The planned follow-up conference, scheduled for August 1941, never took place, by then the Nazi invasion of Russia had fundamentally changed the situation and the Communist Party had become amongst the most enthusiastic supporters of the Anti-Fascist War in Britain.

What sort of party?

We have to reject the notion that the British Communist Party in 1939 was a hardened, revolutionary, Leninist organisation. In that respect the negative characterisation of the CPGB ten years earlier by the Comintern official Dimitri Manuilsky as a 'society of great friends' has some validity.[35] The position that the party took in 1939 and 1940, occasionally paid lip service to the Leninist notion of revolutionary defeatism, for example the *Daily Worker* carried a number of adverts for copies of a Lawrence and Wishart edition of *Lenin: On Peace & War*. However in this period the party never actively sought or argued for the military defeat of the British ruling class to hasten the day of the revolution. Special Branch with characteristic caution appeared to take elements of the party's 'revolutionary defeatist' rhetoric at face value. A Special Branch report of a Political Bureau meeting at June 1940 suggested that the CP's advice to members in the case of invasion was to adopt an attitude of 'non-resistance'.[36]

What is it, then, that gave the CP its distinctive feel, and how can we explain its hold on its members during this difficult period? An indication comes in one of the condolence letters to Pollitt on his mother's death. Referring to the old generation of party members (the writer's father and Pollitt's mother had just died) Sidney Walmsley, a party member from Grimsby writes:

> We must carry out where they left off and if we serve as faithfully as they did, then we too will have no regrets when our time comes.

When I think of the struggles they faced, I am pleased they lived to see their own class come to power in one sixth of the world, the tasks they have left us is to play our part in the conquest of the remaining five sixth – may we never fail them![37]

A brief survey of the *Daily Worker* and the output of the Left Book Club and other party imprints confirms the point. Books like Dudley Collard's *Soviet Justice and the Trial of Radek and Others*, Johnny Campbell's *Soviet Policy and its Critics* and the Fabians Sidney and Beatrice Webb's *Soviet Communism, a New Civilisation* show a level of identification with the Soviet Union which ran beyond the party's membership. Support and admiration of the Soviet Union and everything Soviet ran like thick red thread through the entire being of the British Communist Party.

For Harry Pollitt, support for the Soviet Union was simply an extension of his basic, gut class loyalties. In a famous passage which must have spoken for thousands of British Communists he described his feelings:

> The thing that mattered to me was that lads like me had whacked the bosses and the landlords, had taken their factories, their lands and their banks ... These were the lads and lasses I must support through thick and thin ... For me these same people could never do, nor ever can do, any wrong against the working class.[38]

This particular sense of a special relationship with 'one sixth of the world', was to impart to many Communist activists an acute sense that history was on their side. Sheffield party activist Bill Moore elaborates:

> Until Franco finally won in 1939, I can never remember feeling dispirited, I can never remember feeling anything but exhilarated. We felt that we were on our way ... We felt that capitalism was on its last legs and that fascism was the last rat in the corner. If we could defeat fascism then we were really on the way to socialism.

It was this faith in the Socialist Motherland which was to provide above all other factors the ideological cement to keep the party together, faced with the diplomatic and military merry-go-round ridden by Stalin. Ironically those moves in Soviet foreign policy which served to alienate the party from their erstwhile Popular Front supporters; the Non Aggression Pact, the carve up of Poland and the Finnish

War, often worked to bolster the internal cohension of the party itself. Fred Westacoff recalls that the Finnish War:

> Strengthened our argument. Yes, there was some anti-Communist feeling at the time, Finland was presented as a small country being attacked by a bully. But we were able to point out, that we were supposed to be at war with Germany, and the government were doing nothing, but as soon as the Finnish crisis broke they came to life. Chamberlain wasn't prepared to seriously fight Nazi Germany, but as soon as it came to having a go at the Soviet Union by sticking up for Finland, he was all for it.

In this account of the relatively cohesive response of the party to the change of line, a minor role is given to the Comintern itself. That is because it was the authority of the Soviet State itself rather than the Comintern which was mobilised by the party leadership to win support for the new line. David Springhall, the CPGB's representative on the Comintern, certainly used the authority of the Comintern to win over the Central Committee of the party to the new line, however the CPs public statement of the new line 'PEACE or WAR? To the Men and Women of Great Britain'[39] makes no reference to the Comintern whilst drawing on the example and authority of the Soviet Union. Fred Westacott recalls: 'It's only afterwards that we knew what the Comintern line was. There had been hints ... but we didn't know that there had been a line from the Comintern for at least a fortnight'. The replacement British party leadership of Win Rust and Rajani Palme Dutt were aware that an appeal to the traditions of international solidarity of the Comintern would carry less weight than the direct authority of Stalin and the Soviet State. The Comintern as the vital tool of transmitting the foreign policy objectives of the Soviet State to foreign Communist parties had proved to be largely redundant, small wonder then that Stalin was willing to disband the organisation as a gesture to his wartime allies in 1943.

That the party did not turn into a sectarian Stalinist rump in 1940, certain in the correctness of its own line but unable to influence the world around it, was due primarily to the existence of a substantial anti-war mood to which it could orientate. The leftist aspects of the party's anti-war stance did not significantly hamper its ability to continue to lead struggles both within the workplace and within working class communities, although its adherence to Soviet foreign policy dictates did. In the period after June 1941, there is evidence of political forces such as both the small Trotskyist groups and populist groups such as the Commonwealth Party prepared to challenge the social truce then endorsed by the CP, gaining significant if often ephemeral support.[40] In this respect the Communist Party was a living contradiction. On the one hand it was the organisation to which thousands of industrial and social militants looked, people who were determined to rid Britain of the sharp social inequalities of the 1930s, people who, in an age before it was fashionable, challenged Britain's role as an Imperial power. On the other hand it was an organisation in which those aspirations were turned towards uncritical support for the Soviet Union.

June 1941: all change

Operation Barbarossa, Hitler's attack on the Soviet Union on 22 June 1941 was to bring about a radical change in circumstances for the Communist Party which enabled it enthusiastically to recast itself in the mould of the Popular Front of the 1934–39 period. After Barbarossa British Communists undoubtedly had a 'good war'. Despite the dislocation caused by wartime conscription membership grew to a peak of 56 000 in 1942 and although the later war years saw a decline from these dizzy heights the level of membership far outstripped anything known from the pre-war period. Conscription hit the Communist Party particularly hard as the party's membership came overwhelmingly from young working-class men. Some Communist trade union activists who worked in protected industries escaped conscription and in the latter years of the war when conscription was introduced for men in their late 30s and 40s, some individual Communists were passed over for political reasons. Ivor Montague the Communist writer and historian who turned 40 in 1944 was issued with RAF call up papers which were subsequently withdrawn.[41] Despite the practical and organisational problems posed by working under wartime conditions, the political benefits of the war were overwhelmingly positive for the party. In addition to continuing to recruit amongst the manual working-class base of the party, the resumption of a Popular Front approach and the overwhelming popularity of the image of the Soviet Union, particularly the Red Army, made party membership once again attractive to a much wider section of liberal and left opinion from all classes. To the established membership, used to swimming hard against the tide of mainstream political opinion, the experience of 'cutting with the grain' of an anti-fascist consensus was heady. For the first time in its history the prospect of the Communist Party moving from the margins of British political life into the mainstream looked a real possibility. As we have discussed above, the sharp 'Imperialist War' phase of the party's policies had modified significantly as the Phoney War had ended with the debacle of Dunkirk. Harry Pollitt, who had been removed from the party leadership in 1939 had gradually been worked back into taking a prominent role, and the vacant position of General Secretary had not been filled. By early 1941 the party's orientation on a Peoples' Convention with its demands for defence of living standards, trade union rights and for a pro-Soviet foreign policy had replaced the demands for a directly negotiated peace with Germany. Party publications, guided as ever by the key influence of Palme Dutt, began to raise once again the dangers of an anti-Soviet alliance between Britain and Germany. Rudolf Hess's flight to Scotland in 1941 was seen, with some justification, as an attempt on the part of a section of the Nazi leadership to bring about this realignment. Just as in the run up to 1939, the party's pronouncements on the war were characteristically contradictory, garnished with the opacity of Dutt's re-workings of the line emanating from Moscow.[42] Stalin refused to countenance the growing evidence of Hitler's invasion until well after the invasion itself was mounted. Palme Dutt, although constantly worried that the warnings from the British Government of Hitler's plans could be a devious ruse, was prescient enough to warn on the eve of Barbarossa in his famous Notes of the Month in *Labour Monthly* of the 'lull before the storm.'[43] The change of party line in July 1941 once again put paid to a major Palme Dutt publishing project. *The Crisis of the British People*, a major book outlining the party's anti-war policies, was due to go to the press in the summer of 1941, its eventual non-appearance being blamed on printing difficulties.[44]

'The issue is clear: victory over the fascist barbarians ...'[45]

June 22 removed all ambiguity. The announcement of the launch of Operation Barbarossa was made on the BBC on the Sunday morning. With most of the Central Committee away from the party's King Street Headquarters, Dutt was to formulate the official party response in the form of a press release. The fundamental change in the characterisation of the war was immediate; Dutt's statement argued the need for the 'rapid and complete victory over Hitlerism'.[46] Dutt's initial position retained the party's hostility towards the Churchill government dominated as it was by 'Tory friends of fascism and coalition Labour leaders'. Within days the Comintern apparatus had intervened decisively in all the major Communist Parties emphasising the need for complete and unconditional support for the allied governments. The return to unconditional anti-fascism was cemented by Pollitt's triumphal return in early July to his former position of General Secretary. The new line was formally announced in a new manifesto entitled 'People's Victory Over Fascism'. This not only stressed the need for a formal alliance with the Soviet Union but also highlighted the need to 'Organise Production for Victory' which was to become the dominant theme of CP efforts in the coming years. Churchill was not to disappoint on the former issue, in his speech to the nation of the evening of 22 June he outlined his position.

> We shall give what help we can to Russia and to the Russian people. We shall appeal to all our friends and allies in every part of the world to take the same course. The Russian danger is our danger ... just as the cause of any Russian fighting for his hearth and home is the cause of free men and free people in every quarter of the globe.[47]

The response of the party, now personified to a great extent by the figure of Pollitt, was to launch a major propaganda drive to support the war. It is during the war years that Harry Pollitt became a real figure on the British political landscape. He spoke and wrote tirelessly reiterating the basic theme of the need to organise and sacrifice for victory. Criticism of the government continued but was focussed to specific strategic issues, most notably the demand for the opening of the Second Front. The theme of the need for a Second Front, an allied land invasion of Europe to augment the First Front being waged by the Red Army in the east, was repeated time and again by the party press and by Pollitt and other party leaders at numerous speeches. This was the overriding political demand championed by the party up until the Normandy landings in 1944, and there is no doubt that it struck a chord. Large crowds would attend Second Front rallies where a wide platform of speakers often starring Pollit would ram home the message and sharply criticise those politicians who appeared to be dragging their feet. Speaking in Trafalgar Square on 19 September 1943, after the invasion of Sicily, Pollitt criticised the 'gross mishandling of the military and political situation in Italy' which had allowed Mussolini to escape and the Germans to occupy Rome.[48] On the home front the CP was to become a completely uncritical champion of the coalition government in its drive for increased production, stopping to criticise only when ministers and in particular employers were seen as not being fully behind the production drive. It was in industry and in particularly in the crucial engineering and aero industries where the CP had built up a significant base amongst shop stewards from the mid 1930s, that the battle for production was waged.

'Everything for the front must be the rallying call ... '[49]

Since the partial recovery in the British economy in the mid to late 1930s and in particular due to the growth in armaments production, CP activists had begun to establish a solid base of influence within key sectors of the engineering industry, notably aircraft manufacture. The ability of the party to establish a shopfloor base in the new industries of the 1930s, for examples the party's successful attempts to organise at the Morris Cowley Plant in Oxford, was to pay handsome dividends. The establishment of the Aircraft Shop Stewards National Council (ASSNC) in 1935 and the publication of the popular rank and file paper *New Propeller* gave a voice to a small but significant group of experienced CP militants, many of whom like Wal Hannington had been out of work for up to a decade. It also provided a way into the party for a generation of younger shop floor activists, many of whose political allegiances to the party were forged during the height of the anti-fascist Popular Front. This was the group who were to play such a crucial role the CP's new battle for production.

Central to drive for production was the CP's endorsement through the now re-named Engineering and Allied Trades Shop Stewards' National Council (E&ATSSNC) of Joint Production Committees (JPCs). The issue of worker participation had a long and chequered history in the British engineering industry. Twice, in 1898 and in 1922, employers had organised national lockouts to attempt to break the hold of skilled craft workers over the production process and establish hegemony over the shopfloor. However by the early 1940s, both under the influence of liberal variants of management theory, and in the realisation that British arms production remained chronically inefficient, some employers were beginning to favour some degree of worker participation. The theme of greater co-ordination and organisation of war production was one stressed in particular by Labour members of the war time coalition government with the enthusiastic backing of the millionaire publisher Lord Beaverbrook who was charged by Churchill with the task of increasing aircraft production. When a proposal for worker participation on production committees had been floated by Ernest Bevin in December 1940 it had been roundly condemned by the Communist Party press as an attempt by the government to introduce fascist-style corporatism into British industry. Party opposition to initiatives such as worker co-operation had been central to the Peoples' Convention, and had been influential in pushing trade unions such as the AEU into a critical position. After April 1941 the change was absolute with the party becoming the most avid enthusiasts for, and participants in, JPCs.

The Communist Party's strategic position in engineering and in particular the assiduous building up of shop stewards organisation was to prove crucial. In effect the weight of the party through the E&ATSSNC provided a component in the government's campaign to overcome the natural reluctance of both the engineering unions and many employers towards production consultation and the introduction of JPCs. The party's campaign in the late summer and Autumn of 1941 centred on a national E&ATSSNC conference held in the Stoll Theatre in London in October which emphasised the need to re-organise production for the war effort, was heavily critical of management incompetence and stressed the need for the establishment of JPCs. There was criticism from the left, initially from activists influenced by Trotskyist groups but subsequently from within the party from shop stewards who saw JPCs as a form of class collaboration.

The experience of JPCs was mixed. In some factories where there was already well established stewards organisation there is some evidence that management used JPCs to attempt to bypass and weaken traditional trade union organisation with JPCs being known as 'Gaffer's Committees' in the Coventry district. However, equally often factory management fought hard against the establishment of JPCs, and sought unsuccessfully to control them, seeing them as an encroachment on managerial prerogative. At the Rover plants in Birmingham there was a hard-fought campaign in late 1941 over elections to the JPCs which were overwhelmingly won by the CP-influenced stewards. The party's championing of production was also most popular amongst workers in newer engineering centres such as aircraft engineering and motor manufacturing and it is no coincidence that recruits to the party during 1941 and 1942 came disproportionately from this group. The older bastions of heavy engineering and shipbuilding, where there was often a long established tradition of shop stewards' organisation often proved resistant. Older workers in particular had memories of the bitter class battles which had broken out in the engineering industry in the latter years of the Great War. These traditions were readily passed down to younger workers. In areas such as Glasgow where there remained a significant Independent Labour Party tradition the Communist Party began to lose the support of militants:

> They [the Communists] are now emphatic in their insistence upon uninterrupted work at the highest standard of intensity. For this reason they are rather suspect and have lost any influence that they had.[50]

The party's new found enthusiasm for production was also to lead party activists into previously uncharted territory as opponents of shopfloor industrial militancy and as strike breakers. This feature of the party's policy was to set up a significant counter-dynamic to the generalised growth of the party during the war years. There is evidence from the engineering industry both of CP members leaving and more significantly of a layer of previous CP shopfloor sympathisers peeling away from the party's perceived pro-production and pro-management positions. This was to open up space to the left of the party, which for a brief time during the war could be filled by the small organisations of British Trotskyism and the rather looser ILP. Although very few in number the Trotskyists were able to make interventions in a number of wartime disputes, and in particularly in the well-organised and militant engineering industry and in mining. Despite their successes on the industrial front the Trotskyist groups were unable to sustain their challenge to the position of the CP as the credible left-wing workers organisation – it was to be another quarter of a century until the CP's dominant position on the far left of British politics was to be challenged and eventually taken.

As we have seen up until July 1941, despite no evidence of a national policy of fomenting industrial unrest, party activists had often been at the forefront of strike activity. From July the culture of the party changed dramatically. Strikes, especially in industries which could be deemed as vital to war production, and in a campaign for a 'total war' which the party advocated that covered just about everything, were now frowned upon. At the 1942 Communist Party conference Harry Pollitt went out of his way in his address to the delegates to praise a Communist docker in Hull who had broken a strike: 'When the rest of the dockers struck work, he fought against it because he believed that the course of action he recommended would get what was wanted without a strike. What courage, what a sacred spirit of real class consciousness, to walk on the ship's gangway and resume his job ... '[51] While strikes remained localised, brief and small in scale, the party's hostility to strikes posed local difficulties for individual Communists or small factory party groups. However these problems were not insurmountable, in some cases Communist shop stewards supported and even led strikes in contradiction of the official line in order to retain their credibility with the rank and file. However as soon as strikes spread and took on a district wide aspect as in the case of the 'Total Time' strike in the Tyneside shipyards in October 1942, the reputation of the party as a national organisation was on the line. In the case of the Tyneside strike, the party mobilised significant resources to defeat the strike, condemning the strike in the pages of the *Daily Worker* as a 'disgrace to all concerned'[52] and dispatched Harry Pollitt to personally persuade leading party stewards to disassociate themselves from it. The pattern of strike activity was to increase, in line with experiences of the First World War, as the threat of military defeat subsided. Grievances amongst workers included perennial problems over pay rates, and disputes in particular over equal pay for women as women gradually took on more and more jobs in engineering and in armaments production. Communists naturally supported equal pay for women as a socially progressive ideal, but typically, as in the case of the 1943 strike at Rolls Royce Hillington factory in Glasgow, argued against strike action to achieve it. The Communists at Hillington found themselves in a doubly embarrassing position due to the influence of organised Catholic trade unionists, who traditionally had been derided by Communists as being both socially reactionary and 'soft on the bosses', actively supporting the strike.

Both Fishman and Croucher suggest that as the war drew to a conclusion the party's concern to maintain the 'no strike' position was subtly amended. Whether this was, as Fishman suggests, due to the 'tolerant guidelines' laid down for by Pollitt and Campbell for members to follow and the 'shrewd forbearance' of the party's interpretation of the pro-production line is open to question.[53] In a lengthy and closely argued political letter to the party membership in September 1943, Pollitt warned strongly against the notion that 'the worst is over and the end is in sight', raising the spectre of fifth columnists and Tory die-hards conspiring to undermine the war effort. The imminent release from prison of Oswald Mosley, the pre-war fascist leader, the rash of strikes which 'divide and confuse the working class' and the activity of the Trotskyists were pulled together by Pollit to present a picture where Communists had to continue to ' ... call for the greatest production that is possible-to make sacrifices and enforce sacrifices on others. To support every measure to win the war-however irksome it may be.' In a deliberate reference to Lenin's famous April Theses, written to win over the Bolsheviks to his point of view in April 1917, Pollitt called on Communists to 'patiently explain' to their fellow workers the need for continued sacrifice.[54] Although it is clear that the threat to the CPs position in engineering from its left-wing critics was not sustained, the party did not continue the dramatic level of growth into the later years of the war that it showed in the 18 months after Barbarossa.

Despite problems in holding the productionist line amongst industrial militants many British Communists have looked back on the war years as a golden age. Party leaders such as Harry Pollitt became, if not household names, then at least a left-wing point of reference for British politics. The popularity of Russia and the image of the heroic struggle of the Russian people against nazism led to the establishment of Anglo-Soviet friendship societies in which CP members were to play a prominent part. The *Daily Worker*, banned in January 1941 during the period of the CPs opposition to the war, was eventually freed from restriction in August 1942 and was back in daily publication by September. The campaign to remove the ban had involved a highly successful campaign within the trade unions and the Labour Party culminating in a resolution narrowly carried at the 1942 Labour Party conference calling for an end to the ban. However the party still faced stiff opposition from within the Labour Party, with Herbert Morrison the Home Secretary in the coalition government taking a keen and hostile interest in the activity of the CP.

The electoral truce

The Communist Party's position as a loyal supporter of the National Government also led the party to support the electoral truce that was declared for the duration of the war between Labour, Liberals and the Conservatives. Under the terms of the truce, a by-election caused by the death or resignation of a sitting MP would be contested by a National Government supporting a candidate from the same party as the outgoing member. Whereas as we have seen, in the pre-1941 period the Communist Party fought numbers of by-elections with varied success, in the post-1941 period the party not only abstained from all independent electoral activity, but went as far as calling for a vote for Conservative candidates. Of the 25 by-elections held between

Operation Barbarossa, which marked the beginning of the CP's adherence to the electoral truce, and the end of the war, all but one, a Liberal, were held by Tories. This meant that not only were the Communist Party calling for a Tory vote but that the Labour Party did not offer up an electoral alternative at all. The electoral truce opened up a significant political vacuum on the left which was exploited both by the Independent Labour Party and the short–lived Commonwealth Party led by Richard Acland which won three wartime by-elections. Whenever the Independent Labour Party stood candidates the CP were quick to leap to the defence of Tory candidates, issuing leaflets denouncing the ILP as 'associating with Trotskyists who were publicly convicted as acting as Hitler's agents in every country in the world'. During the Cardiff by-election in 1942 the ILP candidate Fenner Brockway was attacked as an agent of Hitler, with a CP election leaflet declaring 'better a vote for Sir James Grigg [the Tory candidate] an honest capitalist than a false socialist'.[55] However holding this line was evidently distasteful for some party members, and the relative success of anti-National Government candidates such as those supported by the ILP and Commonwealth, who reflected to some extent popular discontent with aspects of domestic policy, was worrying to the party. Herbert Morrison's decision to release the pre-war fascist leader Oswald Mosley from prison in November 1943 caused a brief breach in the electoral truce. When a by-election was announced in Acton and the Executive Committee (EC) voted that feelers should be put out to the local Labour Party to put up a suitable Labour candidate rather than supporting the Tory. In the end a Tory stood and the Communist Party dutifully attacked the ILP candidate who challenged him. However when the Tories put up the son of the Duke of Devonshire, the owner of the Chatsworth estate, in the rural West Derbyshire constituency in January 1944, left-wing and democratic opinion was outraged. The Communist Party called for a vote for the Independent left-wing candidate who won the seat.[56] The breach did not last long but remaining tensions caused by the policy in the party led to the EC formally writing to the all three of the major coalition parties in June 1944 urging either joint selection conferences of the pro-coalition parties or freeing the parties from their obligation not to run candidates against each other in by-elections: ' ... failing adoption of such an agreed solution ... we must reserve our freedom of action as a party in future by-elections.'[57] No agreed solution was reached, yet the party's threat to break with the coalition turned out to be idle.

Paradoxically, whilst abstaining from standing parliamentary candidates during the war, the Communist Party's overall policy on parliament and the possibility of a parliamentary road to socialism was shifting decisively. The party's 1935 programme with the revolutionary-sounding title *For Soviet Britain* had, despite its generally Popular Frontist tone, rejected the notion that socialism could be achieved through parliamentary methods. The CP's forays into the electoral field were conceived primarily as opportunities for propaganda, and the role of CP MPs was to use their position to further the revolutionary goals of the party. In 1943 the party established a Parliamentary and Local Government Commission which came up with proposals for proportional representation on the Single Transferable Vote model, and the party's 1944 draft programme *Britain for the People* envisaged a 'twin track' policy whereby Communist and Labour MPs in parliament would work in conjunction with an extra parliamentary movement to bring about the establishment of socialism. For the rest of its effective life the CP was to chase the chimera of a parliamentary road to socialism with no real success. Caught in the trap of its inability to come to an electoral agreement with Labour to stand 'progressive' candidates, and the extreme difficulty of making an electoral breakthrough using the First Past the Post electoral system, this key element of the twin track strategy was never to get off the ground.

By the final year of the war the political truce was coming under further strain. Within the Labour Party in particular, attention was focused on the real possibility of a postwar majority Labour government which could begin to redress the long standing grievances built up by workers through the lean years of the 1920s and 1930s and start the construction of a socialist Britain. These demands for 'no return to the 1930s' had been reflected within the political elite as early as 1942 with the drafting of the Beveridge report and its demand for the ending of the 'Five Giants'; Idleness, Ignorance, Want, Squalor and Disease. The Communist Party in its full-blown productionist mode post-1941 had studiously refrained from any concerted engagement with questions of postwar society. As the party's own official historian Noreen Branson admits, 'party leaders had regarded talk about what should happen after the war with some suspicion, believing it could be used as diversion from the war effort.'[58] It was not until 1944 that *Britain for the People* was to emerge. Once again we have the party placing itself significantly to the right of much of left-wing British opinion during this period. This was further evidenced by the failed attempt by the CP to call for a continuation of the wartime alliance with Churchill and the Tories into postwar Britain.

There is little doubt that the key figures within the leadership of the CP went along wholeheartedly with the significant shift to the right implied by their new line. No longer would the struggle for socialism require revolutionary organisation, but rather a gradual progression towards a planned society could be built by consensus out of the experience of wartime planning. Pollitt's enthusiasm for the continuation of the wartime alliance was however strongly prompted by the line emerging from Moscow. Two key events marking a significant rightward shift in the international Communist movement were the dissolution of the Comintern by Stalin in June 1943, and the Tehran Conference in December 1943, the first of the wartime conferences which were to bring together Stalin, Churchill and Roosevelt. The communique issued from Tehran included the pledge of all three leaders to 'work together in the war and in the peace that will follow' and 'banish the scourge and terror of war for many generations'. The CP press trumpeted the new spirit of international co-operation heralded in by the 'Spirit of Tehran'. Palme Dutt went so far as to detect in the Bretton Woods agreement of 1944, which did much to underpin the economic hegemony of the US in the postwar world economy, a new phase of international economic collaboration. The most extreme case of the influence of the spirit of Tehran within the international Communist movement was the decision of the CPUSA under the leadership of Earl Browder to dissolve itself, a decision that was initially approvingly commented on by Pollitt and Dutt.[59]

'Browderism' as this policy of liquidationism came to be called, was not taken up in the British party. Indeed there is some evidence of tentative moves towards ending the party's support for the coalition at the end of the war with the appearance of the slogan 'Smash the Tories' in party material discussing a possible postwar election. However after the Yalta conference in February 1945, the party's position shifted abruptly to the right. Now the call was for National Unity, a continuation of the war time coalition based on a 'Labour and progressive majority' but including progressive Tories.[60] Aggregate meetings of the party membership were held in March 1945 to endorse the new position. Members at the meetings raised serious and searching questions. One member asking 'What are the fundamental differences between Tehran and Crimea [Yalta]?'[61] With neither the Labour or Conservative Parties seriously considering a long term continuation of the National Government, the party unsurprisingly failed in the attempt to hold together the wartime alliance. Attention was then turned to a campaign for a joint 'progressive' slate for the forthcoming General Election which would draw together Labour and Communist voters behind locally agreed candidates. The narrow defeat of such a proposal for Progressive Unity at the May 1945 Labour conference shows significant support for this idea amongst both trade unionists and Labour Party members. However it was vigorously opposed by the Labour leadership, long used to rebuffing CP-inspired calls for unity. As part of the campaign for Progressive Unity the party offered to reduce the number of seats that it intended to challenge Labour for from a notional 52 to just 22, issuing a press release to that effect in April.[62] However there is no evidence in the archive material that there was ever any serious discussion at a national level to stand more than 22 or 23 candidates.

The party's approach to the 1945 election was a disaster. Boosted by its high-profile role in campaigns over production and the Second Front, the party both overestimated its own support and seriously underestimated the level of working-class support for Labour and the deep desire amongst millions of people radicalised by the war to kick the Tories out. Palme Dutt characterised those who argued that Labour could win an outright election victory in 1945 as 'dangerously unrealistic'.[63] As one rather more perceptive member put it at the time of the debate over National Unity in April 1945; 'Is not this whole policy [of calling for national unity] a completely defeatist attitude towards the possibility of Labour and progressive forces wining a victory? There is a big swing to the Left in the country, many people are hoping to get rid of Churchill and the Tories, and our proposals will be very unpopular.'[64] The party's approach to the election combined the worst elements of sectarianism towards the Labour Party and opportunism towards the notion of national unity. The post-mortem that the EC carried out into the election reveals that many members were confused by the party's position, and in numerous cases were unwilling to campaign for Communists standing against Labour candidates.[65] Historians sympathetic to the Communist Party such as Noreen Branson skate over the embarrassing mistakes of the election in their portrayal of the party in its 'finest hour'. The sharp volte face after Yalta once again begs the question as to what extent the party leadership were obeying direction from Moscow or at least interpreting the mood music coming from Stalin at Yalta? The Yalta Conference marked the highpoint in the relationship between Churchill and Stalin, featuring as it did the notorious exchange of a scrap of paper on which the two war leaders had sketched out the division of postwar Europe into spheres of influence. Stalin was involved in diplomatic realpolitik at Yalta and if keeping Churchill on board could in any way be helped by the British Communist Party taking a conciliatory position towards Churchill's pretensions to lead postwar Britain, then so much the better.

In the event the Communist Party stood their 22 candidates at the 1945 election, winning just two seats as Labour swept to a 146 majority landslide. The two seats they won reflected specific localised bastions of party strength. Willie Gallacher the lone Communist MP during the war years was re-elected in West Fife, one of the remaining Little Moscows, and Phil Piratin won the Mile End constituency with 5075 votes. Piratin won Mile End, which prior to the workings of the modern day Boundary Commission was one of the smallest and most compact constituencies in the country, on the basis of a Jewish East End vote. The party still enjoyed enormous credibility amongst East London Jews going back to its success at the Battle of Cable Street, which was celebrated in Piratin's 1948 book, *Our Flag Stays Red*. During the war the party also benefited from the high standing of Russia, which was seen as the main force resisting Hitler's anti-semitism. The party famously raised far greater sums through the Jewish Fund for Soviet Russia than did the Board of Deputies in its campaign to raise funds for the war. As Harry Srebrnick has argued, 'the Stepney Communist Party served as the vehicle for the political aspirations of a sizeable section of Stepney's working-class Jewish population.'[66]

Harry Pollitt received a creditable 45 per cent of the vote in the Rhondda but just failed to win a seat. Palme Dutt fighting the Birmingham Sparkbrook seat against the Colonial Secretary L. S. Amery on the platform of support for Indian independence came a poor third with only 7 per cent of the vote. Despite the problems and the disappointing outcome the 1945 election marked the highpoint of the CP's electoral success, subsequent election results showed a steep and relentless decline at a time when the party was to stress more and more the possibility of a parliamentary road to socialism.

Conclusion

Although sharply isolated from official culture, mildly repressed by the state and shorn of many of its pre-war Popular Front allies due to its 'About Turn' in policy in October 1939, the Communist Party survived the early years of the war. In fact it found itself able to swim in a current of working-class opinion which was hostile to the Chamberlain government and cynical about demands to tighten belts because 'there's a war on'. Campaigns such as that around the People's Convention showed significant potential to build the party. However there is no doubt that both the leadership and the rank and file saw the opportunity to return to a 100 per cent anti-fascist orientation after Barbarossa as liberating.

The period 1941–45 when the party embraced 'social patriotism' saw the CP experience rapid growth and enjoy its own 'finest hour'. The numerical growth of the party depended largely on a general sense of well-being felt by many of the left towards the Soviet Union and its war effort and many of the new members put on during the war years were not to remain active. But although support for the Soviet Union was a positive asset in the aftermath of Barbarossa, the twists and turns in party policy during the war years as the British party leadership sought to interpret the latest foreign policy objective of the Soviet state was ultimately, as we have argued throughout this book, highly corrosive. By 1945 membership had once again declined from its peak in 1942, and the target of 100 000 members set by Pollitt in 1943 was a mirage. The favourable international situation which had enabled the CP to swim for a short while in the mainstream of British politics was soon to come to an end. Although the party remained rooted in the industrial working class throughout the war, the experience of working for production and acting as a brake rather than a spur for rank and file workplace militancy was to change further the culture of the party. Although the party was to shift leftwards again under the impact of the Cold War, the Second World War marked the final end of any pretence that the CPGB remained a revolutionary party.

4
Past its Peak: 1945–56

Coming out of the war, the Communist Party seemed to be at the height of its power. Largely as a result of its politics of left patriotism, it had gained a level of respectability. In the difficult conditions of war, with its members ever likely to be called up, the party held together a large membership of between 35 000 and 56 000 members. These members were overwhelmingly drawn from manual industry. Of the 754 delegates to the 1944 party congress, over half were members of the five main manual unions. One hundred and ninety three were members of the AEU engineer's union, 81 were members of the TGWU transport workers' union, 52 were members of the miners' NUM, 33 were members of the electricians' ETU, 32 were members of the rail-workers' union, the NUR. At the Labour Party Conference in May 1945, the Communist Party's motion calling for 'Progressive Unity' was supported by the delegations of the AEU, the NUM, the ETU, the firefighters' union, the painters union, the vehicle builders' union, and the train drivers' union ASLEF. The party-backed engineering workers' paper, the *New Propeller*, had a circulation of 94 000. In 1945, the party had two MPs, Willie Gallacher and Phil Piratin, and one member, the bus worker Bert Papworth, on the General Council of the TUC. The best sign of the CP's strength was its newspaper. During the years 1945–51, the Daily Worker had a circulation of over 100 000 and in March 1945, the party's membership stood at 45 535. Most party members were still young, the average age of delegates to the 1944 conference was just thirty-two. At the same time, the CP's tactic of applying for membership to the Labour Party seemed to be on the verge of taking off. In June 1943, a motion at the Labour Party Conference calling for 'Progressive Unity' with the CP was defeated by 712 000 votes to 1 951 000. In May 1945, a similar motion lost by just

1 219 000 to 1 314 000.[1] As the logical consequence of this shift, the party adopted a new programme in 1944, *Britain for the People*. The programme argued that with a new parliament, Britain could progress directly to Socialism, without going through a revolution first.

Yet beneath the surface, there were frustrations among the party's industrial cadre. The drive for production saw the party supporting uninterrupted work in the factories at the highest level of intensity. Meanwhile, the CP had established a layer of officials within the machinery of several of the larger unions. Arthur Horner was president of the South Wales miners, Abe Moffat was president of the Scottish miners, Joe Scott and Gilbert Hitchings were on the AEU executive, Wal Hannington and George Crane were national organisers for the AEU, Tim Burns was on the executive of ASLEF, Jim Gardner was general secretary of the Foundry Workers' Union, John Horner was general secretary of the FBU. It was not worth jeopardising the position of these officials, merely out of any commitment to the interests of ordinary workers. The perspective of building an independent rank-and-file movement was shelved. Not surprisingly, the Communist Party began to loosen its hold on its periphery of left-wing stewards in the factories. In 1944, for example, the party's Executive Committee complained of the 'very low level of factory group life'. In response, the party briefly dissolved its factory groups, and instructed its members to join residential branches in their home area. According to one observer, Robert Emmett,

> As the CP members at factory and job level began to find that their CP comrades in the top jobs of their unions were another bunch of trade union officials, differing hardly at all from the official Transport House variety, disillusion spread rapidly and the CP began to lose the real base it ever had – in the factories and particularly among the shop stewards.[2]

The direction was established, even if it would be some years before the party's industrial decline became clear.

The changing international situation set the limits inside which the Communist Party of Great Britain operated. As the Second World War drew to a close, the leaders of Britain, Russia and America agreed to divide up the world into two spheres. The deal was signed at the Yalta conference in February 1945. In return for a free hand in most of Eastern Europe, Stalin renounced any plans to spread Russian influence across the rest of the world. The mass Communist Parties of Greece,

France and Italy (possessing 70 000, 500 000 and two million members respectively in 1945) were instructed not to go too far. Mass armed resistance movements contributed to the defeat of fascism. Factory and local committees sprang up. Yet as the French Communists entered General de Gaulle's government, the Italian party turned its back on mass insurrection. The upsurge was held in check.

As Ian Birchall has argued, the postwar Communist Parties of Western Europe became much less important to Moscow than their predecessors of the 1930s. This was not just true of the small British party, but even of the mass Communist Parties in France and Italy. The declining global importance of the western CPs was a product of several factors. Through the late 1940s and into the 1950s, the defence of the Soviet Union was increasingly based on nuclear arms, and there was little to be gained by threatening the West with the spectre of working-class revolt. Meanwhile, increased working-class prosperity fitted well with the prevalent attitude of do-it-yourself syndicalism. Party militants in Britain could win support on the shop-floor, but there was no chance of any significant growth in the party's electoral support. Splits within the Soviet bloc reduced the automatic loyalty and discipline of the Western Communist Parties. In addition, Communist militants believed that there was a similarity between planned 'capitalism' in the West and planned 'Socialism' in the East. This justified their desire for rapprochement between the Communist and Socialist parties. For all these reasons, the Western Communist Parties came to look more and more like the Social Democratic Parties which existed in Europe before 1914. They shared the old emphasis on gradualism, the ideology of mechanical and abstract Marxism, the emphasis on the success of building the organization of the movement, the same hostility to workers' power.[3]

The effects of these changes in Britain was to polarize convinced Communists in one of two directions. One large group remained ultra-loyal to the Soviet Union, the first Socialist state. Another group saw a contradiction between the reformism of the Popular Front era and loyalty to Moscow. These latter Communists stressed their loyalty to British traditions and to the broad class alliances of 1935–39. The moment that individual Communists came to work out their own individual response to these rival poles of attraction, they began to step beyond the bounds of party loyalty. All sorts of rival traditions were to flourish in the space between Stalinism and Social Democracy, including Titoism, New Leftism, Maoism and Eurocommunism. A number of Communists joined rival parties. In the 1980s, the party itself would eventually be torn apart by the contradiction between the two strategies, expressed as it was in the rivalry between the *Morning Star* and *Marxism Today*. Although it would be some years before the full extent of the contradiction was fully felt, the period after 1945 did see a number of crises in which the tensions were made clear, and the party was unable to continue as the monolithic body which it had been before 1939.

Revolutionaries and labour

The crucial task for the British Communist Party in the immediate aftermath of war was to relate in the most effective way possible to the Labour government. Here, as before, the party aimed to navigate between the two extremes of sectarianism and capitulation. The challenge was to relate to what Labour actually did. The 1945–51 Labour government did achieve real reforms. The National Health Service was set up. The railways, mines, gas and electricity were all nationalized. The government built 200 000 houses a year. Unemployment never rose above 250 000. Given Labour's successes, it was imperative for the Communist Party to operate as a friendly critic. If the CP had simply attacked Labour for not introducing workers' power, then most workers would have seen the party as a sect. The party's influence would have withered. But if it had withdrawn all criticism, and welcomed everything Labour did, without calling for any more left-wing measures, then the party would have been side-lined. If the party had simply acted as a cheerleader for Labour, then it would have been incapable of offering any alternative politics. The need to argue a consistent line grew as Labour's reforms petered out after the winter of 1947–48. Certainly for the last three years of Labour government, there was a space to the left of Labour, provided the CP could exploit it.

In practice, the Communist Party veered from one extreme to the other. As we have seen, the party had a disastrous start in the 1945 election. The party overestimated its own support, and underestimated the level of working-class support for the Labour Party. Rather than calling for a clear class vote for Labour, the CP suggested an alliance between the CP, Labour, and the Conservatives, leading to a 'Labour and progressive majority'.[4] Historians sympathetic to the Communist Party, such as Noreen Branson, have downplayed the events of the election, but the Communist Party's decision was an embarrassment. It made things easier for anti-Communists in the Labour Party, and meant that the CP took little gain from the swing left. Labour won with a huge majority of 146, yet just two Communist MPs were elected, Willie Gallacher and Phil Piratin.⁵

Having called for a Labour–Tory pact in the election, the Communist Party determined to not repeat its mistake afterwards. From the election of 1945 until late 1947, the party acted as the most loyal prop to the government. The Labour Party was now immune from criticism. Five days after the election, strike-breaking troops were sent into the Surrey Docks. The *Daily Worker* refused to condemn them, and gave a neutral account under the headline, 'Troops take over London Docks'. In 1946, there was a renewed attempt to affiliate the Communist Party to Labour. Harry Pollitt wrote an obsequious letter to the secretary of the Labour Party, Morgan Phillips, stressing the common position of the CP and Labour. Unity 'would afford the opportunity for the special contribution of our party, with the devotion and campaigning enthusiasm of our membership, to be made in a constructive and helpful fashion to the common tasks of the Labour movement in this period.'⁶

After July 1945, the party returned to its war-time theme of increased production. Writing in *Labour Monthly*, J. R. Campbell described the Labour government as though it was already socialist, 'The trade unionists must recognize the fact that they are operating in a controlled economy which is being steered by a Labour government. They will have to consider the bearing of any wage policy which they put forward on the entire economic policy that the government is pursuing.' Any obstacle to increased production would have to be resisted. Campbell pointed to the slow rate of work in London's blitz repairs, insisting that Social Democracy should be defended against the interests of workers. Being a socialist meant opposing the best activists in the class. In his words: 'A minority of building workers did not play the game and this scallywag minority was not combated sufficiently by the active trade unionists on the jobs. Sabotage of the Labour Government may come not merely from the class-conscious employers but from the class-conscious in the ranks of the workers.'⁷

The impact of Communist support for Labour in 1945–47 was felt most strongly in the workplaces. Although the Communist Party did not break strikes, as it had in 1941–45, it did do everything to stress that Labour policies had removed the need for protest. Arthur Horner, now general secretary of the miners' NUM, insisted that nationalisation had solved the need for workers' control,

> Everything now depends upon an adequate supply of coal to keep the present industry active. Production is the key, not only to a

prosperous mining industry, but also to an expanding and vigorous British economy ... The main fight of the future will not be between management and men, it will be a struggle against Mother Nature.[8]

The CP continued to insist on the need for Joint Production Committees. There was little emphasis on the need to build the unions from below, far more weight was put on the need to change unions from above. More left-wing officials were needed. More trade unionists should be appointed onto the several boards running the nationalised industries. As in 1941–45, Communist Party propaganda stressed the need to replace strikes with visits to government ministers, delegations, and appeals for outside intervention.

The party's postwar production drive has recently been defended by the historian James Hinton, who argues that increased production was the only way to save British capital from its inevitable postwar decline, 'the Communist Party was a potential agency of capitalist modernization ... between 1941 and 1947 this was indeed the role that it sought: making capitalism work, first to win the war and then to consolidate the peace.'[9] Hinton's idea seems to be that by restraining their power, workers were also demonstrating their independence. The result would be a reduction of managerial control. Such an argument must rest on several questionable foundations. One is the productivist notion that capitalist crisis is caused by workers' greed. In other words, build partnerships, increase profits and everyone benefits. Yet in the late 1940s profits did rise more quickly than wages, in Britain at much the same rate as elsewhere. High profits were not enough to fight off the competition of rival companies. A more likely explanation of the relative postwar decline of the British economy is that many British firms were simply undercapitalised. Too many firms relied on low wages to guarantee profits, when they would have done relatively better to invest more quickly in new machinery. A yet more important criticism comes to mind. If the great historic task of British Communism was to rescue capitalism, then what had happened to the vision of the party's founders? If the Communist Party of Great Britain had dropped the revolutionary socialism of the early 1920s – and the authors of this book would argue that it had – then this transformation was not acknowledged in the party's own literature. As one leaflet of this period proclaimed, 'The Communist Party is based upon Marxism, the scientific socialist theory which shows that the capitalist system exists through the expropriation of the working class ... that the way to Socialism lies through the intensification of the class struggle against the capitalists and through the seizure of power by the working class.'[10] If the Communist Party of Great Britain was now different from what it had been, then the party itself would not acknowledge the change.

Whatever the merits of a strategy of increasing production, there was little chance for the party to impress with its new line. In 1947, the party was still demanding increased production. Under the pressure of the Cold War, however, the CP was forced to turn rapidly to the left, and within a year the party would again denounce increased production as a bosses' trick.

The Cold War (1)

In March 1947, President Truman announced US intervention against the left in Greece. He established what became known as the 'Truman Doctrine', the idea that America could intervene abroad against any radical movement which it considered threatening to its interests. In June 1948, Marshall Aid was announced, economic support was offered to the countries of Europe, provided that they distanced themselves from Communism. In October 1947, the CPs of East and West Europe formed the Cominform, or Communist Information Bureau, a regular gathering of Communist parties to co-ordinate political activity. Although not a member of the Cominform, the British party was expected to follow its decisions, communicated via the comrades in France. Compared to the earlier epoch of the Comintern, the mechanism of control were now reduced. Yet authority within the International had always been about self-discipline and internalised authority. National leaders were expected to think themselves into the mind of the Moscow apparatus. Being a 'good Communist' in a local branch meant obeying orders – before they were given. The British party had no difficulty in turning left, as was now required.

As the Cold War began, Labour shifted to the right. The government stressed the need for deflation. Chancellor Stafford Cripps announced a wage freeze. In 1948, wage increases were held to 4 per cent, against an inflation rate of 5 per cent. In the following year, wage rises were held to 2 per cent, against inflation of 4 per cent. As Labour attacked on the wage front, so other reforms were toned down. The nationalisation of steel was dropped, and there were no new reforming bills on the scale on 1945–47. At the same time, the TUC General Council attacked the role of Communists in the trade unions. In July 1949, the TGWU conference passed a rule insisting that no union positions could be held by members of the CP. Eight members of the TGWU's executive were sacked. Bert Papworth was removed from the General Council of the TUC. Other officials were removed from posts in the AEU, the shopworkers union USDAW, and the Civil Service Clerical Association. Labour's Cold War offensive against ordinary workers culminated in a series of strikes, in which the government used both troops and wartime anti-strike legislation against the trade union movement. The most bitter disputes came on the London docks.[11]

In the worsening climate at the start of the Cold War, the Communist Party talked first to the left. The party's room for manoeuvre was limited. It would have been absurd to continue the earlier message of increased production for the Labour government, while the same government was busy purging Communists from the Civil Service and the teaching profession. The clearest sign of its new politics was the party's renewed hostility to increasing production. Why should workers make the bosses rich? George Allison defended the change of line:

> The wage-freeze, the speed-up and the war alliance with big business provide no problems concerning the British workers and their powerful trade union movement. Resistance to all these measures, the development of class solidarity, the fight against profits and for the burning needs of the people, is the only line of development for the working-class movement.[12]

In the 1940s, the CPGB was still the largest force on the British left. Its politics exercised significant influence on a milieu of shop stewards and radical workers. It was no doubt a step forward for the trade union movement when the party reversed its support for increased production. Yet the conversion would have been more impressive if it had been flavoured with humility, or perhaps an admission that the old line had been wrong.

The Communist Party changed tack in the winter of 1947–48, but the party returned not to the left, but to the sectarian habits of 1929–34. The political message was slightly different. The party coloured its sectarianism with a different touch of left patriotism. Yet the effect was the same, the Communist Party separated itself from majority opinion on the left. So in 1949, Koni Zilliacus MP was expelled from the Labour Party for his opposition to Attlee's leadership. Although he was favourable towards Russia, he was also a supporter of Marshal Tito in Yugoslavia, who had now fallen out with Stalin. *Labour Monthly* accused Zilliacus of 'frantically treading water in an ocean of lies'. The anti-Tito line was backed up by James Klugmann's *From Trotsky To Tito*, a profoundly dishonest book written by a former champion of the Marshal's wartime exploits. No alternative to the Russian clique was allowed. What was true of politics was also true of cultural life. In 1948, the Soviet geneticist Lysenko received official backing from Stalin for his idea that changing environment would lead to inheritable genetic modifications. The British party followed suit, antagonising the leading party scientists, including J. B. S. Haldane, who filed his last report for the *Daily Worker* on 9 August 1950, and quit the party soon after.[13]

The Communist Party's new line can be seen at its worst when it came to immigration. The *Daily Worker* did welcome Jamaican immigrants, sending journalist Peter Fryer to report the arrival of the *Empire Windrush* in 1948. But, as a result of its Cold War politics, it opposed the immigration of 'fascist Poles' and East Europeans to Britain. Welsh miners' leader Arthur Horner insisted 'We will not allow the importation of foreign – Polish, Italian, or even Irish – labour to stifle the demands of the British people to have decent conditions in British mines.' Harry Pollitt's *Looking Ahead*, combined left-wing rhetoric with nationalist attacks on migration, 'Does it make sense that we allow 500 000 of our best young men to put their names down for emigration abroad when at the same time we employ Poles who ought to be back in their own country?' The crime of these Poles was to have chosen not to return to the self-proclaimed Socialist state established by Russian tanks at the end of the war.[14] Such xenophobia became common currency within the party in the late 1940s. J. R. Campbell's speech to the 20th Congress of the party in February 1948, announced that the CP was 'the patriotic British party above all others.' The US workers' movement was attacked for its capitulation to capitalism, the American Federation of Labour was 'the chosen instrument of Wall Street'. American capitalism became 'fascist big business'.

Similarly, the 1951 version of *The British Road to Socialism* combined left attacks on the Labour Party with an unpleasant chauvinism, 'The Communist Party declares that the leaders of the Tory, Liberal and Labour Parties and their spokesmen in the press and on the BBC are betraying the interests of Britain to dollar imperialism. Our call is for the unity of all true patriots to defend British national interest and independence.' Patrick Goldring followed this up with an article for *World News and Views*, on 'The Menace of the Comic Strip'. 'American comic strips, now being widely distributed in the country in the form of "comic books", are a dangerous drug which is debauching the minds of our children.' 'Not all US comic strips are 'evil', Goldring confessed – but most were.[15] When comics were not attacked, it was the turn of electric music, another baleful American influence which threatened the minds of British youth. Not only was this bad socialism, it was also a flawed way to build a left-wing party. There were plenty of rival forces, right-wing Labourites, Conservatives and even fascists, which could easily outbid such right-wing populism.

Indeed the period 1945–51 witnessed a brief revival in the fortunes of one such populist force, British fascism.[16] After 1945, and despite the enormous unpopularity which the fascists enjoyed, the former members of the British Union of Fascists set up a new organisation. First, Oswald Mosley published two books; one, *My Answer*, to provide an apology for his past, the other, *The Alternative*, to act as a programme for the future. Then, there was a Mosley paper, the *Mosley Newsletter*, which could be bought under the counter at W. H. Smiths. Next, a network of Mosley book clubs were set up to provide a forum to discuss the leader's ideas. Finally, in November 1947, Mosley held a large meeting, attended by the British League, the book clubs, and about 50 organisations all told, where he announced that he would soon form a new political party, the Union Movement.[17]

Events in Palestine may have helped the fascists. Following the bomb attacks on the King David Hotel, and the killing of the two British sergeants at Natanya, there were large anti-Jewish riots in August 1947 in Liverpool, Eccles, Salford and Manchester, and smaller incidents in Plymouth, Birmingham, Bristol, Cardiff, Swansea, Devonport and Newcastle. The Merseyside Docks was covered with the slogan, 'Death to all Jews'. Slaughtermen in Birkenhead came out on strike against the employers responsible for the production of kosher meat, the Liverpool Shechita Board. In August 1947, the *Morecambe and Heysham Visitor*, a North Lancashire paper with a circulation of around seventeen thousand copies, ran an editorial welcoming the riots and insisting that British Jews had earned the hostility of the crowd.[19] By now, the fascists were on an upward curve. Mosley's supporters claimed to be holding thirty-four public meetings each week. The total weekly audience at fascist meetings stood at around 6000.

Different organisations responded to the fascist threat in different ways. Labour was in government, and was thus in the best position either to change the law or to demand that the police act against anti-Semitic speakers. Between 1945 and 1951, however, there were no Labour-sponsored demonstrations against fascism, no changes in the law, neither to ban fascist parties, nor to outlaw anti-semitic propaganda. The failure of the Labour Party to take a lead in the street campaigns against Mosley meant that there was a gap on the left, which was partly filled by the Communist Party. As well as the Communist Party and the National Council for Civil Liberties, the rest of the left was also involved in the anti-fascist campaigns, as far as resources permitted. In particular, the Trotskyists of the Revolutionary Communist Party (RCP) played a valuable part. Alongside the left, there were also a number of Jewish groups which organised against the fascist threat. The best documented of all is the 43 Group, as a result of Morris Beckman's book of the same name. At its peak, the 43 Group had around 2000 members. It published its own newspaper, *On Guard*, and sent infiltrators into the Mosley Book Clubs and the Union Movement. The Group seems to have specialised in turning over fascist platforms. A typical 43 Group 'commando' might close down 13 fascist meetings in one Sunday's work.[19]

To the fascists, the combined activity of these different anti-fascist groups working at a local level, without much official co-ordination, must have felt much as it would have if the separate organisations had been consciously working together. In the local areas, the 43 Group turned over fascist platforms, while the Trades Council and the Communist Party organised petitions and anti-fascist demonstrations. What the fascist speakers experienced was a single anti-fascist opposition. One arm of the movement won the local community to the politics of anti-fascism, while the other arm attacked fascist street meetings. Together, they made it increasingly difficult for the Mosleyites to hold their meetings in public. By the spring of 1948, the fascists were on the retreat. In 1951, Mosley left the country, promising never to return. Because the overwhelming majority of people were clearly hostile to British fascism, the Union Movement was always doomed to failure. Yet the CP can also claim some credit for having helped to hasten fascism's demise.

The party in crisis

Because the Communist Party failed to carry through any consistent or principled relationship to the Labour Party in government, the years 1945–51 saw a decline in the strength and influence of the Communist Party. The CP's membership fell dramatically, though with a blip in 1947 as the CP re-launched its factory branches and enjoyed a brief, fading, moment of revival. Party membership, which stood at 38 579 rose to 43 000 in April 1948, before falling again to 38 853 in May

1950, and 35 124 by March 1951. The best sign of the withering away of the Communist Party is in its decline as an electoral force. In 1945, the party stood 22 candidates, of whom 9 reached the 12.5 per cent needed to save their deposits. In total, the candidates won 102 780 votes. In the 1950 election, the CP stood 100 candidates, of whom just three saved their deposits. In total, the 100 candidates received just 91,815 votes, which was noticeably less than the 22 candidates in 1945. G. J. Jones in Hornsey saw his vote fall from 10 058 in 1945, to 1191 five years later Howard Hill's vote in Sheffield fell from 4115 to 1081. The two Communist MPs, Phil Piratin and Willie Gallacher, both lost their seats.[20]

The party lost elections and failed to win new members. Meanwhile, a large number of Communists began to criticise the party's politics, and especially its stampede to the right between 1945 and 1947. Kenny McLachlan, an activist in the Scottish engineering union, hung on, but 'only in the belief that whatever had been wrong would be rectified. Loyalty to a vision can be stretched a long way.' Brian Behan, chair of the rank-and-file building workers' movement, and a member of the party's national executive, felt that the CP was stagnating, 'All we did is hold our own. Our membership never rose above 30 000, and this was only kept up by frantic recruitment drives in which, like the runner in the escalator, we kept running mad just to stay in the same place.' At the 1946 conference, Eric Heffer moved a resolution on behalf of the Hertford branch, accusing the leadership of having betrayed Lenin, 'the perspective of proletarian revolution has been abandoned'. He was expelled. Harry McShane left in 1953. He had been a leading Communist for many years, but he felt that CP's lurch to the right had gone too far. It was 'a complete departure from all the Marxist fundamentals'. Each of these dissidents was encouraged by the 'Australian letter', a message from the Australian Communist Party printed in *World News and Views,* accusing the British Communists of betraying the key ideas of Marxism. Douglas Hyde of the *Daily Worker* and C. H. Darke the trade unionist also quit the party at about this time, although they were both moving to the right. Rose Osment and Les Moss resigned in 1947, while Claud Cockburn ceased to write for the *Worker,* citing the party's diminishing returns, 'We ran faster and faster and seemed to remain almost exactly in the same place'.[21]

Edward Upward's autobiographical novel, *The Rotten Elements* (1979), describes how Alan and Elsie Sebrill (Edward and Hilda Upward) came into conflict with the CP's hierarchy in 1946 and 1947. The book describes the argument that the Upwards used to justify their opposition. They only wanted to restore the party to its earlier vigour, 'During the years when [the leaders of the party] had led the struggle against unemployment and against fascism they had been leaders whom the rank and file could ... be inspired by'. Alan, in attacking them as they were now was defending them as they had formerly been. Such frustrated loyal opposition was to become increasingly frequent over the next thirty years.[22]

In 1947, the Communist Party established a National Cultural Committee.[23] This co-ordinated the work of a diverse range of groups, including a science committee, a novelists' group and also numbers of poets, playwrights and other writers. The most famous of these cultural bodies today is the Communist Party Historians' Group (CPHG). It was established around a talented generation of historians, including Eric Hobsbawm, Rodney Hilton, John Saville, Edward (E. P.) Thompson and Christopher Hill.[24] Often in opposition to the hierarchical and top-down politics of their party, they transformed the way in which history was written, pioneering the method of history from below, the notion that the past should be studied through the actual lived and creative experiences of real people. Hill's accounts of the English revolution, Thompson's *William Morris* and *The Making of the English Working Class*, and Hobsbawm's books, *Age of Revolution, Age of Capital, Age of Empire* and *Age of Extremes*, covering the period from 1789 to the present day, remain some of the most powerful works of history yet written from within the Marxist tradition.

The CPHG was formally established out of a party Historians' Conference in 1946, held to discuss a new edition of A. L. Morton's *A People's History of England*. Over the next ten years, members of the group published widely. Dona Torr worked with Christopher Hill, Edmund Dell, Max Morris and J. B. Jefferys, as the general editor of a series of document-books, 'History in the Making' (1948), which were intended as an entire history of the development of British capitalism.[25] In 1955, E P. Thompson brought out his famous biography of *William Morris*. In the following year, Hill, Saville and Thompson published an important collection, *Democracy and the Labour Movement*. The last collective venture was Torr's *Tom Mann and his Times*, which appeared in November 1956, and included chapters written by Christopher Hill and A. L. Morton.[26]

Previous Marxist histories, including almost all written from within the Communist Party tradition, had tended to describe the past simply in terms of the succession of new classes, and new ways of organising production. According to this model, within each society production grew until it could grow no further. At that moment there was a revolution and a new form of society came into being. Societies grew and declined according to mechanical laws, almost independent of what people did to organise against them.[27] From such a fatalistic theory, it followed that the task for socialists was simply to wait until the level of protests rose and capitalism necessarily collapsed under the weight of its own contradictions. In this way, there was a connection between the history from above which dominated within the Communist Party, and its political strategy, socialism from above, which adapted Marxist politics to the practice of the Labour party, waiting for alliances with left Labour MPs.

The Communist historians formulated an alternative way of looking at the past, which came to be known as 'history from below'. Their argument was that meaningful change in society comes from below, and that is shaped and often led by working people and their political movements. It is ordinary people who have changed the course of the past. What began as a historical argument was not restricted to that sphere. History from below also opened up the vision of an alternative and more radical politics, in which society had been changed by ordinary people, and could again be shaped by workers, creating the political possibility of a socialism that would come from below. Not surprisingly, the historians' work was to take most of the historians outside the narrow confines of the CP.

The CPHG effectively collapsed as a result of the turmoil within the party in 1956. As early as 8 April that year, a 'full and extended' meeting of the historians' group condemned the British Communist Party for its failure to raise at its own annual conference Kruschev's secret speech, which criticised 'the cult of personality' in the USSR and revealed some of Stalin's crimes. Many of the party historians resigned in 1956 and 1957. Christopher Hill was invited onto the Commission on Internal Democracy within the Communist Party. The minority report which he co-signed concluded that there was no democracy in the party at all. John Saville and Edward Thompson began a stencilled newsletter, *The Reasoner*, which was a bridge along which former Communists joined the New Left, which grew outside the CP and often in opposition to the old party.[28]

Although the Communist Party failed to offer any consistent alternative to Labour, it would be absurd to suggest that the party got everything wrong. So in 1946, the party took an active part in the London squatters movement, when working-class families faced with the housing shortage occupied empty blocks of luxury flats, such as the

Duchess of Bedford House in Kensington.[29] Similarly, in 1947–48 Communists were centrally involved in the fight against fascism. Ordinary members of the CP were the backbone of the anti-Mosley movement. Again, in 1951, Communist dockers played an honourable part in the dock strikes which led to the repeal of Order 1305, wartime legislation which had banned strikes and was still enforced by the Labour government.[30] These campaigns are distinguished by the open and unsectarian way in which ordinary Communists did work with other forces, while fighting for specific gains. In the 1951 strike, for example, the four arrested stewards included not only three communists, but also one docker, Albert Timothy, who was a Catholic and a member of the Labour Party. This tells us something about the Communist Party. No matter how opportunist or sectarian its leadership, the CP remained a mass workers' party. Among its ordinary members there was a real desire to change the world. Communists often acted against or despite their formal politics, and the majority played a positive role, building trade unions, and also often promoting the interests of the rank and file.

There is a way in which the CP could have grown – especially after 1947 as the government turned rightwards, and positioned itself against the people that had voted Labour into power. There is no iron rule which demands that left-wing parties must do badly under a Labour government. Indeed Communist failure in 1945–51 and 1974–79 contrasts with success in 1964–70. The strength of the party as a whole depended on the success of the party's argument at the most local level. British Communism was a matter of individuals and branches, and its argument was won or lost at the grassroots. There are times when left parties can recruit thousands quickly; indeed for the CP, autumn 1941 was such a moment. But most often success has been about winning small numbers of campaigners, often people who have been around the movement a long time. This was often a slow process of patient argument and explanation – ideas would be advanced, considered, maybe rejected, advanced again. A local branch would tend to succeed if its members argued with supporters in a clear and consistent way, and if their morale was high. Yet neither of these factors were in place. Instead, the twists and turns of Communist tactics actually widened the gap between Communists in the factories, and their supporters around them.

The Communist Party had a tendency to zigzag, to shift from right-wing politics which glossed over and concealed the party's differences with reformism, to an ultra-left-wing politics which stressed the CP's differences, as a point of principle, and which antagonised ordinary workers who remained attached to the Labour Party. This was not a healthy way to organise, as one old activist recalls, 'the party's acrobatic twists and turns on policy matters left members perplexed and somewhat bewildered.'[31] Yet, in the campaigns where the party had its greatest success, such as the squatters' campaign, or the dock strike of 1951, the method was very different. In these struggles, ordinary members of the party successfully worked together with other people, in temporary alliances, without either liquidating their politics, or degenerating into sectarianism. In these cases, the British party returned to the politics of the United Front. The tragedy of the CP in the years from 1945 to 1951 is that the positive examples are few, while the negative examples are many.

The Cold War (2)

In June 1950, as North Korean troops crossed the demarcation line into South Korea, the Cold War took an awful turn for the worse. A Third World War seemed imminent. American and United Nations troops pushed the North Koreans back, before Chinese troops entered the war in October 1950. The Labour government sent troops to support the US, a move which deepened the government's financial crisis and precipitated the resignation of Nye Bevan in April 1951. The Communist Party opposed the war, but its basic approach was to call for a compromise between the superpowers. Soviet peace initiatives were widely trumpeted in the party press. The party campaigned not for American defeat but for East-West *rapprochement*. Thus the British party hosted the second World Peace Congress in November 1950. As it turned out, this initiative was not the success it could have been. The Labour government opposed the Congress, with the Home Secretary James Chuter Ede barring most of the foreign delegates from travelling. Of 20 leading delegates, 19 were not allowed into the country. Only one third of the foreign delegates who applied were given visas. The organisers responded as best they could holding a public meeting in Sheffield Town Hall, with speakers including the Dean of Canterbury and Pablo Picasso. Three thousand people attended the meeting and another 1500 listened to the overflow speeches outside.[32] Meanwhile, the CP's press reflected the British party's shift towards rapprochement. In 1952, the *Daily Worker* remembered the anniversary of the dropping of the atomic bomb. 'The excuse that, in the long run, this bestial action saved lies is worthless. There never has been a crime committed in war which this excuse has not been used to justify.' Jock Haston, formerly a leading member of the Revolutionary Communist Party, and now organiser of the National Council of Labour Colleges, wrote to the *Daily Worker* pointing out that that in August 1945, the paper had defended the bomb in precisely this way. To his credit, J. R. Campbell replied to Haston's letter, 'Dear Sir. We admit that we were wrong about the bomb in 1945. To err is human.' Yet there were limits to the apology. Campbell did not publish the exchange in the party press.[33]

Rapprochement was a policy wholly compatible with loyalty to Moscow. Yet as the 1950s continued, ordinary Communists found their support for the Soviet state undermined by a series of nasty revelations. One of the most shocking was the discovery of the so-called 'Doctors Plot', when it was revealed that the regime was considering the whole-scale slaughter of Russian Jews. Only Stalin's death put an end to this possibility. In the 1930s and 1940s the Russian government had presented itself as a principled defender of minority rights. Much was made of the constitution's ban on anti-semitism, and the success of the Jewish colony in Soviet Birobidjan. Yet the public anti-semitism manifested in the 1953 trials forced British Communists to adopt a more critical perspective on Soviet policy toward its Jewish minority. 'It was found that there was a professional quota for Jews; that Jews had their internal passports stamped "Jew"; that even the Great Soviet Encyclopaedia itself had a distinct anti-Jewish bias.'[34] Along with the historians, the scientists, branch activists and the party's industrial cadre, the Jewish Communists from the 1930s formed yet another group that was becoming disillusioned with aspects of party life.

The Cold War continued to shape every aspect of the internal life of the party. Within the CPGB, the hostility of outside society encouraged an atmosphere of suspicion, as is apparent in the following advice from a *World News and Views* article by Betty Reid, the party's witchfinder general, 'There is a tendency to believe that vigilance merely means keeping ears and eyes open for disruptive activities, and reporting them to the party committee. This is one of the most serious weaknesses we have to fight ... Political differences, if they are not challenged and thrashed out, can over a period become so deep that in the end disciplinary action is the only solution.'[35]

Such paranoia was further encouraged by the defection of Guy Burgess and Donald Maclean to the Soviet Union in 1951. With Kim Philby and Anthony Blunt, they had been part of a left-wing generation of students at Cambridge University in the 1930s. It is impossible to know whether any members of the Communist Party knew that such spies existed. Although leading Communists Percy Glading and Dave Springhall had been convicted for spying in 1938 and 1943, it is most unlikely that the party was involved in recruiting Philby or Blunt.[36] Although Francis Beckett uses the Cambridge spies as a stick to beat the CP, this incident should not detract from the real source of conspiracy and deceit. It was the insular character of the British ruling class which helped the KGB to use Cambridge as a recruiting ground for future spies. 'A combination of class, school and social loyalties', writes one historian, Ann Rogers, 'led the ruling establishment to overlook security risks in its own ranks.' The ruling class 'continued to represent itself as the repository of all that was good and loyal in the British state, even as it harboured the most nefarious and successful Soviet agents'.[37] The major effect of the spy scandals was not to discredit the British Communist Party, but rather to entrench the Cold War way of thinking into the secret services, paving the way for the right-wing conceits of the 1970s.

One positive consequence of the party's nationalistic opposition to American imperialism, is that party members developed a contempt for imperialism and colonialism, including British imperialism. In the 1940s and 1950s, by contrast, Labour Party journals including *Tribune* and *Socialist Commentary* increasingly toned down their criticisms of the British Empire. Clement Attlee, Stafford Cripps, even Nye Bevan argued that the continuance of colonialism in Africa could provide one solution to the economic problems of British capitalism. Whatever its other faults, the CP did not follow the Labour Left's abdication to British imperialism. Instead, Communists kept up their assault on the colonial wars in Malaysia and elsewhere. The party was able to recruit a number of students and other young people from colonial countries, many joining through the International Union of Students and the World Federation of Democratic Youth, or other international bodies. A generation of Nigerian and other West African Communists were recruited this way.[38]

As Britain went into a period of Conservative government after the 1951 election, so it seemed that a new era had dawned. The world economy entered into a boom which was to last for over twenty years. The British economy was also thriving, and even industrial worker's salaries kept up with the pace. On the shop-floor, these were the classic years of wages drift'. National agreements would allow for certain wage rises. Then, in different factories and sections, groups of workers could win additional increases. Conditions were ideal for militant shop stewards. In this way, Communists could win respect for their economic agitation, at exactly the same moment that the ideas of revolutionary socialism had seemingly become irrelevant. The Tory slogan of 'you've never had it so good' fitted the experience of many working people, and the Conservatives were re-elected with increased majorities in 1955 and 1959. A gap grew between the political and the economic mood within the working class, and this gap was reflected in the political agitation of the Communist Party.

The CP's support on the shop floor remained strong among whole numbers of different rank and file workers. The party also retained a strong base within the low-level bureaucracy in the miners', engineers', electricians' and fire-fighters' unions. Yet the political method of this working-class party was to argue for Popular Front alliances with the mythical progressive bourgeoisie. The party's programme was elaborated in *The British Road to Socialism*, the first edition of which was published in 1951. According to Laybourn and Murphy, this pamphlet was inspired by Harry Pollitt's visit to Stalin in 1950 to discuss the British political situation.[39] On his return, Pollitt certainly suggested such a document, and a final draft was agreed by spring 1951. The importance of *The British Road to Socialism* is that it was an open rejection of revolutionary socialism, 'The enemies of Communism accuse the Communist Party of aiming to introduce Soviet power in Britain and abolish Parliament. This is a slanderous misrepresentation of our policy.' Readers of *The British Road* may have been puzzled by this formulation. For if it was not a revolutionary party, then what was the CP? The answer given in *The British Road* was that it was a left-wing parliamentary party, in contest with right-wing Labour, 'British Communists declare that the people of Britain can transform capitalist democracy into a real people's Democracy, transforming Parliament, the product of Britain's historic struggle for democracy into the democratic instrument of the will of the vast majority of her people.' At one level, this reformist politics was merely a continuation of the trajectory of the Popular Front. Yet, at another level, it was the most complete rejection of the party's earlier theory of the state.[40] The new politics also contained within itself important tensions, for if the CP was not a revolutionary party, then what actually was the purpose of its existence?

You might say that the logic of *The British Road to Socialism* was electoralist, but even this formulation begs more questions than it resolves. From the early 1950s onwards, the Communist Party spent more and more time on electoral work. Some of this was support work, canvassing for Labour candidates. Some of this political work was independent, campaigning for would-be Communist councillors and MPs. But in reality neither choice was entirely satisfactory. The support work for Labour candidates had the effect of calling into question the need for a separate party. Yet the independent work was no more viable, as Communist candidates were regularly thrashed and the CP vote declined. Could electoralism work, and if not what should be done? This would be one of the key dilemmas which the party was to face in the postwar period.

In March 1953, Joseph Stalin died. The event was to have enormous repercussions for the world Communist movement. For twenty-five years, Stalin's position had been unquestioned, and his death struck at the very heart of the Soviet monolith. Nobody knew who would rule Russia next, or what strategy they would adopt. Nikita Kruschev eventually emerged out of the power struggle, at about the same time as an end was found to the war in Korea. This was followed by a peace settlement in Indochina in 1954 and reconciliation with Yugoslavia, one year later. Slowly a new *détente* pattern of international relations emerged, in which each of the two superpowers possessed the atom bomb, neither willed a nuclear apocalypse, and both were content to exist together. Nikita Kruschev encouraged a gradual liberalisation within Russia, and a thaw even within the Western Communist Parties. In April 1956, Kruschev delivered his so-called 'secret speech'. Before the 20th Congress of the Soviet Communist Party, Kruschev acknowledged that the party had been 'misled' over Yugoslavia, and also admitted several of Stalin's crimes.

Nikita Kruschev's speech was met with confusion across the Communist movement. The leaders of the Western Communist Parties did not know whether to condemn Stalin or to reject Kruschev. As Ian Birchall suggests, 'The choice that confronted the CPs throughout the period – Stalinism or Social Democracy – was now posed in a particularly acute form.' Harry Pollitt was replaced as secretary of the British Communist Party by John Gollan, while Rajani Palme Dutt insisted that Stalin's errors were merely 'spots on the sun'.[41] The party was already heading for one of the greatest periods of turmoil in its entire existence, when events in Hungary brought the crisis to a head.

5
The Monolith Cracks: 1956–68

1956 was the 'annus horribilis' of the British Communist Party and the Communist movement internationally. Once again it was developments in Moscow which were to impose themselves on the British party. The death of Stalin in March 1953 had been greeted by the party as a great tragedy with the party press given over to eulogising the life and works of 'The genius and will of Stalin, the architect of the rising world of free humanity ...'.[1] However within the Eastern European socialist block Stalin's death had a far more direct, material impact.

Within three months of Stalin's death popular revolts had broken out; firstly in Czechoslovak town of Pilsen and then on a far greater scale across East Germany. With a judicious mixture of repression and partial concessions these risings were put down. The official explanation of the revolts as 'an attempted coup and fascist putch' was broadly accepted by Communists in Britain and internationally. However in 1956 in Hungary and again in Czechoslovakia in 1968, massive popular revolts, crushed by Soviet tanks were to send shock waves reverberating through the British Communist Party which were to wound it profoundly.

The initial destabilisation of the certainties of the Stalinist world-view was to come not so much from popular revolts but from the political re-adjustment within the Soviet leadership after Stalin's death. On 24 February 1956 at a closed session of the 20th party congress of the Communist Party of the USSR, Nikita Kruschev, Stalin's successor to the post of General Secretary, delivered the now legendary secret speech in which Stalin's crimes were outlined to a shocked audience. Visiting foreign communists were kept away from the session. Harry Pollitt and George Matthews, two of the three-strong British delegation were being shown around a condom factory in Moscow at the time of the speech,[2] although Rajani Palme Dutt's whereabouts are less clearly established. Although the detailed allegations against Stalin were made in closed session, the general tone of the conference had been anti-Stalinist; no pictures of the great man adorned the conference hall and the denunciation of the 'cult of personality' had been made without direct mention of Stalin's name. News of the shift gradually filtered through both to British party leaders, and in particular to journalists on the *Daily Worker*. On 10 June after weeks of partial disclosure the full text of the speech was printed by the London Sunday newspaper the *Observer*.

The turmoil within the party gathered pace. In the May edition of *Labour Monthly* Rajani Palme Dutt, in his influential *Notes of The Month*[3] misjudged the mood of his audience by likening criticism of Stalin to 'spots on the sun' and suggesting that those criticising Stalin were 'ivory tower dwellers in fairyland'. The level of negative reaction to Dutt was unheard-of in the British party. He was heckled at a closed party meeting in the East Midlands for his attitude towards the secret speech revelations, and the East Midlands District Committee voted 15/3 to censure his 'serious error'. A fortnight later Dutt again outraged an invited audience of CP-supporting doctors[4] by his refusal to allow any criticism of Stalin, the meeting resulted in the resignation from the party of a number of doctors rather than the hoped recruitment of supporters. For the second time in his life, faced with a political volte face from Moscow, Harry Pollitt resigned as General Secretary. This time however there is no evidence that he was pushed, indeed his resignation on grounds of ill health exacerbated the atmosphere of crisis in the party. Pollitt's biographer, Kevin Morgan suggests that Pollitt was simply unprepared to go along with the criticism and denunciation of Stalin that he felt would have been required by a party General Secretary.[5] Faced with demands from sections of the membership for change and the opening up of inner party democracy the new leadership established a Commission on Inner Party Democracy made up of twelve party full-time workers and five lay members, however by the time it reported to the Executive Committee in December, a new crisis had engulfed the party.

Still reeling from the impact of the secret speech, the Communist Party was now hit by the political backwash of mass revolts in Eastern Europe. On 23 October, mass demonstrations of students and workers led to the establishment of workers councils in Budapest which soon spread to the rest of the country. Russian troops were used to restore order but subsequently withdrew. When the new Hungarian leadership of Imre Nagy formed a National Government and withdrew Hungary from the Warsaw Pact, Russian troops once again took to the streets and put down the movement in a brutal way. Up to 30 000 Hungarians died before the rising was finally crushed. Unlike in 1953, when the revolts could pass without causing much major damage, Hungary was catastrophic. The *Daily Worker* had dispatched a talented journalist Peter Fryer to cover the re-alignment in the Hungarian party leadership in the wake of de-Stalinisation. Fryer filed reports from Hungary throughout 1956 as the crisis in the Hungarian party developed, and the movement took on a mass working-class character. These articles were initially edited and eventually spiked by Johnny Campbell the editor at the *Daily Worker*. Fryer was subsequently to return to Britain, publish his account of the uprising, *Hungarian Tragedy*, and openly campaign against the party's position of support for the new Kadar regime. He joined forces with the Trotskyist group, The Club, led by Gerry Healy and publishing the *Newsletter*. For a brief period the *Newsletter* operated as an umbrella publication around a loose federation of former members and Trotskyist members of The Club before emerging as the organ of the newly formed Socialist Labour League.[6]

The initial position of the leadership was to support the Russian intervention. A statement issued on 4 November reasserted 'support for the Kadar government and the necessity of Soviet intervention to prevent the victory of fascism and counter-revolution.'[7] There was a storm of protest from the party rank and file. Between 4 November and the Executive Committee meeting in mid-December, 219 Resolutions were sent to the EC on Hungary, the vast majority critical of the leadership's stand. However, by the time a special congress was held at Easter 1957, the hold of the leadership on the machinery of the party at least was secure. A minority report from the Committee on Inner Party Democracy criticising the conduct of the party was heavily defeated and Peter Fryer, who had by now burned his boats by aligning himself with the Trotskyists, was expelled.

The haemorrhaging of membership had started in 1956, but after the 1957 conference many of those who had argued to 'stay in and fight', now left the party. Party loyalists argued at the time and subsequently that it was overwhelmingly the middle-class intellectuals who left and the solid workers who stayed loyal. Closer inspection suggests that this sociological approach is a handy myth. Overall membership fell by a third between February 1956 and February 1958. Although no direct statistical evidence of who was leaving is available, there was no notable shift in the occupations of delegates attending national

Congresses in years to come, which one would expect if those who had left had been predominately middle-class intellectuals. The resignation of a number of prominent members of the Communist Party Historians Group, notably Christopher Hill, Edward Thompson and John Saville provides the key evidence of the 'flight of the intellectuals'. Yet other key historians such as Eric Hobsbawm and James Klugmann remained loyal. A number of prominent party trade union leaders resigned including John Horner secretary of the Fire Brigades Union and Les Cannon Secretary of the CP-controlled Electricians Union (ETU). The only member of the Communist Party's Executive Committee to resign was Brian Behan, a rank and file building worker, who like Peter Fryer threw in his lot with the Trotskyist Socialist Labour League. Many of the former trade union officials, notably Les Cannon and Frank Chapple of the ETU were to shift rapidly to the right after leaving the party. Others, including Lawrence Daly of the Fife Miners, who had resigned just prior to the Hungarian uprising and who launched the Fife Socialist League, were to attempt to regroup on the left but with limited success. Although the CP were to suffer some notable setbacks in their trade union work in the post Hungary period, the damage was repairable, with the exception of the ETU, within a relatively short period.

The impact of the Hungarian events was to continue to be felt over the following years and decades. Although many party members continued to identify closely with the Soviet Block, especially against the background of continuing evidence of the iniquities of the imperialist states demonstrated for example by the Vietnam War, there was never again the ringing confidence in the fundamental superiority of the Soviet System. In the wake of both the Krushchev speech and Hungary other ghosts from the past raised their heads. The way in which the CP had swung behind the vilification of Tito in 1948 was re-examined.[8] Both the 'Doctors Plot' and the Slansky[9] trial had raised allegations of anti-semitism at the time, this was now amplified in the uncertain post-1956 atmosphere. Even at the highest levels of the party leadership the doubts were clear. In interviews with party members for her unpublished biography of John Gollan, who replaced Pollitt as General Secretary, Margot Kettle discusses the way in which both the 'Secret Speech' and Hungary fundamentally changed Gollan, who had been a personal friend of Rudolf Slansky.[10] Prior to the events of 1956 and 1957, it was certainly possible for tens of thousands of rank and file British communists to hold genuine, if distorted views about the nature of the 'socialist states'. Senior party figures such as Pollitt and Dutt must have already had to undergo mental and moral gymnastics. After 1956, no senior party figure who paused to think could have retained an absolute faith in the Socialist Motherland. However whatever inner doubts Gollan might have had, the job of running the party went on. Although the leadership of the party retained control of the organisation and new recruitment brought membership levels back above the 1956 level within a few years, no longer would the party be the monolith it once was.

The New Left

One of the lasting legacies of the crisis of 1956 was the opening up of a political space to the left of the Communist Party. Ever since the decline of the Independent Labour Party as an effective force, there had been no significant organised alternative on the left of the CP. The brief flowering of the Trotskyist groups during the war had ended in division and marginalisation. Of the half dozen or so rival far left groups, only one, the faction around Gerry Healy had benefited to any significant extent from the CPs discomfort in 1956. Healy had recruited a number of working-class militants from the party to his group and for a brief period it appeared that a possible alternative was being created. The Communist Party was to retain its dominance as the organised left political force amongst industrial militants for at least another twenty years. The most significant shift was to take place away from the milieu of trade union politics and in the still small but growing world of protest politics which was later to become synonymous with the 1960s.

In July 1956 two adult education teachers from the Yorkshire region of the party, Edward Thompson and John Saville, published an internal party discussion bulletin *The Reasoner*. This was ordered to be shut down by the party leadership. Thompson and Saville were suspended and subsequently resigned their membership in the wake of the Hungarian invasion. Thompson and Saville then established *The New Reasoner*, which was no longer a primarily internal party publication but an attempt to re-orientate a broader New Left. *The New Reasoner* lasted until 1959 and pulled around it a talented group of writers, many of whom had been party members, some of whom like Iris Murdoch and Doris Lessing were on a trajectory which was to take them out of left-wing politics.

At the same time another New Left publication, the *Universities and Left Review* (*ULR*) was founded. As its title suggests, *ULR* was rooted in a primarily academic milieu, but it was able to relate to a new generation of young activists who were to become radicalised by their opposition to atomic weapons and were to flood into the Campaign for Nuclear Disarmament (CND). *ULR* provided an intellectual and cultural focus for many of the new CND activists, and ran a coffee bar for a short period in central London. In 1960 *Universities and Left Review* and *The New Reasoner* merged to form *New Left Review (NLR)*, which survives to the present day. The early *NLR* set out to be more than merely a journal, it aimed to provide, as both of its antecedents had, a political framework through a loose network of left clubs and New Left centres. In the short term these organisations were to pose a significant threat to the hegemony on the left hitherto enjoyed by the CP. Although the New Left made virtually no impression on the CP's position as the organisation on the left within the trade unions, and it was soon to falter, it did pose a challenge to which the party had to respond.

As early as April 1957 the Communist Party's Executive Committee discussed a document entitled *Proposals for a new Theoretical Journal* which clearly identified the challenge posed to the Communist Party by Journals such as *ULR* and the yet to be published *New Reasoner*. A loyalist, heavyweight, editorial board was proposed for the new publication with the author of the document clearly declaring that 'I do not think that we should follow a policy of giving places on the board to people whose attitude is at present vacillating in order to win them over'. Specifically to be excluded as 'vacillating' were the historian Christopher Hill, and the popular scientist JD Bernal. Subjects to be dealt with included 'The Middle Class and Their Problems ... Marxism and Morals, Personal Liberty ... Trotskyism at work in Britain Today ... The Intellectuals and their Role in the fight for Socialism'.[11] Thus was conceived the journal to be eventually known as *Marxism Today*. It is a matter of supreme irony that this journal, prepared as a defence of the party's orthodoxy, was to play such a key role thirty years later in unravelling the tortuous theoretical contradictions of British Communism.

The following year the attention of the party leadership was once again drawn to the emerging New Left when Eric Hobsbawm presented some notes to the EC on the *Universities and Left Review*. He emphasised that *ULR* and the CND were attracting around them an audience of 'people who have never been in politics before and would like to be ... especially youngsters'. Worryingly from the party's point of view he suggested that attitudes to the CP amongst this group ranged from hostility, especially in the wake of Hungary, to disinterest. 'There is simply no talk about the party at all among them'. Hobsbawm was to suggest that the CP should gear up its intervention amongst this group.¹² There is evidence in the years to come of a concerted effort by the party to engage with the emerging protest politics which were to characterise the 1960s, despite the difficulties that the party's adherence to the foreign policy priorities of Moscow posed. By 1963 Fergus Nicholson the party's student organiser could report to the EC that although the party only had 500 student members, 'we have more than recovered from the difficulties of 1956'.[13]

The Campaign for Nuclear Disarmament

Both at the time and in retrospect our view of the protest movements of the 1960s is symbolised by Campaign for Nuclear Disarmament (CND). The iconic power of the CND logo bears witness to the impact that this movement was to have in ruffling the complacent atmosphere of 1950s Britain.

The Communist Party's position on atomic weapons was from the start determined by the wider foreign policy preoccupations of the time. So the *Daily Worker*, still at that time in deeply pro-war and super-patriotic mode greeted the dropping of the bomb on Hiroshima and Nagasaki with the headline 'Japs still try to haggle.'[14] In the Cold War atmosphere of the late 1940s and early 1950s, however, the position was to change: by 1952 the use of atomic weapons against Japan was criticised in retrospect as a 'beastly action'. In 1953, the explosion by the Soviet Union of its first atomic device was once again to change the situation. Communist Parties around the world were mobilised to support the initiatives of the Stockholm Peace Conference which attempted to pressurise western governments to enter multilateral peace negotiations. It was this emphasis on multilateralism that was to bring the CP into conflict with the new young radicals being pulled into activity during the early CND protests. For the first two years of CND's existence the party vehemently opposed the unilateralist line of CND which had paradoxically won significant support from the very 'trade union and Labour lefts' that party policy was orientated towards.

CND was officially launched in February 1958, the coming together of a number of ad hoc protest groups which had been established in the wake of Britain's first H-bomb test on Christmas Island in 1957. The anti-H-bomb movement drew on a number of differing political traditions from traditional Labour leftism to small groups of protestors influenced by Gandhian principles of Non-Violent Direct Action, including the prominent philosopher Bertrand Russell. At the 1957

Labour Party conference the erstwhile hero of the Labour left Anuerin Bevan dismissed opposition to nuclear weapons as an 'emotional spasm' and came out in favour of the party leadership's pro-nuclear deterrence position. This was enough to convince numbers of Labour party activists of the need to campaign outside the party for unilateralism. CND was to soon set a trend for street-based protest politics of a kind not seen in Britain since the 1930s. The first Aldermaston march at Easter 1958 was a huge media success, with thousands participating. CND was on a sharp upward curve, by 1960 there were 500 CND groups around the country and a full time staff of seven.

Unilateralism made swift headway within the trade unions. At the 1958 TUC a unilateralist motion was defeated heavily, but several smaller unions had already adopted a unilateralist position. By 1959 the normally right-wing General and Municipal Workers' Union had adopted unilateralism, with the National Union of Mineworkers conference only rejecting it after the intervention of Communist Party-influenced votes. 1960 marked the high water mark for CND support within the official trade union and Labour movement with both the TUC and the Labour Party conferences passing unilateralist motions, prompting the party leader Hugh Gaitskell to pledge to 'fight, fight and fight again' to reverse the policy, which by the following year the right in the party had achieved. Although CND was to remain a significant mass protest movement throughout the rest of the early 1960s, the reversal of Labour Party Policy at the 1961 conference marked a turning of the tide and by 1964 the movement was beginning to decline. CND was to continue as an effective but relatively low key pressure group through to the present, and in the early 1980s was to burst back into life again as a mass protest movement.

Despite frequent and repeated allegations from the right-wing press and opponents of unilateralism that CND was a Communist Party front organisation, the party missed out on the development of CND as a mass movement. It was not until 1960, after considerable pressure from within that the party dropped its opposition to unilateralism and urged members to participate in CND and began to put its significant weight within the structures of key unions behind CND. Prior to 1960 the CP's trade union muscle had been used to marginalise the unilateralists. So for example at the 1958 TUC when the unilateralist motion from the Fire Brigades Union was defeated heavily, it became apparent that some delegations from unions which did hold a unilateralist position had cast their votes against the FBU motion. How had this come about? The Labour left newspaper *Tribune* thought it had the answer:

'What happened within these union delegations? The answer is simple: The Communist party members within them urged this course of action in line with the policy line plugged by the *Daily Worker*'.[15] Prior to the change of line in 1960 there is also evidence of serious division inside the party on this question. In a hard fought argument at the 1959 NUM conference Abe Moffatt, who had rejoined the party after his resignation in the wake of Hungary, led the argument to defeat the unilateralist position put by Bert Wynne of the Derbyshire NUM, also a party member.

By early 1960 the line changed dramatically, the party was very well represented on the 1960 Aldermaston march and the organisational and political skills that party members brought to CND was to ensure that by the mid-1960s the CP were firmly ensconced as a key force within the movement. However the growth of the CP's hegemony within CND coincided with the decline of the movement. As the movement declined Communists were firmly associated with the more conservative forces within CND, wishing to pull the movement away from the Direct Action tactics of militant rank and file members towards the model of Popular Front which had typified the party's activities since the 1930s. Greater CP involvement brought with it attempts to tie the campaign closer to the pro-Moscow international peace movements which had marked the CP's initial forays into the issue of arms control and also an unhealthy dose of nationalism, particularly anti-German feeling with slogans such as 'No German Finger on the Trigger'. To push home the anti-German message the party printed 27 000 copies of a pamphlet, *The German Menace,* and a three-colour poster depicting a jackboot being planted on Britain bearing the slogan NO GERMAN BASES.[16] Natural allies were found, not so much with the radical activists of the Committee of 100, but with the significant numbers of Christians who had joined CND, many of whom such as John Collins and later Bruce Kent were to play a prominent role. Veteran CP stalwarts were to keep CND organisation ticking over in a rather genteel atmosphere of Communism and Christianity until a new influx of anti-bomb activists as to shake the organisation up again in the early 1980s.

The downward trajectory of the mass movement in the 1960s effectively isolated those left elements within CND who favoured a more activist and confrontational politics. However a pattern in the party's relationship to the politics of protest had been established in the case of CND which would be repeated later in the decades of 1960s, 70s and 80s. Rather than the 'red ogres' of anti-Communist rhetoric, intent on spreading radical and possibly violent protest, the CPs influence on the protest campaigns which were to follow in CND's wake was very much that of the 'respectable left'.

Immersion, albeit belatedly, into CND did bring the party much-needed recruits and the possibility of consolidating the process of regroupment and rebuilding which was taking place after the debacle of 1956. Membership which had bottomed out after the Hungarian events in 1958 at 24 670 began a slow but steady process of recovery reaching 26 052 by 1960 and after the decision to join CND increased at a rapid rate until the 1964 figure of 34 281. This meant that membership had now recovered from the fall-out over Hungary. With the benefit of hindsight we can now see the 1964 figure merely as a respite on a generally downward trajectory, but at the time, encouraged especially by evidence of recruitment successes of the Young Communist League, it must have appeared to the party's leadership that the tide was shifting in their favour. Political ideas in Britain appeared to be shifting leftwards. The Tory Party, after '13 years of misrule', was on the way out with a Labour Party led by a dynamic leader from the left, Harold Wilson, on the way in. The party could take particular satisfaction that from its position of relative strength within the trade union movement it could continue the process of 'strengthening of left trends within the Labour Party'[17] that the *British Road to Socialism* called for.

Building in the unions

Despite the image of the 1950s as an era of social peace, political conservatism and growing working-class living standards, the Communist Party was able to maintain and extend a significant if localised influence within workplaces and within the structures of trade unions. The party controlled the Electricians' Union (ETU), and held leading positions within unions such as the National Union of Mineworkers (NUM) and the Fire Brigades' Union. Within the Amalgamated Engineering Union (AEU), where the battle for influence and control was fought out between well organised left and right wing 'parties', the Communist Party remained the key group shaping the strategy of the left in the union and retained powerful influence in a number of key localities. Prior to 1956, although there were clear efforts made to capture key positions within the trade union apparatus, the party also maintained an activist orientation on rank and file workers in the workplaces, maintaining factory based branches. The party continued to act both as a forum for rank and file trade union militants and attempted to use its position in the trade union bureaucracy to shift the Labour Party to the left. Individual Communist Party members played key roles as trade union shop stewards and convenors, and sales of the *Daily Worker* organised by factory party branches in individual factories were often impressive. A report to the 1955 party congress claimed that 'Our best factory branch in Scotland has a regular sale of 300, our best Sheffield factory branch a regular daily sale of 120, our best Lancashire factory branch a regular sale of 135, our best Middlesex branch a regular sale of 210 and our best Midlands branch a sale of 350 daily'.[18]

The fact that party members were continuing to gain and retain high profile positions within the full-time leadership of trade unions was to open up a problem in the party's trade union work which would remain throughout the rest of its existence. The existence of fundamental antagonisms between trade union full time officials and rank and file workers, and in particular rank and file union militants, has been addressed by sociologists and social theorists, both Marxist and non-Marxist.[19] However within the orbit of official Communist doctrine, the issue had never been fully addressed. The notion of a fundamental structural contradiction between trade union officials and workers was rejected in favour of a political division between left and right. If trade union leaders 'sold out' workers' struggles it was because they were right wingers, influenced by right-wing, social democratic political ideas. The key way for workers to make progress was to elect left-wing union officials to replace the right wingers. Ideally the left candidates should be Communists, if not they could be 'progressives', Broad Left candidates supported by the party. Once left officials took up their positions within the structures of the unions they were however subject to all the pressures to compromise and moderate their positions. Holding a Communist Party membership card would not render the union official immune to moderating pressures.

The significant and growing number of Communist Party members taking up leading positions within the unions in the 1950s and 1960s was inevitably to lead to situations where full-time party trade union officials would come into conflict with rank and file trade union activists, who themselves might well be CP members or sympathisers. The potential for these conflicts of interest were heightened by the significant growth in the post war period of workplace based shop stewards organisations, notably in industries such as engineering and motor manufacture. The image of the militant Communist-influenced shop steward as portrayed rather benignly in the film *I'm All Right Jack* and in a more sinister vein in *The Angry Silence*[20] may have been caricatures, but caricature often works precisely because it does reflect a reality, albeit in a distorted fashion.

The growth of strong workplace-based shop stewards movements had its roots in the long boom of the 1950s and 1960s, where despite the relatively weak position of the British economy, the general expansion in the world economy meant that order books for manufacturing companies were full, unemployment low, and the bargaining position of workers strong. In the engineering industry in particular, demand was strong and employers were eager not to lose production through strike action and were therefore willing to conclude local pay deals with plant based shop stewards. In addition there existed throughout the industry extensive use of Payment by Result (PBR) or piecework systems. These had the effect of driving local wages in well organised factories significantly above the national rates which were negotiated nationally between employers organisations and the national unions.[21] So for example in 1968 the national negotiated rate for an engineering fitter was £12.75 per week, the actual average earnings for fitters were £22.75.[22] Under the PBR systems the unofficial shop floor movement led by shop stewards became of crucial importance, explaining the quite marked differentials between well organised shops and those with less well developed shop stewards, even within the same establishment. Although PBR had been introduced initially by management as a way of controlling the shop floor, under conditions of strong demand and a tight labour market, well organised groups of workers could turn PBR to their advantage. The class struggle on the shop floor, in a situation where good organisation could make a real difference to workers material well being threw up a whole new generation of workplace based shop steward activists, a significant minority of whom, if not joining the Communist Party, would orientate to the party as a community of militants. The party had been actively involved in building stewards organisation since the 1930s, but the scope and scale of these types of organisation was to grow significantly in this period. Workers would often look to CP members a the 'best stewards', without necessarily endorsing the politics of the party as a whole. So for example when the CP attempted to replicate the success its industrial militants were having in workplace trade union elections by standing them as candidates in General, council or by-elections, they generally received few votes.

The 'British Disease' of militant shop floor trade unionism not unnaturally led to a clamour from employers' organisations to restore 'management's right to manage' and to curb the power of workplace trade unionism. It was this battle which was to dominate British politics in the 1970s, a battle in which Communist-led and influenced trade unionists played a key role. However, earlier in the 1960s significant steps were being taken by employers to replace PBR systems with methods of measuring and rewarding workers' output which did not allow workers' control over the production process. Productivity deals aimed at bringing about a fundamental shift in the culture of the workplace and in particular to reduce the direct control that rank and file organisation could have on wages, thus reducing the power of shop stewards. In 1960 unions and management at Esso's Fawley Oil Refinery near Southampton agreed what was to be a trail-blazing productivity agreement. The key signatory for the deal for the union side was Frank Foulkes, a Communist Party member and President of the Electrical Trades Union. At the same time rank and file shop stewards organisations were busy opposing productivity deals, often led by Communist Party members. Productivity deals were supported by trade union officials because they curbed the power of shop stewards whose growing influence was eroding the power of full-time union officialdom. In this battle for power within the trade unions Communist Party members were clearly to be found on both sides of the barricades. In November 1960, Frank Foulkes declared at the TUC that 'Unofficial bodies are not in the best interests of the union'[23] and supported the banning of the Power Workers' Combine, a rank and file body whose secretary was George Wake, another prominent CP member.

The engineering union, the AEU, had always played a key role in the party's trade union strategy. It was skilled metal workers above all who had formed the backbone of the revolutionary workers' movement of the last years of the First World War and which had given birth to Communist Parties around Europe.[24] As we have seen, the party built a substantial base in engineering during the late 1930s and wartime years, a base which was retained through to the 1960s and replenished by a new generation of activist shop stewards. However the leadership of the AEU had remained since the war in the hands of a well organised and explicitly anti-communist right-wing grouping. The leadership of the union, notably its president throughout much of the 1950s and 1960s, William (later Lord) Carron, was openly hostile to the growing power of shop stewards and in particular the growth of unofficial strikes. The number of strike days 'lost' annually in the engineering industry had grown from 441 700 between 1947 and 1955 to 1 206 700 between 1965 and 1968 with approximately 95 per cent of these being unofficial.[25] Carron who once described unofficial strikers as 'werewolves' went as far as to blame management for unofficial strikes 'because they gave in easily and allowed the men to derive benefits from industrial action'.[26]

The atmosphere that the left including the Communist Party operated within the AEU for much of the 1950s was of a constant low level witch-hunt which took its toll on CP representation within the official structures of the union. By 1959 the right wing in the union could boast that 'Communists inside the union have had some very severe setbacks in the last couple of years. Now the only communist on the Executive Committee is Claude Berridge, he must find it very lonely'.[27] Six of the seven EC seats were held by the right, as was the Presidency (Carron) and the General Secretaryship (Jim Conway), only one of the two Assistant General Secretaries, Ernie Roberts, was on the left and the right would normally control a majority on the lay National Committee. In 1963 the leadership estimated that out of a total of 160 full time officials of the union only 42 supported the left.[28]

The 1961 Communist Party congress was to usher in a significant tactical shift for Communists operating within the AEU and other trade unions. The congress detected a leftward shift in the Labour Party and the CP moved towards supporting left Labour candidates for electoral positions within the unions and away from standing open CP candidates. In the engineering industry the Communist-run rank and file newspaper *Metalworker* was closed down as was the Engineering and Allied Trades Shop Stewards National Council which had carried the party's intervention in the industry since the heyday of the late 1930s and 1940s. There is evidence of some significant disagreement within the party at this shift in orientation away from an open party intervention and towards a Broad Left strategy. In the 1964 Presidential elections for the AEU the party still ran their own candidate, Reg Birch, a member of the AEU EC. Birch received over 42 000 votes, significantly reducing the majority of the incumbent Carron. In those areas where the party had a solid implementation in the local union, such as Sheffield and North London, local party leaders argued against a move towards Broad Leftism. To what extent this opposition was based on political principal is questionable, key party activists in a few strongholds who had build up a significant base within the union locally may well have been unwilling to give up their positions. In the case of North London, Reg Birch was to look to alternatives to left of the CP, eventually leading a small pro Peking breakaway group, the Communist Party of Britain (Marxist–Lennist).

The Broad Left strategy did bring positive electoral results and in the short to medium term weakened the grip of the right within the union. In 1967 Hugh Scanlon, an ex-party member, and former convenor of the giant Metro Vickers Plant on the Old Trafford estate in Manchester, beat the right-wing candidate John Boyd in the Presidential election by 52.4 per cent to 47.6 per cent with active CP support. The victory was particularly sweet for the left in the union as Scanlon had been dragged through the courts by the right wing in 1961 in an unsuccessful attempt to invalidate his election to the EC. By 1972 the position of the left in the union had been further secured with four of the seven EC seats, the presidency (Scanlon), both the assistant secretaries and an estimated 62 of the then 180 full time posts.[29] This general shift to the left in the structures of the union communists were well represented, for example within the powerful Manchester District by the early 1970s the CP had gained significant influence with the Divisional Organiser, John Tocher, and two of the three District secretaries being party members.[30] However as we shall see in the next chapter, when large scale disputes blew up in the engineering industry in the 1970s the network of CP officials often did not act as a coherent body, with contradictory policies being pursued in different regions of the union. Neither did the election of Broad Left allies such as Hugh Scanlon to the leadership of trade unions guarantee support for Communist Party initiatives. When in 1971 *Labour Monthly*, the influential journal edited by Palme Dutt, was preparing a special 50th anniversary edition, invitations were sent out to leading figures in the Labour and trade union movement asking for greetings messages which could be displayed. Dutt's appeal to Scanlon was met by a curt refusal.[31]

The one trade union where the CP had established solid control of the bureaucracy in the postwar period was the powerful Electrical Trades Union (ETU). In the wake of Hungary two leading Communists, Les Cannon and Frank Chapple, resigned from the party and rapidly shifted across to become standard bearers for the well organised and resurgent right-wing opposition within the union. Frank Chappell won election to the union executive as an anti-Communist candidate and the control that the CP held over the union's electoral machine was threatened. In 1959 the Communist incumbent Frank Haxell narrowly survived a challenge from John Byrne, the standard bearer of the right, in an election for the General Secretaryship. It was in the wake of this election that allegations of ballot rigging, which had been doing the rounds since the late 1950s, hit the headlines in both the popular press and in one of the earlier examples of TV investigative journalism. The allegations suggested that Communist union officials had tampered with ballot returns to disqualify votes from branches which were thought to be anti-Communist. A lawsuit followed with the case being heard in the High Court in the summer of 1961. The court ruled that the election of Haxell as General Secretary had been fraudulent and there was evidence of ballot rigging. Byrne was declared to be the rightful General Secretary. The TUC followed up the court case by demanding that the President Frank Foulkes, who had been named as party to the fraud by the court, submit himself to re-election. When Foulkes refused the ETU was expelled from membership of the TUC. In the atmosphere of witchhunt and recrimination that followed, the right wing were able to gain electoral control of the union, and the successor organisations to the ETU remain to the present bastions of 'moderate' trade unionism and a fortress of the right within the TUC.

Although there is no evidence that ballot rigging as practised in the ETU was typical of the behaviour of Communist trade union activists, the outcome of the ETU ballot rigging scandal was a severe blow to the party. There is also no direct documentary evidence that the ballot rigging was sanctioned by any of the leading bodies of the party, indeed one of the features of the detailed minutes of Executive and Political Committee meetings during this period is how little formal discussion took place within the party leadership of the details of party trade union work. Not surprisingly, the party sought to distance itself from the scandal and Frank Haxell, the villain of the piece, resigned his membership. Willie Thompson's claim that despite having 'searched for many years' he has never found any 'evidence implicating King Street in the affair' are no doubt correct.[32] However the case reveals real problems in the party's trade union work. Faced with the loss of part of its base in the ETU in the wake of Hungary, the Communist leadership could only hold on to power by ballot rigging. Party organisation within different unions and industries was carried out in the main by the relevant Advisory Committees. Bodies of leading Communist trade union activists and officials in each union who determined the broad outlines of party policy in the relevant unions. There is some evidence that we will deal with below that during the later 1960s and 1970s as both the level of working-class struggle rose and the implantation of the CP within the bureaucracy of the trade union movement grew, that a more co-ordinated and centralised approach by the party's industrial department developed. However in practice trade union work was marked by a form of devolved federalism in which the big hitters within the various unions effectively determined policy within their unions.

The alleged prominence of Communists in the growing industrial militancy of the later 1960s was highlighted during the seaman's strike of 1966. The seamen's strike was the first major all-out national strike by a British trade union since the railway workers strike of 1955, and in retrospect can be seen as marking the onset of a period of strike activity which lasted through the 1970s to the great miners' strike of 1984/85. Briefed by his intelligence advisors, the Prime Minister Harold Wilson denounced the organisers of the strike as a 'tight knit group of politically motivated men', accusing the Communist party of orchestrating the dispute. One of the ironies of the accusation is that the CP's influence within the seaman's union at the time was on the whole moderating, with Bert Ramelson the party's industrial organiser arguing for a return to work.

As we have seen above, one of the features of the 1960s was the growth of workplace militancy focused on shop stewards' organisations. As a response to management attacks on shop stewards, and in particular the attempts by the Labour government to introduce Incomes Policies which would limit the power of stewards' organisations to determine wages, groups of shop stewards in some industries, notably engineering and construction, began to form joint committees. One example of these was the London Shop Stewards Defence Committee (LSSDC) formed on the initiative of members of the International Socialists, one of the small revolutionary organisations which was having some limited success in attracting seasoned rank and file industrial militants away from the orbit of the CP. The tensions within the party over trade union strategy meant that Reg Birch, at that time still a leading CP member, and Jim Hiles, secretary of the building workers' Joint Sites Committee, officiated at a conference called by the LSSDC in January 1966. In March of that year a lobby of Parliament in defence of trade union rights was called by a number of shop stewards-based organisations, most of which were still influenced by the CP and thus was born the Liaison Committee for the Defence of Trade Unions, which was to become a key component of CP industrial strategy during the big battles over anti-trade union legislation in the late 1960s and early 1970s.

Moscow or Peking?

The victory of the Chinese revolution in 1949 added greatly to the feeling amongst Communists that the march of history was on their side. Although Soviet Russia, as the cradle of Bolshevism, retained its prime position in the affections and esteem of party members, the coming together of the two most populous states in the world under the banner of Marxism–Leninism was an enormous boost. The first indications of a growing ideological rift between Moscow and Peking came in the wake of the Kruschev's secret speech in 1956. For many years the dispute remained submerged beneath the niceties and diplomatic language which characterised relations between Communist parties in the post-Comintern period. However in 1962 the dispute flared into the open both as a result of Kruschev's perceived climbdown over the Cuban Missile crisis and armed border clashes between China and India, at that time closely aligned with Moscow. Unsurprisingly Moscow refused to support the Chinese and accusations of revisionism were levelled against the CPSU by the ideologues of the Chinese party. The leadership of the British party, despite some initial evidence of sympathy for the Chinese position by Palme Dutt,[33] came out explicitly in support of the Moscow line. In a rather touching overestimation of the influence which the British party could have on the affairs of the international communist movement, delegations were despatched to both Moscow and Peking to seek to mediate and an Executive Committee document, *Restore the Unity of the International Communist Movement*, was published.

How closely rank and file Communists followed the argument is debatable, however the doctrinaire and orthodox defence of essentially Stalinist positions being put forward in statements from Peking did attract a small following within the party. A small opposition grouping headed by Michael McCreery formed a Committee to Defeat Revisionism: For Communist Unity. Support for the pro-Chinese position was limited however to a small number of party branches, primarily in London and Oxford. The EC document was put to a vote of party branches and was endorsed by an overwhelming majority of the membership who attended their branches to vote, with five branches in London and one in Scotland dissenting.[34] McCreery and his supporters were duly expelled from the party, and the committee disappeared into the morass of British left-wing sects. Of rather greater significance was the departure from the party in 1967 of Reg Birch, following a trip to Peking. Birch, who had briefly worked with members of the

International Socialists in the engineering industry,[35] formed the breakaway Communist Party of Great Britain (Marxist–Leninist) which, although faring better than the McCreery grouping, never seriously challenged the hegemony of the party in its trade union heartlands.[36]

The significance of the Sino-Soviet split was not primarily to be felt in the organisational short term, rather it introduced one more element of doubt and uncertainty in the minds of CP activists. Just as with the Krushchev denunciation of Stalin, and the invasion of Hungary, the infallibility of the international communist movement and its leading body the CPSU was called into question. The ideological cement which played such a crucial role in holding the party together was and would continue to crack.

Party life in the 1960s

For active party members in the post-1956 period the key stress was placed on the task of party building. In this the party showed significant resilience and some success. By 1964 membership was back up to over 34 000, significantly higher than that recorded before the haemorrhaging of members in 1956. Each week party office holders in the branches and districts would receive the *Weekly Letter* from the Political Committee, written usually by John Gollan. The *Weekly Letter* invariably started with an item entitled 'The Situation', which gave an overview and digest of the preceding week's key news stories from the party's perspectives. Issues dealt with would range from world affairs, the broader political situation in Britain, trade union issues, and a persistent concentration on the foreign policy objectives of the Soviet State. During the early 1960s in particular, despite the shock of Hungary the emphasis on the scientific and technological achievements of the Soviet Union stand out. For example in August 1961 The *Weekly Letter* opened: 'The most dramatic news during a news packed holiday week was undoubtedly the epoch making space flight of Major Titov. With every circuit around the world the simple fact of socialist scientific and technological superiority over capitalism was being driven home to millions who until now have been doubters'.[37] Recruiting to the party might be hard work and new recruits difficult to integrate into a level of political activity, sales of the *Daily Worker* might be showing an inexorable downward slide, but a reiterated faith in the socialist motherland continued to act as a key motivator for party members.

For those party members active in the branches, party activity during the 1960s consisted of an unremitting diet of recruitment and *Daily*

Worker sales drives. Although membership did pick up significantly from the trough of 25 313 in 1959 to reach a new peak of 34 281 in 1964, two factors stand out. Firstly, the level of political activity amongst the newer membership remained fairly low. This can be seen in particular in respect of sales of the *Daily Worker*, which continued to decline through the period. Secondly there was a high turnover of membership, with the party struggling to retain many of its new recruits. After a succession of unsuccessful attempts to turn around the sales figures of the *Daily Worker* the party decided in 1966 to re-launch the paper under the new masthead of the *Morning Star*, however there was no significant upturn in sales and the long decline continued.[38] The decision to drop the title *Daily Worker*, leaked in the *Guardian* in December 1965,[39] was taken to shift the party away from a perceived identification with the working class at the expense of other groups in society. A letter to branches sent out in January 1966 explicitly argued for the dropping of the term 'worker'.[40] There was an immediate and overwhelmingly negative reaction from party rank and filers, with over 20 letters and telegraphs to the party centre, calling for the retention of the *Daily Worker* title. A party circular sent out in February 1966 canvassed a range of possible titles including: *New Herald*, *Peoples Press*, *Peoples Daily*, *Clarion*, *Unity*, *New World*, *New Age*, *Today* and the eventually chosen *Morning Star*.[41] Recruitment figures being recorded in the *Weekly Letter* through the early 1960s suggest that the party was often recruiting over a hundred members a week, with significantly higher numbers during particular membership drives. Although the party was able to recruit and sustain some layers of newer and younger activists, particularly through the activities of the Young Communist League and through campaigns such as the CND, the feature of an ageing party which was to become all apparent during the 1970s and 1980s was already establishing itself.

It was however possible in this period for branches and districts of the party to buck the generally downward trend. One of the features of party-building both before and during this period was that persistance and dedication could bring some albeit modest success. Very often the presence of one or two talented and dedicated party cadres (typically a married couple) could make a difference. So for example the small rural Suffolk town of Leiston gained a reputation as 'Red Leiston' and returned Communist councillors. In small towns in the East Midlands such as Mansfield and Chesterfield, where the party's regional organiser Fred Westacott and his wife Kath lived, the party could build up a small but significant presence. In Mansfield for example an anti-

Vietnam War meeting organised by the party in March 1967 attracted 130 people – no mean feat for a cold March evening in Mansfield.'[42] In Chesterfield the legacy of a significant Communist Party presence lived on well into the 1990s, through events such as the Chesterfield Trades Council's annual May Day rally, which remains one of the largest such events in Britain, and with for example the participation of large numbers of former and existing party members in campaigning activity against the 1999 Kosovo war and the 2001 bombing of Afghanistan.

In much of the material which has been written about the decline of the CP in its later years, much is made of the political splits between Stalinists and Eurocommunists, which we will cover below. However, during the period of the late 1950s and early 1960s an arguably equally significant but less dramatic division was establishing itself within the party between the political party activists who kept the local branches together, organised the political routine of the party's life, sold the *Daily Worker* and other party publications, and the industrial militants and trade union officials who held a party card but whose active participation in the life of the party remained marginal. The large scale selling of party publications in and around workplaces was in decline, very often the *Daily Worker* or the new *Morning Star* would be block ordered by a shop stewards committee or local union branch, with copies piling up undistributed and unread in union offices. Although it is too simplistic to argue that Communist trade unionists in this period all uniformly opted out of playing a wider role in the party, the relative autonomy of the various Advisory Committees, reinforced the notion of the party in industry acting as a semi-formal information and organisational network for industrial militants rather than a campaigning revolutionary party.

The parliamentary road

Ever since the publishing of the *British Road to Socialism* (*BRS*) in 1951 the party had been committed to a specifically parliamentary road to socialism. During the 'thirteen years of Tory misrule' the party had reverted back towards a more concilliatory approach to Labour which had been temporarily abandoned at the onset of the Cold War. Throughout the early 1960s the emphasis on an alliance of left forces, which underpinned the party's campaigning work in campaigns such as CND and its trade union work with the emergence of a Broad Left strategy, carried over into the electoral field. During the debates which had wracked the party during the dark days of 1956, the question 'why do we exist?' had been asked openly and had to be replied to. The notion that the party was to be more than a left-wing 'ginger group' had to be tested in the electoral arena outlined by the BRS. Consequently as the party moved though the 1960s the focus on the centrality of the party's electoral intervention grew. One indication of this shift was the decision taken in July 1963 to shift the date of the party's annual Congress from the usual Easter slot to the Autumn, to co-ordinate with the major party conference season and a likely General Election. The move was initially opposed by a majority of party districts, however their arguments against the move centred mainly on the ability of delegates to get time off work to attend a conference away from the traditional Easter holiday period.[43] On the electoral field the party not only faced the formidable technical barriers that the first past the post electoral system places in the path of smaller parties, but also the political problem of its relationship with the Labour Party. If electoral success at General Elections was to prove elusive, local elections to a range of municipal authorities provided an arena where local party branches could mount credible campaigns and some prospect of electoral success could be counted on.

The coming General Election of 1964 set an enticing target for the party, which had recovered from 1956, and had a strong track record both in mass campaigns such as CND and in trade union work. The energy and resources devoted to electoral campaigning in 1964 were enormous for a small party with a small activist membership. In the run up to the General Election in October the party not only stood candidates in all the divisions in the Greater London Council election in May, but put up more than 900 candidates across the country in the municipal elections. The party recorded 92 323 votes in the London poll and claimed over 200 000 votes in the May municipal elections. Although no seats were won in London, 24 Communist local councillors were elected across a range of English, Welsh and Scottish local authorities, an overall gain of four seats.[44] All of the council seats were in the party's few small electoral heartlands, the remnants of the 'Little Moscows' of the 1930s where there remained localised traditions amongst workers of voting Communist in significant numbers. Often in these areas Communists won local council seats after many years of unsuccessful campaigning.

Where the party did have some local support and influence in local government, any distinctive radicalism on their part is difficult to discern. In the early 1970s the party had three seats on Clydebank Council at a time when the Rent Act which entailed a sharp increase in council rents provoked mass protests, notably in Clay Cross in Derbyshire where left-wing Labour councillors faced disqualification from office by refusing to increase rents. Jimmy Reid one of the councillors, prominent in the campaign to save the Upper Clyde Shipbuilders, defiantly outlined the party's opposition to the Rent Act:

> We are issuing this call today that in no circumstances will we implement this Tory Rent Act, whatever the consequences... We are answerable to no courts – only the courts of the working class on Clydebank. I would rather sup on porridge with my principles than dine on smoked salmon and caviare without them.[45]

The following month the three communist Clydebank councillors voted with the Labour majority to implement the rent increase.

Whatever modest electoral gains were made were not however turned into visible growth for the party on the ground or expansion of the sale of the *Daily Worker* which continued to fall throughout the campaign, as a frustrated John Gollan pointed out to branch secretaries in the *Weekly Letter* 'the rate of recruiting to the party is still not reflecting the job of work done by the party in the local elections'.[46] In the run-up to the 1964 General Election Gollan wrote the by now customary letter to the Labour Party requesting a United Left slate at the election and the putting forward of an agreed list of candidates for which both the Communist Party and Labour would campaign. The customary reply from Labour politely but firmly declined the offer and the party put forward 35 candidates, all in Labour strongholds.

The election campaign took up a significant portion of the party's resources. Twenty-two full-time officials were diverted from their work at the party centre or their responsibilities in districts where no seats were being contested to run the campaigns. Leading comrades in the branches were encouraged to take time off work to participate in the campaign. An election fighting fund of £30 000, a considerable sum by 1964 standards, was set up. An election broadcast filmed at the party's expense but never put out by the BBC was taken round the country in a 'film van' and over half a million copies of a special coloured broadsheet distributed in the constituencies. The launch of the campaign was a national rally in Hyde park on Sunday 13 September, 'a mighty send off for our 35 Communist candidates',[47] which was attended by a claimed 10 000 supporters.

Unsurprisingly, given the level of enthusiasm on the left for Harold Wilson's anti-Tory campaigning, the distinctive message of the CP failed to make a significant mark during the election campaign. In all the CP heartlands Communist votes declined from previous benchmarks in the 1950s. In some of the areas where there was not a CP electoral tradition, a few thousand votes were picked up here and there. The low level of support for CP candidates might have been tolerable if the party had entered the elections with a clear headed and realistic assessment of the potential, and if the party had built its branches and influence through the elections. But the effect of the campaign as an organising drive for the party was abysmal, only 96 membership applications were received by the party centre during the entire election campaign, about one quarter of the average for 1963/64 and the party centre sent out increasingly shrill exhortations to the branches to turn the contacts made during the campaign into regular *Daily Worker* readers, all with no perceptible results.

Despite the poor results and the negative impact on party building, abandoning an electoralist perspective would entail ditching the central thrust of the *British Road to Socialism* and therefore could not be contemplated. Without an electoral strategy the party would confirm itself as the 'ginger group' of its worst fears. So the electoral strategy was continued, 57 candidates were put up in the 1966 elections with a further fall in the overall vote, although it is notable that the 1966 campaign was not planned and organised for in quite the lavish way as that of 1964, even if this time round the party did get a five minute Party Political Broadcast on TV. As the party was to move into its period of terminal decline in the 1980s, one of the features of party policy which was to unite both Eurocommunist and traditionalist wings of the party was the shared allegiance towards a doomed electoral strategy. One of the great ironies of the party's aspirations to be represented at Westminster was that after the loss of the party's two seats in the House of Commons in 1950, the party was to gain a parliamentary representative, in the House of Lords in the person of Wogan Phillips who inherited a peerage in 1963. Phillip's elevation to the peerage provoked a debate on the Executive Committee as to whether he should take up his seat. After debate the EC voted by 27 to 6 that Phillips should take his seat and make a maiden speech outlining the party's opposition to the House of Lords.[48]

A further feature of the party's electoral aspirations and illusions was the highly detailed approach to policy making taken by Communists. Records of the leading committees of the party through into the 1990s show evidence of this engagement in a stream of highly detailed policy papers. The system of Advisory Committees which had been set up to co-ordinate the work of Communists in different industries, unions and professional groups were closely involved in this process. As late as July 1991, months before the formal dissolution of the party, the Further and Higher Education Advisory committee was submitting evidence to the Secretary of State for Education on Further Education policy.[49] Royal Commissions, Green Papers and Speakers Conferences all regularly received input from the party, on issues ranging from electoral reform[50] to teacher training. How closely the politicians and senior civil servants who received this documentation read and digested this prodigious output, we can only speculate.

For a radical left-wing party operating within the straitjacket of the first past the post system the numbers of votes won during some of the CPs electoral forays in the 1960s were not negligible if seen as left-wing protest votes. But the illusions within the party that it was actually possible to win a number of Communist MPs who would then play a crucial role in strengthening the forces of the parliamentary left within the Labour Party to bring about a transition to socialism were a serious error. Over 90 000 Communist voters in the GLC elections of 1964 provided a significant pool of left-wing opinion in the capital. If the party could have tapped into and mobilised a portion of that support through its branches and campaigning activity, firmer roots could have been laid down so that as the curve of working-class militancy and protest campaigns grew during the late 1960s and 1970s, Communists could have been better placed to lead and influence those fights. But the electoral illusions of the party pulled against that type of activist perspective, so when in the period after 1968 the level of working-class political activity grew decisively in Britain, the party was unable to capitalise fully on it.

Conclusion

Despite suffering a heavy blow as a result of the Russian invasion of Hungary, the party survived and to an extent thrived during the early part of the 1960s. By relating, albeit belatedly, to the radicalism engendered by CND, the party was able attract new and young recruits who could revitalise what was already an ageing party. Communists continued to play a significant role within the unions leading strikes and despite losing control of the ETU, party members continued to play a significant role within the leadership of a number of unions. However the tendency for the party to become in practice a loose federation of socialist and trade union activists continued to develop and the party's electoral aspirations which were central to the strategy laid out in *The British Road to Socialism* were to fail.

6
Not Fade Away: from 1968 to Dissolution

1968 marked a significant turning point in the fortunes of the Marxist left across Europe. The radicalisation of the 1960s was expressed in anti-Vietnam War protests, student struggles and by a growing willingness of younger workers to take militant forms of industrial action including factory occupations, mass political strikes and the use of flying pickets. This trend was most visibly demonstrated in the May '68 events in France where mass student revolt sparked of a general strike. The views of many of the social theorists of the 1950s and 1960s who had argued that workers had been thoroughly incorporated into the culture of bourgeois society, looked decidedly flimsy seen through the prism of the newly born radicalism of the late 1960s and early 1970s.[1] This process of radicalisation was to throw up many new leftist political formations, and give a significant boost to the fortunes of small groups of revolutionaries of a Trotskyist, Guevarrist or Maoist complexion. Tiny organisations mushroomed into sizeable if often unstable and ultimately short-lived parties all of whom defined themselves clearly to the left of established Communist parties. This trend was most clearly observed in southern European states; Italy in the wake of the 'Hot Autumn' militancy of 1969, and Spain and Portugal after the end of their respective periods of dictatorial rule in the 1970s.[1] In Northern Europe and in Britain this phenomenon was also seen with the Communist Party facing significant forces to the left off it which were able to tap into and exploit the mood of popular radicalisation. However 1968 did not simply see a swing to the left. 1968 was also the year of mass disillusionment amongst Labour's traditional base and that feeling often swung sharply rightwards. The Conservatives won spectacular local and by-election victories and Enoch Powell's infamous 'Rivers of Blood' speech tapped into and helped formulate a racist anti-immigrant sentiment. The certainties of the postwar world in the western liberal democracies, the Bustkellite[2] postwar consensus based on Keynesian economics and a commitment to state welfare, was beginning to unravel.

Three international events in 1968 were to shape elements of the revolutionary movement, which crystallised that year. In February the Tet offensive by the National Liberation Front in Vietnam struck a mighty blow against US imperialism, shattering the myth of US invincibility and providing a spur to the anti-Vietnam War protest movement in the US and across the world. The boldness of the Tet offensive was to give a sharp impetus to young leftist radicals who took their inspiration from Mao and Che Guevarra. The notion that with enough effort of will the left could 'make two, three, many Vietnams'[3] was to lead to much of the super-optimism which marked many on the new revolutionary left. The May '68 events in France, which saw a mass student movement initially dismissed by the French Communist press as the work of 'false revolutionaries (who) must be energetically unmasked', led to the largest general strike in history, involving mass occupations of factories which echoed and exceeded the activism of the Popular Front period of 1936. May '68 was to challenge the notion that the western working class had been written off as an agent for social change. This was to lead to an attempt by some British groups to the left of the CP, notably the International Socialists, to focus their organisational energies on trade union work, which was an area hitherto of CP hegemony.

In August 1968 Warsaw Pact troops invaded Czechoslovakia to halt the reform movement in the Czech party associated with Edward Dubcek, in what appeared to be re-run of the Hungarian events twelve years previously. The revolutionary groups were virtually unanimous in their condemnation of the invasion, for the post-1968 left opposition to 'Stalinism' was to become the norm. For the Communist Party of Great Britain the crushing of the Prague spring was a decisive moment. The party press had enthusiastically reported on the reform process in the Czech party, seeing the development of 'Socialism with a Human Face' as being in step with the constitutional thrust of *The British Road to Socialism*. The reaction of the party leadership, in line with many other Communist Parties was to criticise the invasion. George Matthews, representing the party's NEC spoke to reporters outside the King St Headquarters of the CPGB describing the invasion as 'a violation of socialist legality'.[5] However within the party ranks the enthusiasm of the leadership for the Prague Spring and the open criticism of the actions of the Socialist motherland in 'restoring socialism' opened up bitter divisions which never healed and instead formed the battle lines between different wings of the party through to its final demise in 1991. Traditionalists within the party, many of them based around the Surrey district organiser Sid French, but with the support of the remaining Old Bolshevik, Rajani Palme Dutt fought a rearguard action to save the party from 'revisionism'. The 1969 Communist Party conference saw the 'tankies', as supporters of the Soviet invasion of Czechoslovakia were dubbed by their opponents, lose the vote but muster a significant 28 per cent of the delegates.

Yet there was to be no repeat of the debacle of 1956, no mass exodus from the party, no prominent resignations. The relatively smooth passing of the Czech crisis pointed to a new feature of the nature of the party and its relationship to its members and its broader constituency on the British left. Prior to 1956, party membership had implied a higher level of political commitment, an adherence to a tough and oppositional set of values and beliefs in a Cold War atmosphere. That party had effectively fractured on the impact of Hungary, and the party which had emerged in the aftermath was more open, softer and to a degree pluralistic, susceptible to a widely diverging set of political interpretations, tactics and values. For some within the party, this new and more open culture was of itself a positive move away from the orthodoxy of the past, however the growing fragmentation was to spell danger for the party's continued long term existence as a united, campaigning organisation.

The hopes of the newly formed Marxist revolutionaries for immediate revolutionary change in Europe were in the main disappointed as by the mid-1970s relatively stable liberal democratic polities were established in Southern Europe. The main beneficiaries of the radicalisation of the 1960s and early 1970s were resurgent social democratic parties and to a lesser but significant extent the communist parties. The late 1970s were the hey day of the southern European Communist Parties with the Italian, Spanish and French Parties continuing to consolidate both a significant electoral base and an ability on occasions to mobilise large protest movements. For the Communist Party of Great Britain the dynamic was slightly different, far smaller than its southern European comrades it lacked the electoral base and strategic positioning within the working-class movement enjoyed by many of the European parties. But the challenge to the party from the left had emerged during the 1960s and was to continue through the 1970s and 1980s especially amongst students, social movements such as women's liberation and black rights and others attracted to the politics of protest. This proved a significant problem for the party and one that it felt it had to address. Although the party had for a while produced internally distributed and debated material on the threat of the ultra left,[6] in 1969 a document which had originally been prepared for discussion at the EC by Betty Reed[7] was updated, revamped and produced as a five shilling pamphlet, *Ultra Leftism in Britain*.[8] However just as in Europe the Communist Party of Great Britain was to also find itself the beneficiary of the generalised radicalisation that followed 1968, both amongst workers who were moving into a sustained phase of militancy which was to last through the 1970s, and also amongst students and radicalised intellectuals who dismissed the Trotskyist and Maoist groups as 'ultra left', especially after the initial euphoria of 1968 had died down. Some within the party leadership did recognise the 'genuine base of radicalism' of the spirit of '68 and the need on the part of the Communist Party for 'some degree of constructive engagement' with the radical groups which were emerging.[9] As we shall see there is evidence that faced with growing radicalisation both from protest politics but also amongst industrial workers some Communists did steer leftwards.

Street-fighting man: students and the anti-Vietnam War protests

It has long been a cliché to label the 1968 protest movements as being composed solely of young, middle-class student radicals and in subsequent decades generations of journalists stuck for a story have regularly filed copy along the lines of 'Why today's students aren't as radical as they were in the 1960s?' Nevertheless the mid-1960s did begin to see a number of significant shifts in student politics to the left. In the pre-Second World War period universities had by and large been the training ground for a relatively narrow stratum of the sons of the upper and upper middle classes. This did not mean that left-wing students didn't exist, but as David Widgery argued:

> the rowing and burning of eights, the perfection of classically parsed love verses, elegant drunkenness, pink silk parasols, and membership of the Communist Party were all possible because none of them mattered ... The gap between students and the rest of the world was unbridgeable. Socialists were simply more polite to their servants.[10]

In the 1950s and 1960s that gap was fast closing as the social composition of university students changed. The proportion of young men and women in higher education grew from 1.5 per cent of their age group in 1950 to 15 per cent in 1972.[11] The growth of new universities and the establishment of the polytechnics changed the whole atmosphere of student life. The image of a collegiate and liberal environment often clashed with the experiences of students themselves. The emerging student movement of the 1960s was by nature dynamic and inchoate and not conducive to the well worked out and formalised analyses of either the Communist Party or of the small groups of revolutionaries.

Communist Party students had been active within the National Union of Students (NUS) for a number of years, attempting to break the hold on the union of a well organised and well funded group of right, wing Labour students. Student and youth movements had been the focus of much Cold War instigated manoeuvring, and the NUS was affiliated to the International Students Conference, the Washington-backed counterpart to the Moscow-sponsored International Union of Students. In January 1967 the party initiated a form of Broad Left organisation the Radical Student Alliance (RSA) along with Labour left wingers and Liberals. In the spring of 1967 the RSA organised a campaign of demonstrations and one-day students strikes against increases in fees for overseas students. However when in March of 1967 students at the London School of Economics occupied in protest at the appointment of Walter Adams, the former director of University College Rhodesia, and reputedly a supporter of the racist Smith regime, it was a Conservative who proposed the motion and 'ultra left' revolutionaries who took the limelight. The wave of student protests and occupations through 1967 and 1968 which intermingled with protest over the Vietnam War and racism presented a challenge to the Communist Party. Individual members were involved in some of the protests for example the seven week occupation of Hornsey Art college, but the running was made by the revolutionary left. It was during this time that Tariq Ali of the International Marxist Group came to national prominence as a representative of student radicalism, despite the fact that he was no longer a student himself. However the attempts of the revolutionaries organised in the Revolutionary Socialist Students Federation to form the leadership of a radicalised student movement fell apart amongst sectarian infighting and ultra-leftist high-jinks. Even the more tactically astute elements of the far left had initially tended to write off operating within the right wing and bureaucratic NUS[12] and to an extent, left the field open to the Communist Party whose longer term strategy of shifting the NUS leftwards and of gaining some element of control over it was to bring success. In 1970 the Broad Left won control of the NUS executive and in 1971 Digby Jacks, a Communist, was elected as president. For much of the 1970s the NUS was to remain under the control of a Broad Left which was to varying degrees effectively run by the party. Elements of leftism in the party's approach to student work did continue into the early 1970s. A 1973 Communist Party pamphlet by Dave Cook entitled simply *Students*, while critical of the 'political immaturity of the ultra left', talked about 'the fight for socialist revolution' and argued the formation of campaigning Socialist Societies in the colleges bringing together all left wing groups as a counterweight to the electoralist Broad Left strategy.[13] Communist Party students played an active role in organising solidarity with striking miners in 1972, helping to erase the folk memory of 1926 when students had been mobilised to act a strike breakers. However as the seventies progressed, and once in control of the union machine, the CP-led Broad Left tended to steer the NUS into the waters of 'constitutional struggle'. Yet the persistence of an appetite for militancy amongst students shown in successive waves of student occupations throughout the 1970s continued to make student politics fertile ground for the revolutionaries of the International Socialists and the International Marxist Group.

Student politics were to provide a training ground and test bed for a new generation of Communist activists in the 1970s. Although sharply differentiated from the 'ultra lefts', many of these Communists were also touched by the anti-authoritarian and liberal culture of the 1960s and as such often rubbed along uneasily with the highly traditional and often socially conservative group who made up the leadership of the party. Many of the Communists active in student politics were to become enthusiasts for what became known as Eurocommunism, and gathered around the journal *Marxism Today*. The term Eurocommunism was a form of shorthand. It was initially coined to describe developments in key European parties, notably the Spanish and the Italian Communist Parties, who after 1968 were moving away from a slavish pro-Moscow line and beginning to develop a more pluralistic approach to politics. In the context of the CPGB it refers to the groups of mainly younger reformers who sought to take the party away from its traditional workerist orientation towards a more pluralist approach.

The party took student work seriously, initiating a weekly *Student World* column in the *Morning Star* every Friday. The Communist University of London, an annual week-long seminar which was inaugurated in 1969 on the instigation of Fergus Nicholson, did much over the next decade to develop an intellectual periphery for the party. Many of this generation were to play a significant role in the increasingly bitter internecine battles which were to mark dying years of the party in the 1980s. Although the majority of party students orientated towards Eurocommunism, Nicholson, the then student organiser, was to emerge as a prominent traditionalist.

The student radicalism of the mid sixties was in large part provoked by outrage at the war in Vietnam. By 1966 television news coverage of the war regularly featured reports which were highly critical of the US war effort and sceptical of claims that the war was being won. The Communist Party was quick off the mark in launching campaigning over the issue of Vietnam drawing on the wide networks of peace activists which it had built up around its work in CND. The British Council for Peace in Vietnam (BCPV) was the chosen Popular Front body fronted by the left-wing Labour peer Fenner Brockway. The BCPV operated on the tried and tested lines of Popular Frontist international campaigns. In its work the BCPV stressed the need for a negotiated peace, and called on the UN to intervene to uphold the terms of the 1954 agreement which had originally divided North from South Vietnam. Petitions, rallies and meetings brought together the classic components of the Popular Front from 'bishops to brickies'. The launch of a rival campaign the Vietnam Solidarity Campaign (VSC) in January 1966 initially caused little concern to the party. With its slogans of 'US Troops Out' and 'Victory to the NLF' the new movement caught the mood of a radicalising minority. A VSC organised demonstration of 10 000 outside the US embassy in October 1967 surprised both the organisers and the police and nearly succeeded in storming the building.[14] For the following year the VSC and the BCPV were in competition to such an extent that rival anti-war demos were held on successive weekends in March 1968. The fact that the respectable BCPV pulled far fewer onto the streets than did the radical VSC was finally to persuade the Communist Party that to continue to oppose the VSC was counter-productive. It was, as we have seen, at the May Executive Commitee following these events that a document calling for constructive engagement with the far left was discussed. By the time October came around and the 100 000 strong VSC demonstration was held the Communist Party had adopted a new line, mobilising members and supporters and going as far as providing an escort of 'tough looking and burly ... London dockers ... sent by the Communist Party' for Tariq Ali who had been beaten up the previous day.¹⁵ Although as we have seen above the party carried on an often impressive level of mobilisation over Vietnam in towns and cities across the country, by and large the newly radicalising young protestors were mobilised by the revolutionary left. For the CP another challenge had to be faced. If in reality left electoral politics were an unassailable bastion held by Labour and the politics of protest were being led by new and radical forces, what role could the party play? The growth of militant class struggle was to provide an arena in which the party had an established track record where Communists could continue to feel relevant.

The British Disease – industrial militancy

Despite the common predictions that class struggle was a thing of the past, the early 1970s saw British workers displaying a level of industrial militancy not seen since the years following the First World War. The number of days 'lost' through industrial disputes in the years 1970, 1971 and 1972 were 10 908 000, 13 589 000 and 23 923 000 respectively.¹⁶ The strike wave not only encompassed traditionally militant sections of the blue-collar working class such as miners, railway workers, dockers steelworkers and engineers, but militant trade unionism found an echo amongst previously poorly organised workers in industries such as chemicals, glass production and textiles. Public sector workers in health and local government took strike action, as did post office workers, and the 'disease' of militancy spread to encompass white-collar workers such as teachers, civil servants and local government clerical workers. Although strike figures were never again to reach the heady heights of 1972, the British Disease lingered well on into the 1970s and even in a defensive mode into the 1980s with periodic large scale set-piece confrontations between unions and employers epitomised by the year long miners strike of 1984/85.

Two particular events illustrated the new militant mood of the early 1970s: the Upper Clyde Shipbuilders (UCS) 'work in' of 1971 and the national miners' strike of 1972, the former in defence of jobs, the latter in support of an aggressive wage demand by a group of workers who felt left behind in the 'affluent society'. Communist Party activists were active in both disputes but as we shall see their influence was as often to moderate the tactics of workers rather than to attempt to encourage more militant forms of struggle.

On 24 June 1971, 100 000 workers struck in Glasgow over the threat to jobs at Upper Clyde Shipbuilders (UCS). When a month later the Conservative cabinet minister John Davies announced that 6000 of the 8500 jobs at UCS would go, the workers occupied the yard. There was significant solidarity action including a one-day strike in the West of Scotland on 18 August culminating in a mass rally in George Square. Communist Party activists were centrally involved in building the occupation and the solidarity action which supported it. UCS, which became a national cause celebre attracting widespread and often sympathetic media coverage, heralded a wave of factory occupations, in the main as with UCS, defensive occupations against the threat of closure and redundancy. By the beginning of 1972 groups of employers were beginning to note with increasing worry the popularity of occupation as a tactic. UCS had been led by a CP-influenced stewards committee, which had emphasised that the occupation was a 'work in' with production being maintained, although in practice little actual productive work was carried out in the yards during the sit-in.[17] The tactics adopted by the CP and articulated through the dispute by Jimmy Reid, the chief spokesperson for the dispute and a prominent Glasgow CP activist, consciously attempted to mobilise the broadest possible base of public support for the work in. As a CP pamphlet published at the time of the dispute noted:

> A strike could play into the hands of the employers when they were set on closure anyway. A sit-in would have been difficult to maintain for long enough It would have also given the employers a good excuse to attack the workers by arguing that the sit in made it impossible to fulfil any contract and aggravated the bankrupt situation. This would have helped the Tories to alienate public opinion from support of the UCS workers.[18]

UCS ended with a qualified victory. The majority of the 6500 threatened jobs were saved, but the deal included a four year no strike deal with the new owners. However occupations in the North-West region of England which encompassed Greater Manchester and Merseyside, tended towards full scale 'worker occupations' where workers effectively barricaded themselves into the factories and refused management access.[19] Without the moderating influence of a well organised CP presence in many North-West factories, workers tended towards the more militant forms of occupations, occasionally as in the case of the Fisher Bendix sit in on Merseyside with the encouragement and support of left-wing groups such as the International Socialists. It is not the case as Willie Thompson argues that UCS style 'work ins' became the norm, rather UCS acted for a short period as inspiration for other groups of workers to adopt factory occupations as a valid tactic.[20]

The miners' strike of 1972, which was characterised by the extensive use by striking miners of the tactic of the flying picket, marked a significant shift in the stance of the National Union of Mineworkers (NUM). Communist Party activists played a proud role in the 1972 strike. Party miners were often at the forefront of picketing, and party trade unionists in other industries were crucial in organising the impressive solidarity which brought victory. The miners' victory at the key pivotal action of the 1972 strike, the 'Battle of Saltley' in February, owes a great deal to the network of industrial militants under the organisation of the Communist Party in the West Midlands. Saltley, a coking depot picketed by striking miners, had been kept open by a large police presence, arrests and injuries mounted. Arthur Scargill who was co-ordinating the NUM pickets worked alongside Frank Watters, the Communist Party's full time Birmingham District secretary, to organise solidarity action from Birmingham engineering workers. It was the network of activists buildt up by the party in and around the West Midlands car and engineering industry which delivered the action. On Thursday 10 February striking miners on the picket line were joined by an estimated 10 000 workers. Faced by the size of the protest the Chief Constable of the West Midlands ordered the Saltley gates locked, and the miners had won.[21]

The aftermath of the 1970s strikes, the strike of 1984/85, and memories of the General Strike of 1926, conjure up an image of miners as a particularly militant group of workers. However the leadership of the NUM had followed a policy of co-operation with management since nationalisation in 1945 and the rank and file of the union had, until a spate of unofficial strikes in 1969 and 1970, broadly accepted the moderate policies of the union's leadership. Within the leadership of the NUM the Communists, although often differentiating themselves on ideological questions from others in the leadership, did not push for a significantly different strategy over pay or pit closures, which were the two big issues affecting miners and their communities in the postwar period. 'Communist Party members in official positions around the coalfield continued to advocate continuity in the union's policy of co-operation with the NCB.'[22] The party had established a significant base amongst miners in the pre-war period, especially in the Scottish, Welsh and Kent coalfields and elements of that tradition were maintained and migrated with miners who moved to pits in English coalfields. The party's strong position in the NUM had been reflected in the election first of Arthur Horner (1945–59) and then Will Paynter (1959–68) as General Secretary, both prominent party members. On Paynter's retirement the then General Secretary of the party John Gollan praised his 'brilliant service to the miners and the Communist Party' in pages of the *Morning Star*.[23] Gollan was not alone in praising Paynter's contribution to the miners; Lord Robens, the Chairman of the National Coal Board, was to fondly remember Paynter's role in the 1964 national wage negotiations.

> Paynter was still a Communist, which made his speech all the more remarkable, but his devotion to the union and the men whose wellbeing was his responsibility, as always, came before his party affiliations ... He told his hearers that he accepted the board's offer of 9/6 per week on the minimum was the most the industry could afford ... Paynter saved the day.[24]

Horner and Paynter's periods as General Secretary had seen no official strike action and had coincided with a period during which miners living standards had declined significantly when compared with other groups of manual workers. In 1948 miners' wages were 29 per cent above the average pay of manual workers, by 1960 wages were 7.4 per cent above the average and by 1970 wages were 3.1 per cent below the average.[25] The introduction of a national bonus scheme in 1966, the National Power Loading Agreement, with the support of Communist NUM officials had the effect of equalising down pay rates, by ending locally negotiated bonuses which had allowed miners at well-organised pits to push up wage rates.[26] Shortly after his retirement Paynter was to resign his party membership and take a job in the government's Commission on Industrial Relations.

As in many of the other areas of industrial conflict in the 1960s and 1970s, CP policy was pulled between a priority of focusing on establishing alliances with left wingers in the union leaderships and building within the rank and file. In the NUM there also arose a specific phenomenon of former CP members and supporters such as Lawrence Daly and subsequently Arthur Scargill who moved away from a direct relationship with the party, but who unlike many of the ex-party members in unions such as the electricians did not move to the right but remained on the left. In the case of Scargill this was to lead in the strike of 1984/85 to the CP criticising a Labour Left trade union leader for being 'ultra left'. The tensions inherent in the party's position of developing an uncritical relationship with trade union leaders who could be characterised as left was to resurface time and again in the mining industry. One example was during the unofficial strikes of 1969 and 1970 when upwards of 100 000 miners took strike action over pay. Whilst CP activists in the coalfields were busy trying to build and extend the action, party members on the NUM's national executive were accepting a revised pay offer from the National Coal Board. Communist miners in those regions of the union where the right wing were in control, such as Yorkshire, were more likely to engage in a form of rank and file work which during the late sixties and early 1970s chimed with a rising sense of grievance and militancy amongst miners. In 1967 the Barnsley Miners Forum a semi-official group of lay branch officers was formed with the active participation of local party members both to act as a counterweight to the right wing leadership of the Yorkshire NUM and to become an organising focus for unofficial action over pay. The Forum played a crucial role in the unofficial action in 1969 and 1970, in pushing for forms of militant rank and file activism in the 1972 strike such as the mass picketing of the Saltley coking works in Birmingham, and acting as a launching pad for the swift rise of Arthur Scargill, a former member of the Young Communist League, through to the leadership of the NUM.

The experience of Communist Party activism in the mining industry is instructive. From the immediate postwar years when the party leadership had continued to push for a drive for production, through the period of closure and the decline of miners living standards of the 1950s and 1960s, the party's strategy must be judged a failure. Miners as a group of workers lost out during the era of the 'affluent society', and although Communists and others left-wingers were well established in the leadership of the union, it took the emergence of a new generation of militants schooled in the unofficial strike movement of the 1960s to shift the union decisively towards the more combative approach. By the late 1950s the existence of a distinctive party line in the NUM had virtually disappeared, so although new generations of militants in the pits did join or at least look to the Communist Party for a sense of political lead, the party they joined was by now a looser confederation of activists and officials, bound together by a general sense of loyalty to an idea of socialism, but within which quite divergent practices and strategies were followed.

How divergent these practices were was illustrated by the Paynter case. It is too easy to merely brand Paynter a turncoat, but for years the experience of senior party trade unionists was one where their loyalty or commitment to a distinctive party line was rarely if ever tested. Membership implied a willingness to be quoted in the *Morning Star* and the lending of one's name to whatever the party campaign of the moment was. It is hardly surprising therefore that when stark choices which did hinge on party membership were posed, resignations sometimes followed. Paynter's resignation from the party was followed in 1970 by the resignation of Dave Bowman an EC member and senior trade unionist in the National Union of Railwaymen (NUR). Bowman wished to stand for the presidency of the NUR and the NUR's rules explicitly forbade a Communist holding that position.[27] Paynter and Bowman's resignation from the party along with the resignation of a number of ETU officials after the banning of Communists holding office following the ballot-rigging scandal illustrate the shift in party culture which had taken place. In 1948 when Bert Papworth and eight other members of the TGWU executive were barred from their positions, they kept their party cards and resigned their union posts.[28]

Up against the law: fighting the Industrial Relations Act

The sharply political character of trade unionism in the early 1970s was demonstrated by the clash between the growing militancy of significant groups of workers and the attempt by the Conservative government of Edward Heath to introduce and apply the 1970 Industrial Relations Act. As we have already seen, the Communist Party had already cut its teeth in the battle to defend trade union rights against legislative threats in the form of Labour's *In Place of Strife* proposals in 1969. The chosen vehicle was a form of rank and file organisation, the Liaison Committee for the Defence of Trade Unions (LCDTU). The LCDTU had been launched in opposition to the policies of a Labour government, and in part in response to worries that CP militants might be outflanked to the left. With the election of a Conservative government, any tactical hesitancy on the part of the CP that they were somehow taking action against a 'left' government disappeared. In response to the publication of the Industrial Relations Bill, the LCDTU convened a national conference on 14 November, which received wide backing from a range of union bodies including the national executives of a number of trade unions. The LCDTU called for unofficial strike action against the Bill in December 1970, and the strike call was met by significant support, with the Department of Employment estimating 350 000 strikers and the LCDTU themselves claiming 600 000.[29]

It was the biggest 'political' strike in living memory and played a significant role in creating a momentum for active resistance to the Industrial Relations Act which was reflected in further stoppages in 1971 and 1972 involving engineering and other workers. However although CP militants and, in particular in the case of the engineering union, left wingers involved in Broad Left alliances, continued to organise strike action against the Act, the momentum of the LCDTU waned at a time when working-class militancy itself appeared to be growing. The Liaison Committee, despite its origins amongst wider left-wing forces than the CP itself, was very much under the political control of the party, and as such remained subordinate to the broad political strategy of *The British Road to Socialism* with its stress on a parliamentary road and its perspective of building up of a electoral alliances within the trade unions to pressurise Labour towards more left-wing positions. Thus the LCDTU was never to develop into a fully-fledged militant rank and file organisation, and played little role in the big industrial battles of the 1972–74 period, involving engineers, dockers and miners. So for example when in the summer of 1972 five London dockers were jailed in Pentonville prison under the provisions of the Industrial Relations Act, the LCDTU played little direct role in the mass mobilisations which secured their rapid release in one of the most humiliating climbdowns of the Heath government. When in April 1973 the LCDTU conference chairman refused to allow a discussion of the dockers' struggle the previous summer, the London Port Shop Stewards delegation, previously regarded as a CP stronghold, walked out of the conference.[30]

The LCDTU, the party's chosen vehicle for campaigning against the attempt by successive governments to restrict trade union activity by law, did not feature in the campaigns in the docks. Bitter class battles in the ports through the 1960s and 1970s involved Communist Party dockers, and we can observe some of the tensions inherent in the party's overall Broad Left strategy towards the unions, when groups of militant workers sought to take action which went far beyond that sanctioned by trade union officials.[31] The situation facing party activists in the docks, where there was a strong tradition of rank and file activity was complicated by the fact that the majority union in the docks, the TGWU, had in 1948 placed a ban on Communists holding union office which was not lifted until 1968. This 'confined Communist dock-workers to a purely unofficial outlet for their industrial activity'.[32] This meant that Communist dockers were central to the building of shop steward based committees at first locally and then in 1969 establishing a national shop stewards network linking together key ports with Liverpool and London, both relative party strongholds. Communist Party members along with other socialists were central in spreading the unofficial strike action, which greeted the arrest of the Pentonville Five. On Friday 21 July 1972 Bert Ramelson, the party's industrial organiser, called an emergency industrial aggregate meeting of the London district on Sunday 23 at which party members were urged to 'spread strikes with the aim of pressurising the TUC to call a general strike until the dockers were released'.[33] This willingness of the party leadership to push for unconstitutional action does demonstrate the susceptibility of the organisation to the mood of militancy which existed at the time. However over the weekend the party leadership modified its demands for the TUC to call an open ended general strike, to one of support for a one-day general strike.[34] The impressive solidarity strikes which did take place over Pentonville, such as the psychologically key stopping of Fleet Street and much of the regional press, often reflected the existance of CP or other left wing orientated militants on the ground. In Fleet Street for example CP printers had been central to a significant rank and file movement, whose supporters were vital in delivering strike action.[35] In the event the rapid release of the imprisoned dockers meant that although over 300 000 workers had walked out in unofficial solidarity strikes the issue of a general strike was never put to the test.

The inherent tensions between Communist Party activists playing a central role in dynamic and militant class struggle which went far beyond the norms of constitutional trade unionism, and the core strategy of the party in developing a relationship with 'left' trade union leaders was clear in other struggles. The 1972 building workers' strikes, which involved highly militant strike action and the use of flying pickets, resulted in the imprisonment of two building workers, Des Warren a party member and Ricky Tomlinson the now famous actor, on conspiracy charges. Party members had once again been central along with other left wingers in the creation of a rank and file network of activists around the *Building Workers Charter*, a paper with a circulation of up to 10 000 During the 1972 strike the militant tactics of rank and file activists clashed head on with the constituional approach of the leadership of the main union UCATT. Yet despite the prominance of party members arguing for militant tactics the *Morning Star* not only invited George Smith, the moderate leader of UCATT, to write an article but also uncritically reported 'back to work' deals which had the effect of breaking the unity of the strike.[36]

In those sections of industry where the party had an established base of activists, their role during the strikes of the 1970s was significant if, as we have seen above on occasions, contradictory. However there is little evidence that by the 1970s the party took any co-ordinated attempt to gain an implantation in areas where it had little or no traditional support. In 1969 and 1970 there were a series of significant and quite militant strikes amongst dustmen, British Leyland workers in central Lancashire, and glass workers at Pilkingtons in St Helens. Many of these workers belonged to large general unions such as the GMWU and the TGWU, which had traditionally been regarded as bastions of the right, and where the CP had little organised presence. The reluctance of the party to intervene in these disputes reveals both how far the CP had moved away from a radical activist orientation, and its unwillingness to endorse strike action which was often, as in the case of the bitter Pilkington strike, unofficial.

White-collar workers

One of the key features of trade union growth and development during the 1970s was the emergence of white-collar public sector trade unionism and militancy on an unprecedented scale. Many of the white-collar unions had for years been bastions of right-wing, moderate trade unionism. The growth in militant workers struggles and the success of traditional blue collar unions in winning significant pay rises had the effect of pushing white collar unions towards greater militancy and making the unions easier for the left to operate within. During the 1970s and onwards into the 1980s there was also a steady stream of left-wing activists who had been pulled into some degree of political activity during their student years into jobs in teaching and lecturing, local government and the civil service. Many of these activists, some belonging or close to the Communist Party, others aligned with one or other of the far left groups and others non-aligned or members of the Labour Party, were often to form the organisational cadre of a more leftist and militant layer of trade union lay officials and activists. There is some evidence of Communists in this period developing a rank and filist approach, as in the CPSA civil service union where Communists were briefly involved with other left activists in launching the rank and file journal *Redder Tape* in 1972.[37] In these unions the main arena of party involvement was the lower level of the bureaucracy through the adoption of a Broad Left orientation involving alliances with Labour lefts. In a number of unions, notably the NUT, NATFHE (formerly ATTI), the SCPS and TASS, Communist Party members achieved significant leadership positions. Max Morris, a prominent party member was elected president of the NUT and Ken Gill was elected General Secretary of TASS, and was elevated to the General Council of the TUC in 1984. White-collar unions therefore provided fertile territory for the policy of left advance within the unions mapped out by *The British Road to Socialism*.

The role of the CP within the white-collar unions from the 1970s was primarily focused on the winning of leadership positions and the formulation of a Broad Left strategy. It is therefore not surprising that during a period of growing worker militancy, which as we have seen had a particular impact on white-collar unions, the party and its Broad Left allies should face significant opposition from leftist and radical elements within the unions. Whereas in the traditional blue-collar unions such as engineering, mining and transport, the influence of far-left groups was minor although not insignificant, within some of the white collar unions the far left were able to muster significant influence and support to challenge the perceived timidity of Broad Left leaderships.

Teacher trade unionism had changed significantly during the 1960s with one study concluding, 'teachers have traditionally been reluctant to take strike action, but in the 1960s they resorted to militant tactics with increasing frequency and increasing numbers.'[38] Communist NUT activists were justifiably proud of their record in helping to transform the NUT from a passive and right-wing union in the 1950s to a far more activist organisation, winning affiliation to the TUC in 1970. The Communist Party Education Advisory Group was one of the most prominent in the party and the party journal *Education Today and Tomorrow* had a wide readership. With the union under the control of the right-wing, Communist activity was focused on building amongst an activist rank and file, in particular in taking up the demand for a single salary scale. In 1959 however the party dropped its support for a single salary scale but still was to the fore in the organisation of a militant campaign to pressurise the NUT leadership to fight against the cut in the Burnham pay offer proposed in 1961. Once again as in 1959, having led a militant protest movement within the NUT, the party leadership pulled away from its previously radical positions. By the late 1960s a further bout of teacher militancy found the CP leadership, by now better placed within the national leadership of the union but by no means hegemonic, firmly on the side of constitutionalists. As in some of the other unions the move away from a workplace orientation, towards a Broad Left strategy, caused disquiet among some party teachers and in late 1967 a small group of London based dissident CP teachers produced a journal *Rank and File Teacher*[39] in alliance with a number of members of the International Socialists. For much of the 1970s NUT politics were dominated by clashes between the militant activism of *Rank and File Teacher* supporters and an NUT leadership which had no intention of taking teacher trade unionism beyond 'acceptable' limits of constitutional activism. In those clashes the Communist Party, still a significant force in the union and with a foothold in the national leadership of the NUT best personified by Max Morris, was firmly on the side of the moderate constitutionalists. For example, despite the party's campaign for a Youth TUC, Communists inside the NUT supported the union leadership's decision to close down the Young Teachers Conference because of the influence of *Rank and File Teacher*. One of the features of NUT trade unionism at this time was the pre-dominance of head teachers within the leadership of the union, at one point in the 1970s all the members of the NUT's Executive were heads including the Communist Party members. Morris, himself a head, was later to resign from the party but remained the 'hammer of the Trots', for example using an article in *The Times* in January 1977 to explain 'how Trotskyist wreckers bend democracy'.[40] For the generations of young teacher trade union activists of the 1970s it was the various 'ultra–left' groups such as the IS/SWP or the International Marxist Group who were to form the pole of political attraction.

Communists, particularly those who held positions both as full time and lay officials in the trade union movement were patently a factor during the militancy of the early 1970s. However despite this high profile role, the political growth of the party measured by membership figures or sales of the *Morning Star* was meagre. Dramatic successes in recruiting striking workers such as the claim in the *Morning Star* of 50 building workers recruited in Birmingham in a few weeks of the 1972 were not the norm and were not sustained.[41] This particular success reflects the dynamic role of Pete Carter, a leading Birmingham building worker who played a crucial role in the 1972 strike. Overall the best that can be said for the period of industrial militancy of the early 1970s is that the relentless decline in party membership was halted, then briefly reversed, before resuming its inexorable downward trajectory. National membership stood at 30 607 in 1969, declining to 28 803 in 1971, recovering to 29 943 in 1973 but falling back to 28 519 by 1975.[42] Figures from Sheffield, one of the strongest districts of the CP during this period where party trade unionists had led a successful district wide campaign against redundancies at the Edgar Allen engineering factory, significant strikes against the Industrial Relations Act and called action in support of the Pentonville dockers, accentuate the problem. From 1970 to 1972 membership in the city fell from 744 to 700 as did sales of the *Morning Star* to a level when average daily sales of the paper only exceeded the registered membership by three! The decision taken at the 1971 party conference to abolish the task of annual re-registration, retaining on the membership records all those who had not resigned, died or been expelled from membership erodes the integrity of membership figures post 1971. One can only conclude those membership records after 1971 consistently over-represent any thing approaching 'real membership'. This declining level of commitment to the party can also be seen in the declining base of subscription payments, by 1972 only 62 per cent of Yorkshire members had paid their dues, (considerably higher than the national average of 51 per cent). It was also evident that only a small minority of party members read the party's more theoretical publications with sales of *Marxism Today* totalling 6 per cent and sales of *Comment* 10 per cent of the Yorkshire membership figures.⁴³ The bold rhetoric of the 1964 party congress, which had called for the building of a 'mass party', lay in tatters. In parallel with the political leaders of the country at the time, the leadership of British Communism was in the tricky business of managing decline.

Labour in office

Labour's narrow election victory in February 1974 in the aftermath of one of the most tumultuous periods of class conflict in modern British history was to pose problems for the radical left in Britain. For the Communist Party, Labour's election on one of the most left-wing manifestos in its history, provided evidence of the 'left advance' prescribed by *The British Road to Socialism*. On the eve of the election Dick Etheridge, the retired Communist convenor of the Austin Longbridge factory wrote to John Gollan from his sick bed that 'The trends are now flowing with us'.⁴⁴ Despite the by now customary derisory election results for party candidates, Communists and Broad Left sympathisers held important positions in many of Britain's large industrial unions. The number of left MPs who were prepared to appear in the *Morning Star* and add their weight to CP led initiatives was significant.⁴⁵ Always flattering to the party, numbers of right-wing journalists were busy writing scare stories about how the incoming Labour government would be influenced by the sinister Communists.[46] The noisy ultra-left groups, although troublesome, had on the whole made few significant inroads into the party's trade union base. On the international front there was initially plenty for Communists to cheer. The shock waves of the 1968 Czech crisis had died away, fascist regimes were swept from power in Spain and Portugal by mass movements in which communists played a prominent role, Vietnamese liberation from US aggression was secured and 'actually existing socialism' as typified by the USSR and the eastern block provided evidence of stability and steady progress. It might also be expected that the class combativity and militancy shown by British workers during the late 1960s and early 1970s would continue. Rather than provide a scenario for Communist growth, the period from 1974–79 was to witness the further fragmentation and decline of the party, bitterly divided into factions which was continue through the 1980s to the final dissolution of the party in 1991. During the early 1970s the high level of class struggle and the general radicalisation which was apparent tended to lead to a situation where the theoretical, generational and cultural differences within the party remained primarily beneath the surface. In the post-1974 period the Labour government faced a series of major crises and the simple anti-Tory rhetoric of the 1970–74 period no longer fitted the bill. For a radical socialist organisation to analyse and engage was to take a level of political and theoretical clarification which was to tear the party apart.

On the key industrial and trade union front, so vital for the continued relevance of the party, the question of how Communists should react as the crisis of British capitalism intensified had to be addressed. After 1974 a gap was to open up between the rhetorical opposition of the party leadership and sections of the party press to the inadequacies of Labour's economic programme and the every day practice of the prominent party trade union figures. The gap was most noticeable over the question of the Social Contract, the agreement drafted before the election in 1973 and agreed in 1974 between the Labour government and the TUC over wage restraint. The question of how the party should respond and mobilise over the Social Contract was to open up a sharp debate between traditionalists and the growing Eurocommunist wing of the party.[47] At the heart of the debate was a theoretical discussion as to the causes of inflation, and a developing critique by the Eurocommunists, drawing in particular on a reading of their key intellectual mentor Antonio Gramsci of the 'economism' of the party's traditionalist positions. However, as we shall, see the fault lines opened up by the Social Contract were not to merely lie between the new Gramscian intellectuals around *Marxism Today*, and the party's trade union base. Despite the formal opposition of the party's leadership and its industrial organiser Bert Ramelson to the Social Contract,[48] both the party's Broad Left allies, notably Hugh Scanlon of the AUEW and Jack Jones of the TGWU, and leading party trade unionists were instrumental in selling wage restraint to their members and in isolating militant groups of workers who took strike action which broke the terms of the Social Contract.

The ambiguity of Communists to the Social Contract lay not only in theoretical arguments over economism but in the developing dynamics of workplace industrial relations in the latter half of the 1970s. As we have seen above, during the 1960s a conscious strategy to incorporate trade union militancy, outlined by the 1968 Donovan Report had been followed by some employers with the active support of the Labour government It was only when the Labour government sought, through the proposed introduction of the legislation *In Place of Strife*, to curb the union power through law, that trade unions with the enthusiastic and active involvement of Communists mobilised workers in opposition. The Heath government of 1970–74 had continued and developed this confrontational approach, resulting in the big struggles of those years in which Communist trade unionists played such a significant role. The return of the Labour government in 1974 brought a more collaborative approach to industrial relations, and saw the continuation of a trend towards workers' participation, and the professionalisation of industrial relations whereby shop stewards spent less time on the shop floor and more time in detailed negotiations with management. As early as 1970 Alan Spence writing in *Marxism Today* had approvingly written of the change in shop floor-based industrial relations which was taking place, arguing that 'the traditional meeting ground for the determination of wages has moved from the shop floor to the finance department and therefore the shop stewards must move with it'.[49]

One of the key arenas in which the demands of the Social Contract for wage restraint met the phenomena of workers' participation, the incorporation of shop stewards and a significant leadership role of the Communist Party, was British Leyland, the state owned car company. The nationalisation of British Leyland in 1975 under the terms of the Ryder Plan which introduced participation was greeted by Communists as 'a basis for rebuilding the British-owned car industry'[50] a step forward in line with the process of gradual socialist advance outlined in *The British Road to Socialism*. The form of workers' participation outlined by Ryder was greeted as 'a small step in showing the ability of the working class to become the ruling class, the leading political force in the country'.[51] At the Longbridge factory, the largest in the British Leyland, the key union figure was the Communist Works Convenor Derek Robinson, dubbed 'Red Robbo' by the media. 'Red Robbo' was a keen advocate of participation as outlined in the Ryder plan, and his public statements occasionally displayed a frustration with the Longbridge rank and file's scepticism towards participation:

> We still haven't won the conception amongst the broad masses of people on the shop floor that they've got a vested interest in efficiency no less than we have. It is one of our problems ... if we are able to ... make Leyland successful as a publicly-owned company, then it is self evident that that will be a major political victory.[52]

Leading Communist activists such as Robinson, effectively saw their role as winning the loyalty of the rank and file for a restructuring plan which entailed job losses and speed ups on the production line. Inevitably this was to lead to a situation where the gap between workers and an increasingly bureaucratised layer of full time stewards and convenors grew. In February 1977, skilled toolroom workers at Leyland came out on strike against the terms of the Ryder Plan and the Social Contract. They were publicly denounced by their union leader. The Broad Left, Hugh Scanlon, and Robinson encouraged Leyland workers to cross their picket lines. The traditions of trade union solidarity, built up during the 1960s and early 1970s often under the leadership of Communist union militants were falling apart.

Leyland was not an isolated case. In 1978 shipyard workers at Swan Hunter yard on the Tyne voted down a set of new working practices tied to an order to build ships for a Polish buyer. The Govan shipyard on the Clyde, part of the old UCS, was offered the work. To accept the contract whilst fellow workers were in dispute would be seen as 'scabbing'. Jimmy Airlie the Communist convenor at Govan, who during the UCS work in had declared, 'Are the other shipyards going to accept our orders and let my men starve?' now asserted 'If Newcastle are losing six ships through disputes, we will build them. If we don't the Japs will.'[53] At Heathrow Airport in April 1977, Communist union officials were amongst those encouraging union members to cross the picket lines of 5000 striking maintenance engineers. The toolroom strikers at Leyland, the engineers at Heathrow and maintainance workers in the South Wales steel industry who struck against the terms of the Social Contract were all skilled workers. The criticism of the strikers from the Communist Party leadership centred on their alleged status as 'labour aristocrats', relatively privileged sections of workers who were acting in a sectional and economistic way in defending their status. The criticism of trade unionism as economism and centred on maintaining the privileges of male, white skilled workers was to become one of the key themes of the emerging Eurocommunist critique of militant trade unionists.

For Derek Robinson, the growing gap between himself and the rank and file was starkly displayed after the appointment of a more hardline manger at British Leyland. Michael Edwardes was less concerned with managing through participation and preferred a direct and confrontational approach. 12 500 redundancies were pushed through with only token resistance in January 1978. In November Robinson and the other stewards took a militant turn and attempted unsuccessfully to win a strike against the government's 5 per cent pay limit. Sensing the distance that had opened up between a demoralised membership and the Longbridge union leadership, Edwardes initiated a ballot on a survival plan over the heads of the shop stewards, which was easily won. Weeks later, Robinson was sacked. Although there was an initial and solid walkout in his defence, within a week the union leadership had ordered workers back and the most prominent shop floor Communist in Britain had been silenced.

The case of Longbridge casts a harsh light on the fortunes of the generation of Communist workplace militants who had been at the heart of the mass struggles of the late 1960s and early 1970s. Faced with a Labour government, and a declining level of confidence and militancy amongst the rank and file, Communists found that the forms of 'do it yourself' activism which had appeared to fit in the earlier era no longer worked. The crisis of militancy of the late 1970s was to feed directly into the debates about strategy that broke out in the party from the late 1970s, and contrary to some assumptions it was often Communist trade unionists who embraced the arguments being put forward by the reformist wing of the party.

Anti-racism and anti-fascism: missing the boat

As the political and economic crisis of the late 1960s and 70s developed, it not only encouraged a level of working-class militancy and an opening for the development of radical leftist ideas but also provided a forum where racist and fascist ideas and organisation could begin to gain a foothold. The Communist Party as we have seen had a long tradition of anti-fascists activity stretching back to the1930s and as such would have seemed well placed to put itself at the head of anti-racist and anti-fascist campaigning. Powell's 'Rivers of Blood' speech made in April 1968 had resulted in his dismissal from the Conservative shadow cabinet and protests in his support followed including a strike and demonstration by 1000 London dockers. The dockers' march to parliament in support of Powell came as a shock to the left as the London docks had long been thought of as a Communist Party stronghold. It exposed the extent to which Communist militants, although enjoying support on trade union issues, were often deeply politically isolated from their base in the rank and file. Faced with a wave of populist racism on the shopfloor the response of many party activists was to keep their heads down, hoping it would blow over. Jack Dash the veteran CP dockers leader was off sick at the time and Danny Lyons, one of the leading party militants on the London docks, tried and failed to stem support for Powell by inviting two clergymen, one Catholic and one Protestant to address dockers. The response of the *Morning Star* on the day after the dockers marched was to print a headline proclaiming '60 000 engineers vote against racism', reporting a vote taken at the AUEW NEC which had been critical of Powell. It is far easier to pass a resolution in a trade union meeting than to take on a sharp political argument at a dock gate. The job of carrying an anti-Powell case on the London docks was left to a single docker Terry Barrett, a member of the International Socialists who put out a leaflet arguing: 'Who is Enoch Powell? He is a right wing Tory opportunist who will stop at nothing to help his party and class ... '[54]

Although 'Powellism' as such did not establish itself as a stable political movement in the wake of 1968 the small and demoralised fragments of British fascism began to raise their heads and coalesce into the National Front. The National Front had some success in pulling behind it right-wing Conservatives and anti-immigrant populists who had been inspired by Powell. At the heart of the NF however was a group of experienced National Socialists who had spent the previous decade in the small group world of British Nazi politics. By the mid-1970s the NF was gaining significant votes and establishing heartlands in areas of the East End of London, the Midlands and the North West. In 1976 they won 119 000 votes in the Greater London council elections. The National Front did not merely operate as an electoral machine. Central to their tactics at the time was the holding of provocative marches through areas with large black and Asian populations. The Communist Party press naturally warned against the rise of the National Front and Communists were involved in many of the local Campaigns against Racism and Fascism which appeared in response to National Front activity. Within local campaigns the Communist Party argued hard against those, predominately from the far left who advocated physically preventing the Front from marching and argued instead for legal bans and the re-routing of marches.

The issue gained national prominence in August 1977 at a National Front march through Lewisham in South London which was broken up by demonstrators led by the Socialist Workers Party (SWP).[55] The dominant media reaction was to portray the anti-fascist demonstrators as as bad as the National Front and the SWP were roundly condemned as 'Red Fascists.' On the day of the Lewisham protests the Communist Party had participated in a demonstration called by the All Lewisham Campaign against Racism and Fascism well away from the NF's planned route which explicitly rejected confrontation with the fascists. One difficulty faced by the party was that the SWP explicitly drew on the experience of Cable Street, which had become one of the totemic moments in the party's history.[56] The *Morning Star* initially attacked the demonstrators but a few days later carried a long article which although attacking the tactics of the SWP praised 'the courage and determination of those who took part'.[57]

In the immediate aftermath of Lewisham, the Socialist Workers Party moved quickly to establish an anti-fascist organisation the Anti-Nazi League (ANL) which very quickly grew into a large campaigning movement. Along with Rock Against Racism,[58] an anti-racist music movement bringing together punk and reggae bands which also emerged from the SWP milieu, the ANL organised a number of highly successful Carnivals and protests which mobilised very large numbers of mainly young people in a popular, radical anti-racist movement which played a significant role in shaping popular attitudes towards racism and anti-racism in Britain in the late 1970s. The Communist Party largely missed the boat on mass anti-racist campaigning in the 1970s. Approached by the SWP at the time of the formation of the Anti-Nazi League, the Communist Party declined to get involved but soon found that due to some assiduous lobbying by the SWP of a number of Labour Left MPs, a real alliance of the Left was being formed by the despised 'Trots'. Eventually after the ANL's hugely successful first Carnival in April 1978 the Communist Party came on board accepting a place on the ANL's steering committee.

The attitude of many party activists in the 1970s faced with the rise of racism in society and the growth of groups like the National Front was that racism was a 'difficult issue' to deal with. Party members were of course opposed to racism, but often in the workplace the fear of alienating potential support meant that party members kept their heads down. This attitude fitted in with an analysis prevalent on the left well beyond the ranks of the party, that white British workers were a 'labour aristocracy' who historically had benefited from Britain's imperial past and in whom racist ideas were ingrained. This analysis, often shared and reinforced by black radicals, led many on the left and Communist activists in particular to miss out on significant cultural trends in British society which suggested that, particularly amongst younger people there existed a mass constituency for anti-racism. It was this potential and audience that movements such as the ANL and RAR tapped into in the late 1970s, mobilising a new generation of young radicals into political activity in a setting where the British Communist Party was notably absent.

Gramsci, Eurocommunism and *Marxism Today*

Despite their deep hostility towards the 'ultra lefts' who had been behind ANL and RAR, the notion of building mass popular movements which tapped into elements of mass culture such as popular music was to attract the group inside the Communist Party who were to shape its distinctive ideological trajectory in its final decade. The influence of the ideas of Antonio Gramsci, or more precisely a particular reading of Gramsci's thought, on the development of Eurocommunism during the 1970s and 1980s and in left orientated thought cannot be overestimated. Key Gramscian terms such as 'hegemony', 'civil society', 'subaltern', 'war of position', 'organic intellectual' etc. were the hallmarks of Eurocommunist discourse and have subsequently become the common currency of academic writing. Gramsci, a founder of the Italian Communist Party (PCI) in 1921, had already established a reputation as a revolutionary activist in the radical 'red years' of 1919 and 1920. Imprisoned by the Mussolini's fascist government, Gramsci was to die in 1937 leaving behind a collection of writings in note-form, later published as *The Prison Notebooks*. One of the features of *The Prison Notebooks* is the extremely elliptical language that Gramsci used to put forward his revolutionary Marxist arguments in order to evade the attention of the fascist censors. This leaves Gramsci's writings particularly open to a wide range of interpretations.

The dominant interpretation of Gramsci developed by Eurocommunists was that the Leninist model of revolution, exemplified by the October 1917 insurrection, was not applicable within modern western capitalism. Modern capitalism, propped up by the institutions of civil society through which it maintained ideological hegemony could not be dislodged through an insurrectionary 'war of manoeuvre'. Rather what was required was a long drawn out 'war of position' which would be fought primarily on the cultural and ideological front to challenge the ideological hold of the bourgeoisie. Despite the fact that the European Communist Parties had long abandoned any notion of attempting to replicate the experience of 1917 in their respective countries and had evolved a method of work based on the Popular Front, Gramsci's writings were mobilised by Eurocommunists to criticise elements of traditional Communist thinking and to theoretically underpin a project designed to take Communist Parties away from the perceived political dead end of Stalinism. Reactions to the Russian invasion of Czechoslovakia in 1968 provided the spur to a far more critical position towards the USSR by some of the European parties notably the Italian PCI. For a generation of younger party intellectuals in Britain, many of whom had learned their politics in the more liberal atmosphere of student politics or the Young Communist League (YCL) of the 1960s[60] developments in the more liberal Italian and Spanish parties were to form the inspiration for a fight to transform the British party. *Marxism Today*, set up after 1956 to defend party orthodoxy was to become in the 1970s the forum for debate and argument and by the 1980s the house journal of the remaining Eurocommunist wing of the party and for a significant raft of left opinion well beyond its ranks.[61]

Throughout 1970 there was a running debate in the pages of *Marxism Today* on the issue of Czechoslovakia and the issues raised by the invasion. Although the party had come out against intervention, bigger questions were raised as to the nature of the Soviet Union and on the vexed question of socialism and democracy. Monty Johnstone, compared the defensive and sterile reaction of the East German party the SED at their October 1968 Central Committee to the Czech events to the vision put forward by the PCI at their 12th Congress in 1969 in which they called for 'a pluralistic society which is not centralised, not controlled by a bureaucracy and not identified with the power of a single party'.[62] The publication in 1971 by Lawrence and Wishart, the publisher mostly closely associated with the party, of an English translation of *The Prison Notebooks*[63] was to bring a decidedly Gramscian intervention into the debate on socialist strategies. In late 1971 Martin Jacques, then a relatively obscure young intellectual who was to become *Marxism Today* editor in 1977 and who provides the exemplar of the growth of Eurocommunism within the party, tentatively mapped out a distinct role for intellectuals and wider cultural forces in the struggle for socialism. At this early stage Jacques, reflecting the period of high class struggle, saw intellectuals and wider cultural forces beginning 'to identify with the traditional labour movement and to adopt 'anti-capitalist' positions on a whole spectrum of issues'.[64]

Despite the outward appearance of working-class militancy and combativity, others on what would develop as the Eurocommunist wing of the party were beginning to question whether the working class was on a forward march at all. As early as 1974,[65] Eric Hobsbawm, the most prestigious 'public intellectual' in the party's ranks, was outlining a theme he was to articulate fully in 1978 in his Marx memorial lecture *The Forward March of Labour Halted?*[66] The publication of the text of Hobsbawm's lecture in *Marxism Today* was to spark a running controversy inside the party, with trade union heavyweights such as Ken Gill and Kevin Halpin responding, and supporters of the *Marxism Today* analysis developing the argument.[67]

Hobsbawm's key argument was that the British working-class movement was in the throes of a serious political decline which he dated back to 1951, the year when the postwar Labour government was defeated and thirteen years of Tory misrule were ushered in. The militancy displayed by workers in the 1960s and 70s should not, Hobsbawm argued, be confused for class consciousness in any political sense rather it displayed a narrow economism and sectionalism:

> At the same time the trade union movement became more militant. And yet this was, with the exception of the great struggles of 1970–74, an almost entirely economist militancy and a movement is not necessarily less economistic and narrow minded because it is militant, or even led by the left ... And, as I have tried to suggest earlier, straightforward, economistic trade union consciousness may at times actually set workers against each other rather than establish wider patterns of solidarity.[68]

If the left, and the party in particular, was to remain wedded to narrow economism it would not be able to effectively combat the growing confidence and assertiveness of the right, displayed most graphically in the election of Margaret Thatcher in May 1979. An analysis of Thatcherism was to mark the second distinctive strand of the analysis of the tasks for the British left developed by *Marxism Today*. Stuart Hall articulated the analysis in his *Marxism Today* article 'The Great Moving Right Show'.[69] For Hall and *Marxism Today* Thatcherism represented a 'new political formation', a new and powerful form of popular authoritarianism. *Marxism Today's* editor Martin Jacques was to join with Hall to develop the analysis,

> Thatcherite populism is a particularly rich mix, it combines the resonant themes of organic Toryism – nation, family, duty, authority, standards, traditionalism – with the aggressive themes of a revived neo-liberalism – self-interest, competitive individualism anti-statism.[70]

To simply suggest, as many traditionalists inside the party did, that Thatcher represented a rehash of old fashioned Toryism, of the sort that Heath had represented which could be defeated by traditional methods of class struggle as in 1970–74, was according to the Eurocommunists to underestimate the problem.

What was needed argued the Eurocommunists was a more thoroughgoing counter-hegemonic strategy, a Broad Democratic Alliance of all progressive forces. In its most developed form, particularly in the wake of Labour's disastrous 1983 defeat, the notion of the Broad Democratic Alliance was to embrace 'progressive' Tories and tactical voting for the Liberal Democrats However it's more mainstream formulation suggested an engagement with a whole range of progressive social movements, particularly over issues such as women's' oppression, gay rights, racism and a broader cultural agenda. The notion of a Broad Democratic Alliance had been won by the Eurocommunists for insertion into the re-drafted *British Road to Socialism* endorsed by the party's 1977 Congress. The victory of the Gramscians in 1977 was helped by the defection prior to the Congress of a significant block of the old guard to the newly formed New Communist Party. The breakaway group was led by Sid French, who along with the now deceased Palme Dutt had led the opposition over the Czechoslovak events. However to many party members traditionalists as well as Eurocommunists, there remained a strong element of continuity between the previous formulation of an anti monopoly 'broad popular alliance' and the new notion of the Broad Democratic Alliance. Indeed both formulations can be seen as following on from the Popular Front traditions established in the party in the mid 1930s, which had formed a thread running through the war time period and onwards to the original drafting of *The British Road to Socialism*.

The rise and fall of Bennism

The significance of the analysis developed by *Marxism Today* in the late 1970s and through into the 1980s is less in its direct influence inside the party, although as we have already seen in the crisis of the Social Contract many from what we might expect to see as the traditionalist trade union wing of the party were to incorporate much of the 'common sense' of the *Marxism Today* analysis into their practice. What is of particular significance is the way in which in the second half of the 1980s, at a time when the party itself was in rapid and terminal decline, much of the *Marxism Today* tradition was incorporated into a political project which was to result in the rapid right-ward trajectory of many on the Labour left. In the mid 1980s this move was labelled 'New Realism' and 'Kinnockism' by the mid 1990s the terms 'New Labour' and 'Blairism' had entered the political vocabulary.

The left of the Labour Party had been well represented in the government of 1974–79. Figures such as Tony Benn, Michael Foot and Eric Heffer, all with well-established reputations on the left, served in the government. However the Callaghan years were seen in the eyes of the Labour left as a time of defeat and betrayal. The election defeat of 1979 served to convince a significant section of the left in the Labour Party of a precisely contrary conclusion to that being drawn by *Marxism Today*. Labour had lost in 1979 because in office they had bowed to the pressures of capitalism, most graphically displayed by the intervention of the IMF in the crisis of 1976, and had turned on their working class support. The strikes of low-paid workers during the Winter of Discontent were seen as the precursor to a widespread disillusion with their party by large sections of Labour's natural electorate. The lesson for the left was to steer Labour leftwards towards a more uncompromising set of socialist policies, outlined in an Alternative Economic Strategy designed to withstand the pressures of international capital and retain support amongst Labour's core working class electorate. For Communists the leftward trajectory in the Labour Party in the early 1980s marked out by the rise of Tony Benn and by the left's strong position in local government, would appear to mark a vindication of the strategy marked out in the BRS. But the very success of the Labour left was to cause a fundamental problem for the party. If as suggested in the 1977 draft of the BRS, Communists were seeking to build a broad alliance, and the Labour Party was seemingly transforming itself into a party of the left, what role was there for an independent Communist Party? The fundamental question of 'why are we here?' was harder to answer credibly as membership shrunk, the party's trade union base withered and the party's claim to represent the broader movement outside of parliament became less and less credible. In the early 1980s a vibrant left alternative based around the Labour left posed a clear alternative, many younger activists from the student movement, the womens' movement, including Communists and members of far left groups were joining Labour.

For the group around *Marxism Today* however there did remain a distinctive and decisive role. Communists had always criticised the Labour Party as being weak on theory, the role of the party as Labour shifted leftwards was as Eric Hobsbawm argued to act as a 'political educator'.[71] There was nothing specifically new or Eurocommunist about this proposition, the notion of the party as a powerhouse of ideas for the movement was well established in party culture. What is distinctive about the period of the 1980s is that the group of party members around *Marxism Today* was to exert an influence that was fundamentally rightwards on the existing Labour left. In the immediate aftermath of the 1979 election and during the period of Tony Benn's dramatic 1981 bid for the Labour's deputy leadership, when the left appeared to sweep all before them, the influence of *Marxism Today* remained marginal. However by 1983, especially after Labour's second electoral defeat, the highpoint of the hard left in Labour had passed. Influential members of the Labour left, particularly those associated with the Labour Co-ordinating Committee (LCC), originally established to organise Benn's campaign in 1981, began to distance themselves from hard left positions in the party and sought to create a 'soft left'. Once again Hobsbawm's intervention was crucial, his article 'Labour's Lost Millions'[72] provided the basis on which New Realist ideas took shape on the left of the Labour Party. Two leading luminaries of the Labour left Robin Cook and Harriet Harman shared a platform, jointly organised by *Marxism Today* and the LCC with Eric Hobsbawm and Beatrix Campbell in February 1984 to discuss the article. The Labour left's shift from the hard left positions of 1980/81 to the new realist positions of the mid-1980s, and the transition of numbers of former Bennites into loyal members of the New Labour project in the 1990s was not dependent on the analysis developed in *Marxism Today*. However without doubt, the influence of *Marxism*

Today and the credibility and weight of many of its contributors during this period had a crucial impact. As Alex Callinicos argued in an article written in 1985 as this process was unfolding:

> Of course Labour right wingers don't need to read *Marxism Today* for justifications of their politics. The same is not true, however for a generation of Labour left wingers, some of whom began their politics as revolutionaries, many of whom have moved quite considerably to the right in recent years. Marxist intellectuals such as Hobsbawm and Hall, enjoying as they do considerable and deserved academic reputations, and possessing formidable talents as populisers and polemicists, can exercise a genuine influence by providing impeccable theoretical and historical reasons for abandoning 'fundamentalist' positions. Healey may not need Hobsbawm, but Kinnock does, in order to cover his left flank.[73]

As the membership of the party continued to dwindle alarmingly, beset with terminal and bloody faction fight, unable to either maintain itself as an organisation or initiate any sustained campaigning activity, the influence of *Marxism Today* stands out.

Death throes

The success of *Marxism Today* stands in marked contrast in the 1980s with the terminal decline of its parent body. At the start of the 1980s the party could still claim a significant implantation in the trade unions. For example minutes of the Further Education Advisory Committee claims 12 Communists as members of the NATFHE national executive in 1981/82.[74] However party trade unionists by this time rarely acted as a cohesive block and Communist trade unionists were often reticent in advertising their affiliations as a revealing 1980 memo from the industrial department to delegates to the conference of the AEU shows: 'Please remember that it is already policy of our union to support the *Morning Star* ... so no mention is necessary'.[75] Despite the occasional flurry of activity, for example the 1981 Peoples March for Jobs, Communists were not able to initiate any significant protest activity. Communists were active in building support for CND, which re-emerged as a mass protest movement in the early 1980s. But despite the prominent position of party members in the leadership of the movement and activism from party rank and filers, the party was not able to recruit and to build the organisation as they had in the 1960s.

When it came to the Anti-Poll Tax campaign at the end of the decade, despite some attempts to stir itself, the party's presence on the campaign was dwarfed by the input of the far left Militant Tendency and Socialist Workers Party. The 1980s were a period of unmitigated decline for the party membership halved between 1979 and 1987 and then halved again by the final congress in 1991. The very success of *Marxism Today* was paradoxically a factor in the decline. Since the development of a self consciously revisionist *Marxism Today* in the late 1970s, the centrist group which made up the party leadership, led from 1975 by Gordon McLennan, the General Secretary who would oversee the last period of decline, had played a delicate balancing act between them and the traditionalist wing of the party, grouped around the *Morning Star*. By 1983 the leadership of the party had moved significantly and decisively into the camp of the reformers and relationships between them and the traditionalists who maintained influence on the *Morning Star* was near to breaking point. The developing split was widened by the 'independent' position of the *Morning Star*, run as it was by a management committee, overseen by the shareholders of the Peoples Press Printing Society (PPPS). Within the PPPS, the traditionalists led by the editor Tony Chater held sway and the factional battle raged throughout 1983 and 1984. In January 1985, the party's Executive Committee expelled Tony Chater and a large group of *Morning Star* supporters, further expulsions and resignations were to follow including the expulsion of Ken Gill, the party's only member of the TUC General Council.[76]

The *Morning Star* split coincided with one of the most significant set-piece confrontations between organised trade unionism and the British state in modern history, the miners' strike of 1984–85. The strike, and its eventual defeat were to accelerate the push towards the modernisers' agenda within the party. Although many Communists from both wings of the party were pulled into the organisation of solidarity which mushroomed from the late summer of 1984, attitudes to the strike and to the tactics of NUM president Arthur Scargill, were to lead to further bitter divisions. The strike also exposed the weakness of the party on the ground. Although the party retained some positions in the NUM structure, notably in South Wales, Kent and Scotland, in the wider miners support networks which sprung up around the country, the key activists were as more likely to be members of 'far left' groups, non-aligned activists or members of the Labour Party. The strike support movement spawned some interesting examples of the type of community-based organisation that fitted in with the modernisers' agenda, such as the vigorous Lesbian and Gay Miners Support Group, but party members were thin on the ground. The criticisms of 'Scargillism', which had been relatively muted and coded during the dispute, came out into the open in 1985 as the party, by now rid of the Chater group carried out a post mortem. The lessons drawn from the defeat of the miners appeared to reinforced all of the key assumptions of Eurocommunism; the economism and narrowness of the trade unions epitomised by Scargill, the authoritarianism of the state shown in the hostile press coverage and the harsh policing tactics and hence the need for 'broad democratic alliances' rather than class politics. The natural demoralisation of left wingers and trade union activists at the defeat of the miners was given theoretical and political expression by the analysis coming from the party. However putting forward an analysis which confirms a generally pessimistic and demobilising leftist 'common sense' did nothing to halt the precipitous slide in the party's fortunes.

The defeat of the miners' strike appeared to strike a blow at one of the key underpinning values of British communism, that of class struggle. The crisis of the Soviet system, marked by the dramatic collapse of the East European states and followed by the disintegration of the USSR was to remove another. Although Eurocommunists had been marked by their willingness to take critical attitudes to the Soviet Union and other socialist states, all Communists had an ideological stake in the viability of 'actually existing socialism' however incomplete and flawed the model on offer was. The fall of 1989/90 and the political collapse it brought about was preceded by the false dawn provided by Mikhail Gorbachev's reform Communism. For a short few years it appeared as if 'socialism with a human face', snuffed out in Prague in 1968, was back on the agenda, this time in Moscow. Gorbachev's popular image in the media, and the slogans of perestroika and glasnost chimed with the modernising instincts of the party reformers. Just as Gorbachev was taking on conservative vested interests and sweeping them away, so party modernisers saw themselves as sweeping out the deadwood of former party practice. The notion that it was popular to be a Communist briefly fluttered before the eyes of the reformers. Amongst party lecturers in the Further Education Advisory Committee, where the old guard had been swept aside in a bloodless coup in 1985, minutes of their meetings in the mid to late 1980s abound with discussion on the need to take a 'political turn' and to 'talk politics to our colleagues'.[77] The fiftieth anniversaries of the Spanish Civil War and the Popular Front, coinciding as they did with the Gorbachev years, provided a reminder of better times, with the hope of a possible reprise.

By the late 1980s a more assertive 'post-Marxism' was being aired in the party press. In March 1988 *Seven Days* initiated an iconoclastic and anonymous (mysteriously 'written by a group of Communists in Brighton') column 'socialism 2000' (NB the stylish lower case presentation) questioning 'whether Marxism is a sufficient or necessary basis for progressive politics today'.[78] Critical even of the Eurocommunist formulations in the 1978 version of the BRS, the line of argument being developed evolved into the final draft programme, *Manifesto for New Times*, which was narrowly endorsed by the 1989 party congress. *New Times* drew heavily on the then fashionable notions of postmodernism, particularly the idea that modern economies had moved beyond Fordism, a system of large scale industrial production which brought with it large workplaces and the possibilities of a large and unified labour movement, to Post-Fordism, an economic order typified by small, flexible units of capital which made traditional forms of class based politics impossible. What was therefore needed was a far looser set of coalitions around interests bringing together disparate social movements. The implications of *New Times* suggested the complete abandonment of a party structure, yet paradoxically the manifesto argued for the retention of a distinctive party and a continued independent electoral intervention. Remaining party loyalists could be reassured that the reformers' project was not a complete wind up of the party. The collapse of the East European states was to provide the final impetus towards dissolution.

The initial symptoms of collapse in the Warsaw Pact were covered by the party press in a generally positive fashion. Earlier in 1989, *Seven Days* had commented favourably on the Tiananmen Square movement in China and deplored its bloody repression. This however caused relatively few theoretical problems, since the Chinese Communist Party despite its enthusiasm for Capitalist economic reforms remained, in the eyes of reformist Communists, unreconstructed Stalinists. During the summer and autumn of 1989 the pace of change in eastern Europe was breathtaking, no longer facing the threat of military intervention from the Soviet State, the rulers of both Poland and Hungary conducted round table talks with the opposition, lead to the spectacular victory of Solidarnosc in elections in June and the effective ceding of power by the Polish Communists. In the summer of 1989 Hungary opened its borders with the west leading to an exodus of mainly young East Germans in their battered Trabant cars to the West. When

Gorbachev visited East Germany to mark the fortieth anniversary celebrations of the GDR in October, his rapturous reception and his clear indication that he would not sanction the use of repression against demonstrations led in November to the opening of the Brandenburg gate and the collapse of the Berlin Wall, symbol of the divide between the socialist east and the capitalist west. The sense of collapse was further enhanced by the graphic Christmas Day TV coverage from Romania of the execution by firing squad of the Ceausescus.

In the bleak, midwinter early months of 1990 the remaining ideological underpinning of British Communists came unstuck. Paradoxically for traditional pro-soviet Communists, many now ensconced in the breakaway CPB, the blow was far less shattering. Trained in the tough old school of the Communist movement to disregard the lies and distortions of the bourgeois press, distrustful of Gorbachev and his reform programme at the best of times, for them what was being seen in the Soviet Union was counter-revolution plain and simple. The overthrow of the socialist states might represent a historic defeat for socialism and the working-class movement but it did not entail a negation of traditional and firmly held values and beliefs. For the *Marxism Today* aligned reformists the collapse was primarily ideological. Eric Hobsbawm interviewed in the *Independent on Sunday* when challenged that 'In the Soviet Union it looks as though the workers are overthrowing the workers state' responded, 'It obviously wasn't a workers state, nobody in the Soviet Union believed it was a workers' state, and the workers knew it wasn't a workers state.'[79] A few weeks later it was the turn of Chris Myant, the editor of *Seven Days* to exorcise not just the authoritarian trajectory of the 'workers' states' as they developed but the 1917 revolution itself. Myant's attack on the legacy of 1917, the founding moment not just of the Soviet State but of a distinctive Communist politics fundamentally undermined the entire Communist tradition.

> The time has come when it is now possible for Communists to face a very difficult truth. October 1917, the world event which separates Communists from others on the left, was a mistake of truly historic proportions.
>
> Its consequences have been severe. They have characterised and moulded the great traumas of the twentieth century: a second world war, Hitler's gas chambers; Stalin's gulag; the world of the show trials; the perpetuation of third world fascist dictatorships; the unprecedented, almost unbelievable waste of the arms race in a world of poverty and starvation; the destruction of the Vietnam war ... [80]

Myant's list of the consequences of 1917 fly in the face of even the most benign left-wing interpretation of the twentieth century. The argument, in particular that Hitler's gas chambers were a consequence of 1917, unwittingly echoes the revisionist analysis of the Holocaust which was put forward by the most extreme of conservative German historians in the 1980s.[81] The crimes of the twentieth century which Myant lists, with the exception of Stalin's gulag, are precisely those against which hundreds of thousands of Communist militants worldwide had struggled throughout the century. With the party leadership so intellectually adrift and so fundamentally questioning the entire history and tradition of the movement to which they had dedicated their lives, the continued existence of the party only rested on habit, organisational inertia and the vexed question as to who would inherit the considerable assets.

Dissolution and aftermath

The final ending of the party came at its 43rd Congress in November 1991. Although many of the Eurocommunist reformers who had coalesced around *Marxism Today* in the 1980s had already left the party, the decision to wind up the party and to set up its successor organisation Democratic Left was passed by a clear majority of 2 to 1. As with the preceding two or three party congresses the formulations being put forward by the reformers, by now led by the last General Secretary Nina Temple, were vague enough and made sufficient reference to the traditions of the party to keep the dwindling band of by now shell-shocked members on board. The defeat of the traditionalists was sealed by the fact that many of them who had supported the *Morning Star* in the bitter battles of the preceding years had themselves already left to form the Communist Party of Britain (CPB) which today remains as the bearer of the mainstream CPGB positions as articulated in *The British Road to Socialism*.

At the time of the break of the party in 1991 and later in the 1990s two 'scandals' concerning the party's history received significant press coverage and comment. The first revolved around the issue of Moscow Gold, the second around the question of British Communists spying for the Soviet and other Eastern European States.

The receipt of funds from Moscow by the CPGB, widely assumed to be the case by many on the left in Britain, has been confirmed by recent studies of the now accessible Comintern archives in Moscow, and admitted by some of the key party activists involved. From the outset the party received large sums of money, in 1921 the Comintern's budget commission allocated £24 000 (£500 000 in present day values) to the party.[82] It is possible that the level of funding dried up considerably in the 1930s, although throughout its existence the party has been able to sustain a high level of permanent paid staff and apparatus on a relatively small membership and subscriptions base. The 1991 revelations admitted that direct funding of the party re-started in the 1950s after the Hungary events, and carried on until 1979. Documentation on the (highly Stalinist) CPUSA suggests that funding of the American party continued well into the 1980s, with over $20 million transferred to the party during the decade.[83] The British party owned considerable material assets, including the King Street headquarters in fashionable Covent Garden, whose sale helped contribute to the assets of the party on dissolution, estimated as between £2.5 and 4 million.[84] Indirect funding through a standing daily purchase of up to 12 000 copies of the *Morning Star* continued until 1990.[85]

The fact of a level of 'Moscow Gold' is clear; what is less clear is the impact and effect that the funding had on the party. The ability of the party to build up significant assets and properties, which in turn enabled it to sustain a level of organisation where it punched well above its weight, was to some degree based historically on Soviet funding. A well-funded central apparatus could also lead to an internal financial regime whereby a relatively large proportion of members' subscriptions remained in the local districts and could be used to fund full-time district secretaries. There is no evidence of individual Communist leaders living the 'good life' on Moscow Gold. The one 'perk' open to senior party figures were trips to the 'socialist motherland', when briefly they could be transformed from the workaday organisers of a marginal party in Britain, to feel the equals of major statesmen. As Harry Pollitt was to write on the occasion of a visit to Eastern Europe in 1948 'President Gottwald invited me to his palace to dine, Prime Minister Dimitrov invited me to his palace to dine, so somebody thinks the Old Man is not so dusty.'[86] Pollitt also received medical treatment on three separate occasions behind the Iron Curtain.[87] The issue of the allocation of trips abroad amongst the second tier of the party's leadership was to lead to difficult discussions as to whether husbands and wives could accompany partners unless 'they have a claim in their own right as political workers'.[88] Francis Beckett suggests that in the wake of the party's critical stance on Czechoslovakia, the Soviet print order for the *Morning Star* was cut by 3000 copies as a shot across the bows.[89] However as has been argued throughout, loyalty to a vision of socialism in the Soviet Union was primarily a political and ideological cement which held the party together. Money, although undoubtedly useful to the continued functioning of the party and crucial to establishing the party in its early years, was not the key factor.

The extent to which a sense of political loyalty to the Soviet State could spill over into active spying for the USSR has loomed large in popular conceptions of the British Communist Party. A number of particular cases have been brought to prominence. Kim Philby, the former party member was at the centre of the most notorious postwar spy case. Philby had joined the party as a student at Cambridge in the 1930s, and was to go on to become a fully fledged Soviet spy. Although his party membership may well have provided an entry into working for the soviet regime, Philby was not to maintain his party membership and indeed, continued open membership of the party would have severely dented his credibility as a spy. The revelation in 1999 that Melita Norwood, a long time rank and file party member, had acted as a KGB agent passing on documents that she came across in her work in the Non Ferrous Metals Research Association re-opened the issue in the public mind. However claims that Norwood was the 'most important female agent recruited by the KGB' must be treated with scepticism, as should suggestions that the party itself was involved in spying, although undoubtedly numbers of individuals connected with the party have over the years been involved in some level of intelligence work.

As in any divorce control of the assets remained a divisive issue and it remains a matter of supreme irony that Democratic Left, made up of people who claimed to be horrified by the revelations of 'Moscow Gold', retained the key assets of the party much of which had over the years been bought and paid for with the help of Russian funds. *Marxism Today*, which had played such a significant role in the intellectual unravelling of the party, ceased publication in December 1991, unable to survive without the estimated £50 000 a year subsidy it received from the party.[90] Later in 1998 a special one-off edition of *Marxism Today* was published to analyse the Blair phenomenon. Martin Jacques, who as editor of *Marxism Today* had been the bête noir of the party traditionalists, moved onto to pastures new, establishing the think tank Demos with fellow *Marxism Today* contributor Geoff Mulgan, and following a successful career as a journalist, becoming deputy editor of the *Independent*. Demos has played a role in providing a radical gloss to some of the modernising elements of the Blair project. Charlie Leadbeater, a former Eurocommunist and Demos associate, worked closely with Peter Mandelson during his brief tenure at the Department of Trade and Industry.[91] Democratic Left itself, now named New Times, no longer functions as a political party in any sense of the word, seeing itself rather as a loose organisation organising occasional conferences with other groups, such as Sign of Times. *Seven Days* the weekly paper of the Eurocommunist wing of the party after the coup on the *Morning Star*, changed its name to *New Times* and continued publication throughout much of the 1990s. Significantly when Stuart Hall was to raise some trenchant criticism of the record of the Blair government in the 1998 'one off' of *Marxism Today*,[92] it was an article in *New Times* which leapt to the defence of New Labour.[93]

The various orthodox factions emerging from the party have not been able to do much more than simply survive as declining sects with ageing memberships. The CPB remains as the closest to the atmosphere and style of the post-Second World War party, retaining a basic adherence *to the British Road to Socialism*. The CPB retains the *Morning Star* and the remaining credibility which it brings from an ageing generation of trade union activists. The age profile of the CPB does mean that the party retains some influence in the pensioners' movement. The annual rallies of the Chesterfield Pensioners Action Group, attended by one of the authors, retains the atmosphere of old style Popular Front meetings from the party's earlier days. However with an ageing and stagnant membership the passage of time will inevitably result in the party's further decline. Old habits die hard; in September 2000 the *Morning Star* greeted the overthrow of the Milsosevic regime in Serbia with the headline 'Arson rules in Belgrade'.[94] The CPB also find it difficult to adjust to the experience of being a very small fish in the 'left of Labour' pond. In the May 2000 elections to the Greater London Assembly the party refused to co-operate with other left wing groups in the London Socialist Alliance (LSA) and ran its own candidates receiving a derisory vote, whilst the LSA chalked up some creditable results. Bitter internal power struggles on and around the *Morning Star* were to continue with a destructive faction fight in 1998 resulting in production of the paper being halted by a strike of its own journalistic staff. Earlier breakaways from the party, including the Communist Party of Britain (Marxist Leninist) and the New Communist Party have withered into wholly irrelevant additions to the panoply of British left-wing sects. The one organisation today which trades under the title of the Communist Party of Great Britain, 'Our goal is to re-forge the CPGB as a weapon in the struggle for human liberation'[95] should not be mistaken for the real thing. Originally emerging from a small faction within the party linked to a Turkish Communist group, its journal

Weekly Worker operates as a clearing house for a eclectic range of left-wing groups and is an energetic enthusiast for the regrouping of the British left around the Socialist Alliance. The collapse of the Communist Party of Great Britain was not unique. Larger European Communist parties have also gone into decline. *Unita*, the newspaper of the Italian Communist Party founded by Gramsci in 1924, was finally shut down in the summer of 2000. Many of the European Communist parties have split into social democratic elements and harder-line groupings. In Italy, Rifoundazione Communista, one of the fragments of the break up of the old PCI has established itself as an activist party of radical protest, playing a key role in the anti-capitalist mobilisations in Genoa in May 2001 and the movement against the US bombing of Afghanistan in late 2001. In France the one-mighty PCF is now electorally challenged by the Trotskyists of Lutte Ouvrière and the Ligue Communiste Revolutionnaire. In Britain the organised political space to the left of New Labour has been occupied by organisations who draw their politics to a greater or lesser extent from the Trotskyist tradition derided by the CP in its pomp as either 'Trotsky fascist' or 'ultra left'. The continued move to the right of New Labour opens up intriguing prospects for a re-alignment of left-wing politics in Britain. The recent modest electoral successes of the Scottish Socialist Party, itself an offshoot of the former Militant Tendency, and the Socialist Alliance, a coalition of independent socialists, the Socialist Workers Party, the Socialist Party and other left groups, suggests that in any such re-alignment the fragments of the former Communist Party of Great Britain will play little if any direct role.

7
Conclusion

The collapse of the Communist Party over the winter of 1990–91 provoked widespread press comment. The most common view expressed by journalists at the time was simply that such an end was inevitable. Any one of a number of long-term factors were cited. These explanations included the claim that the moderate character of British history doomed British Communists to isolation; the argument that revolutions are impossible in a prosperous society; the idea that Moscow subsidies demoralised a party which had never sunk deep roots; the belief that 1989 marked the final end for the socialist project in all its forms. Within the Communist Party itself, *Marxism Today* increasingly argued that people were living in 'New Times'. The idea was that the certainties of the Fordist economy had been swept aside by different methods of working in a new global age, and that Marxism was irrelevant to the world of the 1980s and beyond. The fragmentation of the party and of a Marxist 'grand narrative' fitted the vogue for postmodernism and 'end of history' arguments which prevailed then in academic and journalistic circles.

For the authors of this book, the explanations for the demise of British Communism must be found elsewhere. In particular we believe that forecasts of the end of radical opposition to capitalism are misconceived. Instead, the end of the twentieth century has witnessed the re-birth of radical political activism on a worldwide scale. The 'Battle of Seattle' in November 1999 has inspired a new generation of activists whose protests, although often originating in specific issues, target the global system of capitalism. The hold of neo-liberal ideas within the British Labour Party and other traditional social democratic parties has left behind a bitter and disengaged constituency of the left with no political home. In the wake of the collapse of the Communist parties in most countries there is evidence of realignment and the emergence of a new left. Ralph Nader's 2000 presidential campaign in the USA and spread of anti-capitalist ideas are evidence of this change. The emergence of the Socialist Alliances in England and Wales and Scottish Socialist Party, raising a left electoral challenge to Labour on a scale not seen since the Communist Party in the early 1950s also points to the rebirth of resistance.[1] We would argue that the project of building effective socialist organisation in Britain is as valid today as it was eighty years ago. Whilst opportunities for the Communist Party of Great Britain to lead a 1917-type revolution were scarce during the twentieth century, the party's sharp decline was far from inevitable. Rather than looking for any simple, sociological explanation that can be traced back to the party's foundation in the 1920s, we have explained the decline of British Communism in terms of the actual historical practice of the Communist Party.

A number of points which have already been made at different points in this book are worth re-emphasising. The first is that the fortunes of the Communist Party were decisively tied to the fate of the Russian revolution. Although the party sometimes gained prestige from its relationship with Soviet Russia, particularly during the 'Patriotic War', Soviet influence was increasingly negative. As the reality of Stalin's Russia became more and more obvious, defence of Stalinism became a debilitating shibboleth which may have sustained the party faithful but which also cut the party off from large groups of workers and potential left-wing sympathisers. Labour Party activist John O'Farrell describes a Communist meeting which he attended in Exeter in the 1980s. All went well until the man hosting the session began his weekly oration to Comrade Stalin, 'Nobody argued or contradicted him, or pointed out that he was trying to defend one of the greatest mass murderers in history, they just let him finish and then carried on with what they were saying.[2] Shocked by the Stalinism he encountered, and by the apathetic response to it, O'Farrell never attended another Communist meeting. Many activists of his generation could tell a similar story. The legacy of a Stalinised Marxism also meant that the party could never develop a dynamic understanding of Marxist theory to apply as a guide to their political practice in Britain. The Gramscian turn of the 1970s was the nearest the party was to come to a re-appraisal of Stalinised Marxism, but the reading of Gramsci taken by the party was to merely re-enforce the already established Popular Frontism of the party.

Popular Front politics, adopted in 1935–36 and never seriously challenged thereafter, are a second and connected factor leading to the debacle of 1990–91. *The British Road to Socialism*, the Broad Democratic Alliance, Eurocommunism, even New Times, were all continuations of this theme. In each case the argument was put forward that some process of working-class moderation would open up the space for a radical left government. The problem for the Communist Party was that in arguing for diminished expectations, it was attempting to occupy a political space which was already successfully inhabited by the Labour Party. Having chosen not to be a revolutionary party, the CPGB had little success when it attempted reformism. Determined not to become a mere 'ginger group' to the left of Labour, the leaders of the party found themselves in precisely that situation that they were most keen to avoid. The strategies undertaken to surmount isolation were all unsuccessful. Despite sporadic, local successes, the electoral strategy failed to take off. There were no Communist MPs after 1950. In stressing the priorities of the Popular Front the party was often to act as a moderating and conservative influence on groups of left activists within the Labour Party the unions and the broader movements over which the party retained a significant degree of influence.

Despite being shackled with the legacy of Stalinism and Popular Frontism, there were more positive aspects of the party's role. Communist activists were not dilettantes. Despite its weakness the party did at times rise to the occasion. For example in the mid-1930s while the 'Third Period' was forgotten and before the Popular Front orientation fully took shape, party activists did feel their way towards an approximation of the tactic of the United Front, especially in leading a number of key industrial struggles. Communists also played a vital role in the struggles against fascism and mass unemployment in the 1930s. Despite the surge of social patriotism during the war and the tendency to duck issues of race in the 1960s, the party had a proud record of opposition to overseas imperialism. In its dogged and flawed attempt to follow an electoralist road the party did offer a socialist challenge to a Labour Party, which constantly put the needs of capital before the interests of its working-class supporters.

The end of the British Communist Party should not be confused with the defeat of socialism, in Britain or elsewhere. The potential for radical socialists to build in Britain should not be discounted and both socialist activists in Britain in the twenty-first century and students of contemporary politics will benefit from looking critically at the history of an organisation which, despite its many distortions, did attempted to build a mass, activist Marxist party. We end with a quotation from William Morris, a man who lived through the birth, renewal and decline of the first generation of socialist parties in Britain. 'Men fight and lose that battle and the thing they fought for comes about in spite of their defeat, and when it comes, turns out to be not what they meant, and other men have to fight for what they meant under another name ...'³

Notes

Introduction: the Rise and Decline of British Bolshevism

1. C. Bambery 'Introduction', in B. Pearce and M. Woodhouse, *A History of Communism In Britain* (London: Bookmarks, 1995 edn), p. iv.
2. D. Gluckstein *The Tragedy of Bukharin* (London: Pluto Press, 1994), pp. 171–81.
3. R. Darlington *The Political Trajectory of J. T. Murphy* (Liverpool: Liverpool University Press, 1998), p. 136.
4. K. McDermott, 'The history of the Comintern in the light of new documents', *International Communism and the Communist International 1919–1943* (Manchester: Manchester University Press, 1998), p. 33.
5. E. Hobsbawm, *Age of Extremes: the Short Twentieth Century 1914–1991* (London: Michael Joseph, 1994), p. 71.
6. S. Fielding, 'British Communism: Interesting but irrelevant?', *Labour History Review* 60/2 (1995), pp. 120–3; also J. Saville, 'The "Crisis" in Labour History: a Further Comment', *Labour History Review* 61/3 (1996), pp. 322–8.
   A. Thorpe, 'Comintern "Control" of the Communist Party of Great Britain', *English Historical Review* 63/452 (1998), pp. 610–36; J. Klugmann, *History of the Communist Party of Great Britain: Volume 1. Formation and Early Years 1919–1924* (London: Lawrence and Wishart, 1969); J. Klugmann, *History of the Communist Party of Great Britain: Volume 2. The General Strike 1925–1926* (London: Lawrence and Wishart, 1969); F. King and G. Matthews (eds), *About Turn: the Communist Party and the Outbreak of the Second World War* (London: Lawrence and Wishart, 1990).
7. P. Anderson, 'Communist Party History', in R. Samuel (ed.), *People's History and Socialist Theory* (London: Routledge and Kegan Paul, 1981), pp. 145–57; K. Morgan, *Against Fascism and War: Ruptures and Continuities in British Communist Politics 1935–1941* (Manchester: Manchester University Press, 1989), p. 9.
8. N. Fishman, *The British Communist Party and the Trade Unions 1933–1945* (London: Scolar Press, 1995); W. Thompson, *The Good Old Cause: British Communism 1920–1991* (London: Pluto, 1992).
9. H. Pelling, *The British Communist Party: a Historical Profile* (London: Adam and Charles Black, 1958); J. Klugmann, *History of the Communist Party: Volume 1*; and J. Klugmann, *History of the Communist Party: Volume 2*. For Cold War perspectives, see E. Hoffer, *The True Believer: Thoughts on the Nature of Mass Movements* (New York: Harper and Brothers, 1951); and C. H. Rolph, *All Those in Favour* (London: André Deutsch, 1962).
10. F. Newton, *The Sociology of British Communism* (London: Allen Lane, 1969), p. 154; D. T. Denver and J. M. Bochel, 'The Political Socialisation of Activists in the British Communist Party', *British Journal of Political Science* 3 (1973), pp. 53–71.

11. J. Hinton, *The First Shop Stewards Movement* (London: Pluto, 1973); J. Hinton and R. Hyman, *Trade Unions and Revolution: the Industrial Politics of the early British Communist Party* (London: Pluto, 1975); R. Croucher, *Engineers at War* (London: Merlin Press, 1982).
12. Pearce and Woodhouse, *A History of Communism in Britain*; L. Macfarlane, *The British Communist Party: its Origins and Development until 1929* (London: MacGibbon and Kee, 1966); Morgan, *Against Fascism and War*, pp. 6–7.
13. Karl Marx, '18th Brumaire of Louis Bonaparte' in *Karl Marx and Frederick Engels Selected Works* (London, 1968), p. 96.
14. 'Left-Wing Communism: an infantile disorder', in V. I. Lenin, *Collected Works* 31 (London Lawrence and Wishart, 1966), pp. 77–89, 101.
15. Fishman, *The British Communist Party*, p. 8.
16. N. Branson, *History of the Communist Party of Great Britain 1927–1941* (London: Lawrence and Wishart, 1985).
17. K. McDermott and J. Agnew, *The Comintern: a History of International Communism from Lenin to Stalin* (London: Macmillan, 1996); Morgan, *Against Fascism and War*, pp. 5–6, p. 175; S. Bornstein and A. Richardson, *War and the International: a History of the Trotskyist Movement in Britain 1937–1949* (Ilford: Socialist Platform, 1986), p. 26. Such attacks were probably most frequent between 1941 and 1945, interview with Frank Henderson, 10 July 1996; interview with Duncan Hallas, 16 September 1996.
18. Thompson, *The Good Old Cause*; Beckett, *Enemy Within*; K. Laybourn and D. Murphy, *Under the Red Flag: a History of Commission in Britain* (London: Sutton, 1999).
19. Thompson, *The Good Old Cause*.
20. Cited in Hinton and Hyman, *Trade Unions and Revolution*, p. 7.
21. J. T. Murphy, *Preparing for Power: a Critical Study of the British Working-Class Movement* (London: Pluto Press, 1972 edn), p. 219.
22. Thompson, *The Good Old Cause*, p. 8; Pearce and Woodhouse, *A History of Communism in Britain*.
23. Hinton and Hyman, *Trade Unions and Revolution*, p. 73.
24. N. Branson, *History of the Communist Party of Great Britain 1941–1951* (London: Lawrence and Wishart, 1997), p. 198.
25. A. Thorpe, *The British Communist Party and Moscow 1920–1943* (Manchester: Manchester University Press, 2000), p. 5; Thorpe, 'Comintern "Control"', pp. 641–7; see also A. Thorpe, 'The Communist International and the British Communist Party', in T. Rees and A. Thorpe, *International Communism and the Communist International* (Manchester: Manchester University Press, 1998), pp. 67–86.
26. J. Waterson, 'The Party at its Peak', *International Socialism Journal* 69 (1995), pp. 77–85; C. Rosenberg, 'Labour and the Fight against Fascism', *International Socialism Journal* 39 9 (1998), pp. 55–95.
27. P. Cohen, *Children of the Revolution; Communist Childhood in Cold War Britain* (London: Lawrence and Wishart, 1997), p. 61; I. Birchall, 'The British Communist Party'. *International Socialism* 50 (1972), pp. 24–34.
28. Cohen, *Children of the Revolution*.
29. J. Higgins, 'The Minority Movement', *International Socialism* 45 (1970), pp. 12–18.

1 High hopes: 1920–28

1. W. Kendall, *The Revolutionary Movement in Britain 1900–1921: the Origins of British Communism* (London: Weidenfeld and Nicolson, 1969), p. 299; J. Hinton and R. Hyman, *Trade Unions and Revolution: the Industrial Politics of the Early British Communist Party* (London: Pluto, 1975), p. 73.
2. M. Crick, *The History of the Social-Democratic Federation* (Keele: Keele University Press, 1994), p. 7.
3. K. Laybourn, *The Rise of Socialism in Britain* (Sutton: Stroud, 1997), p. 9.
4. The foundation of the SLP is described in R. Challinor, *The Origins of British Bolshevism* (London: Croom Helm, 1977), p. 9, 23. For the ideology of the pre- 1914 left, see L. Barrow and I. Bullock, *Democratic Ideas and the British Labour Movement, 1880–1914* (Cambridge: Cambridge University Press, 1996).
5. Rothstein's activities are discussed in John Saville's 'Introduction' to T. Rothstein, *From Chartism to Labourism: Historical Sketches in the English Working Class Movement* (London: Lawrence and Wishart, 1983 edn), pp. v–xxvi.
6. M. Trudell, 'Prelude to Revolution: Class Consciousness and the First World War', *International Socialism Journal* 76 (1997), pp. 67–108; and I. Birchall, 'The Vice-Like hold of Nationalism? A Comment on Megan Trudell's "Prelude to Revolution"', *International Socialism Journal* 78 (1998) pp. 133–42.
7. D. Gluckstein, *The Western Soviets: Workers' Councils versus Parliament 1915–1920* (London: Bookmarks, 1985), pp. 62–79; for the ideas of the wartime shop stewards' movement, J. T. Murphy, *The Workers' Committee: an Outline of its Principles and Structure* (London: Pluto, 1972 edn); and W. Gallacher and J. R. Campbell, *Direct Action: an Outline of Workshop and Social Organisation* (London: Pluto, 1972 edn).
8. C. Rosenberg, *1919: Britain on the Brink of Revolution* (London: Bookmarks, 1987).
9. The unity negotiations are discussed in L. J. Macfarlane, *The British Communist Party: its Origins and Development until 1929* (London: MacGibbon and Kee, 1966), pp. 47–56.
10. F. Borkenau, *World Communism: a History of the Communist International* (Michigan: Ann Arbor, 1962), p. 205.
11. R. and E. Frow, *The Communist Party in Manchester 1920–1926* (Manchester: Communist Party North West History Group, 1979), pp. 4, 8; D. Burke and F. Lindop, 'Theodore Rothstein and the Origins of the British Communist Party, *Socialist History* 15 (1999), pp. 45–65; W. Thompson, *The Good Old Cause: British Communism 1920–1991* (London: Pluto, 1992), p. 31.
12. *Workers' Dreadnought*, 21 February 1920.
13. V. I. Lenin, 'Left-Wing Communism: an Infantile Disorder', in V. I. Lenin, *Collected Works* 31 (London: Lawrence and Wishart, 1966), pp. 77–89, 85.
14. H. McShane and J. Smith, *No Mean Fighter* (London: Pluto, 1978), pp. 123–5; D. Sherry, *J. Maclean* (London: Socialist Workers Party, 1998), pp. 53–4; N. Milton, *John Maclean* (London: Pluto, 1973), pp. 227–31; N. Milton (ed.), *John Maclean, in the Rapids of Revolution: Essays, Articles and Letters 1902–23* (London: Allison and Busby, 1978), pp. 224–5.

15. T. Bell, *The British Communist Party: a Short History* (London: Lawrence and Wishart, 1937), pp. 67–8; D. Hallas, *The Comintern* (London: Bookmarks, 1985) pp. 43–6.
16. A. Hutt, *The Postwar History of the British Working Class* (London: Victor Gollancz, 1937), p. 56.
17. A. Callinicos, *Socialists in the Trade Unions* (London: Bookmarks, 1995); R. Michels, *Political Parties* (Glencoe, Illinois: The Free Press, 1959 edn).
18. R. Hyman, 'Communist Industrial Policy in the 1920s', *International Socialism* 53 (1972), pp. 14–22, 15.
19. A. Adler (ed.), *Theses, Resolutions and Manifestos of the First Four Congresses of the Third International* (London: Pluto, 1983), p. 202; J. Hinton, *Labour and Socialism: a History of the British Labour Movement 1867–1974* (Brighton: Wheatsheaf, 1983), p. 138.
20. Hinton and Hyman, *Trade Unions and Revolution*, pp. 14, 22; J. Higgins, 'The Minority Movement', *International Socialism* 45 (1970), pp. 12–18, 15. Jimmy Thomas's 'last supper' is recorded in *Communist Cartoons* (London: James Klugmann Pictorials, 1982 edn), pp. 44–5.
21. R. Martin *Communism and the British Trade Unions 1924–1933: a Study of the National Minority Movement* (Oxford: Clarendon Press, 1969), p. 1.
22. Higgins, 'The Minority Movement', pp. 15–16.
23. For example, Lenin's speech to the fourth congress of the Comintern criticised those who would ask foreign delegates to take Russian experience 'like an icon and praying to it', in V. I. Lenin, *Collected Works: Volume 33* (London: Lawrence and Wishart, 19), pp. 418–31. Thanks to Ian Birchall for this reference.
24. B. Pearce and M. Woodhouse, *A History of Communism in Britain* (London: Bookmarks, 1995), p. 77.
25. S. Macintyre, *A Proletarian Science: Marxism in Britain, 1917–33* (London: Lawrence and Wishart, 1980), pp. 91–3, 106–27.
26. Macfarlane, *The British Communist Party*, pp. 85–7; R. Darlington, *The Political Trajectory of J. T. Murphy* (Liverpool: Liverpool University Press, 1998), pp. 105–8.
27. K. Morgan, *Harry Pollitt* (Manchester: Manchester University Press, 1993), p. 1; for the Jolly George strike, H. Pollitt, *Serving My Time: an Apprenticeship to Politics* (London: Lawrence and Wishart, 1950), pp. 111–21; also M. Pollitt, *A Rebel Life* (Ultimo: Red Pen, 1989).
28. J. Callaghan, *Rajani Palme Dutt: a Study in British Stalinism* (London: Lawrence and Wishart, 1993), p. 38; Thompson, *The Good Old Cause*, p. 35. For Palme Dutt's own accounts to convey his distinctive Marxism, see R. Palme Dutt, *Lenin* (London: Hamish Hamilton, 1933).
29. J. Mahon, *Harry Pollitt: A Biography* (London: Lawrence and Wishart, 1976), p. 86; Kendall, *The Revolutionary Movement in Britain*, p. 283.
30. J. Klugmann, *History of the Communist Party of Great Britain: Volume 1. Formation and Early Years 1919–1924* (London: Lawrence and Wishart, 1969), pp. 181–2, 188–94, 353; T. Bell, *Pioneering Days* (London: Lawrence and Wishart, 1941), p. 263. M. Squires, *Saklatvala: a Political Biography* (London: Lawrence and Wishart, 1990), pp. 126–7; M. Wadsworth, *Comrade Sak* (London: Peppal Tree Press, 1998).
31. H. Laski, *Communism* (London: Frank Cass, 1968), p. 45; B. Russell, *The Practice and Theory of Bolshevism* London: George Allen and Unwin, 1920),

pp. 5–6; J. Lucas, *The Radical Twenties: Aspects of Writing, Politics and Culture* (Nottingham: Five Leaves, 1997)
32. Macintyre, *A Proletarian Science* p. 228.
33. K. McDermott and J. Agnew, *The Comintern: a History of International Communism from Lenin to Stalin*(London: Macmillan, 1996); *Inprecorr*, 17 March 1926; quoted in Macfarlane, *The British Communist Party*, p. 141.
34. McDermott and Agnew, *The Comintern*, p. 56.
35. For memories of the Lenin school, *Harry Wicks: A Memorial* (London: Socialist Platform, 1989), pp. 2–3.
36. Mahon, *Harry Pollitt*, p. 90; the Pollitt letter was from Stan Moran to Marjorie Pollitt, and can be found in the Communist Party archives in the National Museum of Labour History in Manchester, at CP/IND/POL/12/1; Pollitt's 1956 boast is in *Daily Worker*, 27 February 1956. J. Callaghan, 'The Communists and the Colonies: Anti-imperialism between the Wars', in G. Andrews, N. Fishman and K. Morgan (eds), *Opening the Books: Essays on the Cultural History of the British Communist Party* (London: Pluto, 1995), pp. 4–22.
37. Darlington, *Political Trajectory*, pp. 128–9.
38. H. Dewar, *Communist Politics in Britain: the CPGB from its Origins to the Second World War* (London: Pluto, 1976), pp. 45–6.
39. For some recent disclosures on the Zinoviev letter, see L. Jury, 'Russia Allows Access to Files on Letter that Helped to Bring down Government', *Independent*, 22 June 1998.
40. J. Klugmann, *History of the Communist Party of Great Britain: Volume 2: The General Strike 1925–1926* (London: Lawrence and Wishart, 1969), pp. 78–9.
41. Hyman, 'Communist Industrial Policy in the 1920s', p. 20; S. Macintyre, *Little Moscows: Communism and Working-Class Militancy in Inter-war Britain* (London: Croom Helm, 1980).
42. Leon Trotsky's writings on Britain at the time of the General Strike include his famous essay, 'Where is Britain Going?' (1925). The pamphlets and speeches are collected together in R. Chappell and A. Clinton (ed.), *Trotsky's Writings on Britain: Volume Two* (London: New Park, 1974). Variations on the Trotskyist approach can be seen in R. Black, *Stalinism in Britain* (London: New Park, 1970); Hallas, *The Comintern*, pp. 115–7; and Pearce and Woodhouse, *History of Communism in Britain*. The emphasis on international developments in shaping the CPGB is criticised from a Trotskyist perspective in Hinton and Hyman, *Trade Unions and Revolution*.
43. There is an excellent short biography of A. J. Cook in P. Foot, *An Agitator of the Worst Kind* (London: Socialist Workers Party, 1986); also T. Cliff, 'The Tragedy of A J Cook', *International Socialism Journal* 31 (1986), pp. 3–68. For the Comintern declaration, see Hallas, *The Comintern*, p. 116; for Palme Dutt, D. Hallas and C. Harman, *Days of Hope: the General Strike of 1926* (London: Bookmarks, 1986), p. 6. Palme Dutt's advice was prone to shift with each message from Moscow. In early 1925, for example, Dutt warned that 'none of these left elements have so far shown any difference in principle from MacDonald and the right wing'. Yet within weeks, his message of 'All Power to the General Council', had been resumed. See *Communist International* 8, pp. 31–3, and the immediate defence of the Anglo-Russian Committee by Losovsky, in *Communist International* 9, pp. 12–3.

44. Higgins, 'The Minority Movement', pp. 16–7.
45. K. Laybourn, *The General Strike: Day by Day* (Stroud: Sutton, 1996), p. 4; for a more detailed history of the strike, see K. Laybourn, *The General Strike of 1926* (Manchester: Manchester University Press, 1993); and M. Morris, *The British General Strike 1926* (London: Journeyman Press, 1980).
46. C. Farman, *The General Strike: May 1926* (London: Granada, 1974); Hutt, *Postwar History*, p.136.
47. Hallas and Harman, *Days of Hope*, p. 17; T. Cliff and D. Gluckstein, *Marxism and Trade Union Struggle: the General Strike of 1926* (London: Bookmarks, 1986), p. 264.
48. J. Skelley, *The General Strike* (London: Lawrence and Wishart, 1976) p. xiii; E. Burns, *General Strike, May 1926: Trades Councils in Action* (London: Lawrence and Wishart, 1976 edn); K. Fuller, *Radical Aristocrats: London Busworkers from the 1880s to the 1980s* (London: Lawrence and Wishart, 1985), pp. 84–8.
49. *Workers Weekly* 19 March 1926; Klugmann, *Volume 2*, pp. 202–5.
50. 'Stand by the Miners', *Workers Bulletin*, 13 May 1926; Klugmann, *Volume 2*, pp. 210–12. Statement by Gallacher *et al.*, 25 September 1926, cited in Hallas and Harman, *Days of Hope*, p. 17. For the expressions of surprise, see Skelley, *The General Strike*, pp. 321, 351; T. Cliff, 'Patterns of Mass Strike', *International Socialism Journal* 29 (1985), pp. 3–62, 15; for Murphy, Jackson and Hardy, Pearce and Woodhouse, *History of Communism*, pp. 148–9.
51. Minutes of ECCI Presidium 17 June 1929, on C. I. Reel 25, in the Communist Party archives in the National Museum of Labour History.
52. I. Birchall, 'Success and Failure of the Comintern', in K. Flett and D. Renton, *The Twentieth Century: a Century of Wars and Revolutions* (London: Rivers Oram, 2000), pp. 117–32; C. Harman, 'The General Strike', *International Socialism* 48 (1971), pp. 23–8.
53. G. A. Phillips, *The General Strike* (London: Weidenfeld and Nicolson, 1976), p. 281; also C. Wrigley, 'Trade Unionists, Employers and the case of Industrial Unity and Peace', in C. Wrigley and J. Sheperd (eds), *On the Move: Essays in Labour and Transport History presented to Philip Bagwell* (London: Hambledon Press, 1991); and Laybourn, *The General Strike of 1926*.
54. For German Communism, D. Gluckstein, *The Nazis, Capitalism and the Working Class* (London: Bookmarks, 1999); there is a similar approach in D. Renton, *Fascism: Theory and Practice* (London: Pluto, 1999), pp. 30–43. Borkenau, *World Communism*, p. 334.
55. Squires, *Saklatvala*, pp. 212–22; for Thorpe, see A. Thorpe, 'The Communist International and the British Communist Party', in T. Rees and A. Thorpe, *International Communism and the Communist International* (Manchester: Manchester University Press 1989), pp. 67–86, especially 74–5.
56. R. Page Arnot, 'The Significance of the Labour Party Conference in Blackpool', *International Press Correspondence*, 13 October 1927; Hutt, *Postwar History*, pp. 192–3; R. Groves, *The Balham Group: How British Trotskyism Began* (London: Pluto, 1974), pp. 17–24.
57. See R. P. Dutt to H. Pollitt, 6 January 1928, and R. P. Dutt to H. Pollitt, 6 January 1928, both in CP/IND/POLL/3/1.
58. Bell, *The British Communist Party*, p. 131.

59. Minutes of ECCI Presidium 13 February 1929, on C. I. Reel 25, in the Communist Party archives in the National Museum of Labour History.
60. CA226, Berlin to Communist Party of Great Britain, 5 March 1931, HW 17/69 in Public Records Office. Martin, *Communism and the British Trade Union Movement*, p. 49. Incidentally, Arnot is often named as a reluctant supporter of Class Against Class.
61. Communist Party of Great Britain, *Class against Class* (London: Communist Party of Great Britain, 1929), p. 8; R. Martin, *Communism and the British Trade Unions 1924–1933: a Study of the National Minority Movement* (Oxford: Clarendon Press, 1969); Losovsky's article is quoted in A. Howkins, 'Class against Class: The Political Culture of the Communist Party of Great Britain, 1930–35', in F. Gloversmith (ed.), *Class, Culture and Social Change*(Brighton: Harvester Press, 1980), pp. 240–58, 242, S. Jefferys, The Communist Party and the Rank and File', *International Socialism* 10 (1981), pp. 1–23, 3–4.
62. Morgan, *Harry Pollitt*, p. 21.

2 The Zig-Zag Left: 1928–39

1. R. Martin, *Communism and the British Trade Unions 1924–1933: a Study of the National Minority Movement* (Oxford: Clarendon Press, 1969), pp. 136–9; N. Branson and B. Moore, 'Labour-Communist Relations, 1920–1951. Part 1: 1920–1935', *Our History* 82 (1990), p. 54.
2. N. Branson, *History of the Communist Party of Great Britain 1927–1941* (London: Lawrence and Wishart, 1985), pp. 31, 83.
3. R. and E. Frow, *The Communist Party in Manchester 1920–1926* (Manchester: Communist Party Northwest History Group, 1979), p. 4; A. Howkins, 'Class Against Class: the Political Culture of the Communist Party of Great Britain, 1930–35', in F. Gloversmith (ed.), *Class, Culture and Social Change: a New View of the 1930s* (London: Harvester Press, 1980), pp. 240–58, 244–9.
4. V. I. Lenin to Thomas Bell, 13 August 1921, quoted in V. I. Lenin, *On Britain* (London: Lawrence and Wishart, 1959), pp. 564–5; J. Klugmann, *History of the Communist Party of Great Britain: Volume I. Formation and Early Years 1919–1924* (London: Lawrence and Wishart, 1969), pp. 72–4; *Party Life* 9 (1929), cited in K. Morgan, 'The Communist Party and the *Daily Worker* 1930–56', in G. Andrews, N. Fishman and K. Morgan (eds), *Opening the Books: Essays on the Cultural History of the British Communist Party* (London: Pluto, 1995), pp. 142–59, 143.
5. K. Laybourn and D. Murphy, *Under the Red Flag: a History of Communism in Britain* (Stroud: Sutton Publishing, 1999), p. 63.
6. Howkins, 'Class Against Class', p. 247; Bambery, *The Case*, pp. 10–15.
7. J. Lowerson, 'Battles for the Countryside', in Gloversmith, *Class, Culture and Social Change*, pp. 273–5.
8. R. Croucher, *We Refuse to Starve in Silence: a History of the National Unemployed Workers' Movement, 1920–946* (London: Lawrence and Wishart, 1987), pp. 38–58; H. McShane and J. Smith, *No Mean Fighter* (London: Pluto,1998), pp. 115–41, 169–76.
9. Croucher, *We Refuse*, pp. 119–21.

10. CB46, Berlin to CPGB, 17 October 1931, in Public Records Office, HW/17/70.
11. See for example minutes of CC of CPGB 16 January 1932, on C. I. Reel 23, in the Communist Party archives in the National Museum of Labour History. There is a very full account of the clashes in Matt Perry's history of European unemployed campaigns, M. Perry, *Bread and Work: the Experience of Unemployment 1918–1939* (London: Pluto, 2000), pp. 116–7.
12. R. Bishop, 'Unemployment Shakes the Government', *International Press Correspondence*, 16 February 1935; W. Hannington, 'British Workers in Action against the New Unemployment Act', *International Press Correspondence*, 23 February 1935; R. Croucher, "Divisions in the Movement": the National Unemployed Workers' Movement and its Rivals in Comparative Perspective', in Andrews, Fishman and Morgan, *Opening the Books*, pp. 23–44; also Croucher, *We Refuse*, pp. 173–95. For the associational culture of the inter-war unemployed, R. McKibbin, *The Ideologies of Class: Social Relations in Britain 1880–1950* (Oxford and New York: Oxford University Press, 1991), pp. 228–58.
13. D. Renton, 'The Man who Turned his Back on Labour', *Socialist Review*, December 1996.
14. Branson and Moore, 'Labour–Communist Relations', p. 56; Branson, *History of the Communist Party of Great Britain 1927–1941*, p. 69; F. Copeman, *Reason in Revolt* (London: Blandford Press, 1948), pp. 43–53.
15. Branson and Moore, 'Labour–Communist Relations', p. 57.
16. *Communist Review*, February 1924, June 1925; B. Pearce and M. Woodhouse, *A History of Communism in Britain* (London: Bookmarks, 1995), pp. 81–2; Communist Party of Great Britain, *The Errors of Trotskyism: a Symposium* (London: Communist Party of Great Britain, 1925), pp. 5–29, 9; R. Darlington, *The Political Trajectory of J. T. Murphy* (Liverpool: Liverpool University Press, 1998), pp. 157–61; the Palme Dutt article is reprinted in R. Chappell and A. Clinton (eds), *Trotsky's Writings on Britain: Volume Two* (London: New Park 1974), pp. 264–80.
17. H. Wicks, *The Balham Group: How British Trotskyism Began* (London: Pluto,1974). p. 43; H. Wicks: a Memorial (London: Socialist Platform, 1989); H. Wicks, *Keeping My Head. the Memoirs of a British Bolshevik* (London: Socialist Platform, 1992); H. Ratner, *Reluctant Revolutionary: Memoirs of a Trotskyist 1936–1960* (London: Socialist Platform,1994), For a CPGB perspective, B. Reid, *Ultra-leftism in Britain* (London: Communist Party, 1969).
18. N. Fishman, *The British Communist Party and the Trade Unions 1933–1945* (London: Scolar Press, 1995), pp. 33–9; K. McDermott and J. Agnew, *The Comitern: a History of International Communism from Lenin to Stalin* (London: Macmillan, 1996).
19. Laybourn and Murphy, *Under the Red Flag*, pp. 64–5.
20. Minutes of ECCI Presidium 29 December 1931, on C. I. Reel 25, in the Communist Party archives in the National Museum of Labour History.
21. Minutes of PB of CPGB, 14 January 1932, on C. I. Reel 4; minutes of CC of CPGB, 16 January 1932, on C. I. Reel 3, both in the Communist Party archives in the National Museum of Labour History.
22. R. Bishop, 'The Strike Movement in Britain', *International Press Correspondence*, 30 March 1935.

23. P. Glatter, 'London Busmen: Rise and Fall of a Rank and File Movement', *International Socialism* 74 (1975). pp. 5–11; K. Fuller, *Radical Aristocrats: London Busworkers from the 1880s to the 1980s* (London: Lawrence and Wishart,1985). For other examples of rank and file trade unionism at this time, see R. Bishop, 'The Class War on the British Railways', *International Press Correspondence*, 8 December 1932.
24. D. Renton, *Fascists, Anti-Fascists and Britain in the 1940s* (London: Macmillan, 1999), pp. 19–20.
25. Labour Party Press Cuttings, *British Fascisti*, undated, in the National Museum of Labour History in Manchester; L. W., *Fascism: its History and Significnce* (London: Plebs League, 1924), p. 7.
26. C. Rosenberg, 'Labour and the Fight against Fascism' *International Socialism Journal* 39 (1988), pp. 55–94; M. Newman, 'Democracy versus Dictatorship: Labour's Role in the Struggle against British Fascism', *History Workshop Journal* 5 (1978), pp. 67–81; N. Todd, *In Excited Times: the People against the Blackshirts* (Newcastle: Bewick Press, 1995), pp. 54–9; D. Renton, *Red Shirts and Black: Fascists and Anti-Fascists in Oxford in the 1930s* (Oxford: Ruskin College Library,1996), pp. 18–20; H. Francis, *Miners against Fascism: Wales and the Spanish Civil War* (London: Lawrence and Wishart, 1984), pp. 87–94; L. W. Bailey, 'Olympia'. *The Times*, 6 March 1996.
27. P. Piratin, *Our Flag Stays Red* (London: Thames, 1948), pp. 5–7; 'Swaffer Says', *World Press News*, 5 August 1943; Branson, *History of the Communist Party of Great Britain 1927–1941*, pp. 120–1; R. Temple, 'The Metropolitan Police and the British Union of Fascists' (PhD thesis, Queen Mary College, 1989), p. 22; *Yorkshire Post*, 9 June 1934; Vindicator, *Fascists at Olympia* (London: Lawrence and Wishart, 1934); D. Cook, *A Knife at the Throat of us all* (London: Communist Party, 1978), p. 17; C. Andrew, *Secret Service: the Making of the British Intelligence Community* (London: Heinemann, 1985), pp. 526–7.
28. J. Strachey, *The Coming Struggle for Power* (London: Victor Gollancz, 1932), pp. 293–4; *Communist Review*, December 1933, January 1934; Pearce and Woodhouse, *History of British Communism*, p. 214; R. Palme Dutt, *Fascism and Social Revolution* (London: Lawrence and Wishart, 1934), pp. 150–76.
29. D. Renton, *Fascism: Theory and Practice* (London: Pluto, 1999), pp. 30–43.
30. Minutes of CC of CPGB 5 January 1934, on C. I. Reel 4, in the Communist Party archives in the National Museum of Labour History.
31. *International Press Correspondence* 17 November 1932; *Daily Worker*, 6 January 1934; R. Black, *Stalinism in Britain: a Trotskyist Analysis* (London: New Park Publications, 1970), pp. 83, 93; Renton, *Fascism: Theory and Practice*,p. 37.
32. Dimitrov's speech is contained in D. Beetham, *Marxists in Face of Fascism: Writings by Marxists on Fascism from the Inter-War Period*(Manchester: Manchester University Press, 1983), pp. 179–86.
33. Branson, *History of the Communist Party of Great Britain 1927–1941*, p. 108; A. F. Brockway, *The Workers Front* (London: Secker and Warburg, 1938), p. 72.
34. Minutes of PB of CPGB 15 November 1934, on C. I. Reel 4, in the Communist Party archives in the National Museum of Labour History

35. Labour Party National Executive Committee to Harry Pollitt, 27 January 1936, quoted in *International Press Correspondence*, 8 February 1936.
36. *Labour Monthly*, February 1936; Dewar, *Communist Politics in Britain*, pp. 117–8.
37. S. Burgess, *Stafford Cripps: a Political Life* (London: Gollancz, 1999).
38. R. Salles, 'Structure, Implantation et Influence du Parti Communiste de Grande-Bretagne dans un Perspective Historique' (PhD thesis, University of Paris, 1978), p. 187; R. Challinor, *The Struggle for Hearts and Minds: Essays on the Second World War* (Newcastle: Bewick Press, 1995), p. 51.
39. H. Dewar, *Communist Politics in Britain: the CPGB from its Origins to the Second World War* (London: Pluto, 1976), pp. 113–7.
40. S. Orwell and I. Angus (eds), *The Collected Essays, Journalism and Letters of George Orwell, Volume 1* (London: Secker and Warburg, 1968), p. 305; also P. Flewers, *'I Know How, but I Don't Know Why': George Orwell's Conception of Totalitarianism* (London: New Interventions, 1999).
41. Pearce and Woodhouse, *A History of Communism*, pp. 138–41.
42. R. Thurlow, 'The Failure of British Fascism' in A. Thorpe (ed.), *The Failure of Political Extremism in Inter-War Britain* (Exeter: Exeter University Press, 1989), pp. 67–84, 76; A. J. Trythall, *'Boney' Fuller: the Intellectual General 1878–66* (London: Cassell, 1977), pp. 181–4; L. Paul, *Angry Young Man* (London: Faber and Faber, 1941), p. 233; Piratin, *Our Flag*, pp. 16–19, 16.
43. This account is based on J. Jacobs, *Out of the Ghetto* (London: Janet Simon, 1978), p. 245; Piratin, *Our Flag*, pp. 19–25; Rosenberg, 'Labour and the Fight against Fascism', pp. 63–4; D. Renton, 'Docker and Garment Worker, Railwayman and Cabinet Maker: the Class Memory of Cable Street', *Jewish Culture and History* 1/2 (1998), pp. 95–108; R. Groves, *East End Crisis* (London: Socialist League, 1937); G. D. Anderson, *Fascists, Communists and the National Government: Civil Liberties in Great Britain 1931–37* (Columbia: Columbia University Press, 1983), pp. 137–68; M. M. Mullings, 'The Left and Fascism in the East End of London 1932–1939' (PhD thesis, Polytechnic of North London, 1984), pp. 251–96; H. Rosen, 'A Necessary Myth? Cable Street Revisited', *Changing English* 5/1 (1998), pp. 27–34; D. Renton, 'Necessary Myth or Collective Truth? Cable Street Revisited', *Changing English* 5/2 (1998), pp. 189–94; P. Catterall (ed.), 'The Battle of Cable Street', *Contemporary Record* 8/1 (1994), pp. 105–132; E. Smith, 'Jewish Political Responses to Political Anti-Semitism and Fascism in the East End of London', in T. Kushner and K. Lunn (eds), *Traditions of Intolerance* (Manchester: Manchester University Press, 1989), 53–71; C. Knowles, 'Labour and Anti-Semitism', in R. Miles and A. Phizacklea (eds), *Racism and Political Action in Britain* (London: Routledge and Kegan Paul, 1979), pp. 50–71.
45. Piratin, *Our Flag*, pp. 25–6; T. Kushner, 'Cable Street: Myth or Reality', paper given to 'Cable Street' conference, London, October 1996; Lebzelter, p. 169; C. Holmes, 'East End Anti-Semitism 1936', in *Bulletin of the Society for the Study of Labour History* 32 (1976), pp. 26–33; P. Cohen, 'The Police, The Home Office, and the Surveillance of the British Union of Fascists', *Intelligence and National Security* 1/3 (1986), pp. 416–34, 429–30; Viscount Simon, *Retrospect* (London: Hutchinson, 1952), p. 216.

46. C. T. Husbands, *Racial Exclusionism and the City: the Urban Support of the National Front* (London: Allen and Unwin,1983), pp. 54–5; C. T. Husbands, 'East End Racism, 1900–80', *London Journal* 8/1 (1982), pp. 3–26, 13; J. Golden, *Hackney at War* (Stroud: Alan Sutton, 1995), p. 11; J. Beckett, 'After My Fashion', unpublished manuscript in the British Union collection in the University of Sheffield, p. 395; J. and P. Barnes, 'Oswald Mosley as Entrepreneur', *History Today* 40/3 (1990), 11–16; F. Selwyn, *Hitler's Englishman: the Crime of 'Lord Haw-Haw'* (London: Penguin, 1987); J. A. Cole, *Lord Haw-Haw and William Joyce: the Full Story* (London: Faber, 1964); C. Holmes, "Germany Calling": Lord Haw-Haw's Treason', *Twentieth Century British History* 5/1 (1994), pp. 118–120.
46. H. Walters, *The Street* (London: Centreprise, 1975), pp. 5–7; H. F. Srebrnik, *London, Jews and British Communism* (Essex: Valentine Mitchell, 1995), p. 15; B. (C. H.) Darke, *The Communist Technique in Britain* (London: Penguin, 1951), p. 44; J. Hepple, '"Jewish Politics" During the Second World War: the National Jewish Committee of the Communist Party of Great Britain', unpublished paper, 1998.
47. E. Litvinoff, *Journal Through a Small Planet* (Harmondsworth: Penguin, 1972), p. 157; R. L. Finn, *Spring in Aldegate* (London: Robert Hale,1968), p. 123.
48. Interview with Chimen Abramsky, 18 February 1997; Cohen, 'The Police, The Home Office', p. 66. Cable Street was of course a static occupation – not a march!
49. Renton, *Fascism: Theory and Practice*, p. 78.
50. Branson, *History of the Communist Party of Great Britain 1927–1941*, pp. 220–39; G. Matthews, *All for the Cause: the Communist Party 1920–1980* (London: Communist Party, 1980), pp. 10–11.
51. M. Kolzov, 'The Trotskyist Criminals in Spain', *International Press Correspondence*, 31 January 1937; *Daily Worker*, 11 May 1937, 17 May 1937; J. Pettifer (ed.), *Cockburn in Spain: Despatches from the Spanish Civil War* (London: Lawrence and Wishart, 1986), p. 184; D. Caute, *The Fellow Travellers: a Postscript to the Enlightenment* (London: Weidenfeld and Nicolson, 1973), p. 171; A. Durgan, 'Freedom Fighters or Comintern Army? The International Brigades in Spain', *International Socialism Journal* 84 (1999), pp. 109–32.
52. Dewar, *Communist Politics in Britain*, pp. 120–2; Branson, *History of the Communist Party of Great Britain 1927–1941*, pp. 188, 191, 218; Caute, *The Fellow Travellers*, p. 3
53. V. Cunningham, 'Neutral? 1930s Writers and Taking Sides' in Gloversmith, *Class, Culture and Social Change*, pp. 45–69.
54. J. Coombes, 'British Intellectuals and the Popular Front', in Gloversmith, *Class, Culture and Social Change*, pp. 70–101, 72; S. Samuels, 'The Left Book Club', *Journal of Contemporary History* 1/2 (1966), pp. 65–86; P. Foot, *Words as Weapons: Selected Writings 1980–1990* (London: Verso, 1990), pp. 116–8; J. Lewis, *The Left Book Club: a Historical Record* (London: Lawrence and Wishart, 1970), pp. 63, 114.
55. R. Davenport-Hines, *Auden* (London: Minerva, 1995), pp. 157–62; S. Spender, *Forward From Liberalism* (London: Gollancz, 1937), p. 27; Coombes, 'British Intellectuals', pp. 79–80; B. Crick, *Essays on Politics and*

Literature (Edinburgh: Edinburgh University Press, 1989), pp. 48–62. There is an excellent political biography of MacDonald in J. Ross, 'Hugh MacDiarmid', in C. Bambery (ed.), *Scotland: Class and Nation* (London: Bookmarks, 1999), pp. 177–99.
56. Branson, *History of the Communist Party of Great Britain 1927–41*, p. 177, 185; *Workers Weekly*, 19 March 1926; Klugmann, Volume 2, pp. 202–5.
57. D. N. Pritt, *The Zinoviev Trial* (London: Gollancz, 1936), p. 24; Pearce and Woodhouse, *A History of Communism*, pp. 226–30.
58. Branson, *History of the Communist Party 1927–1941*, p. 248.
59. K. Morgan, *Henry Pollitt* (Manchester: Manchester University Press, 1993), p. 104.
60. C. Cockburn, *Crossing the Line* (London: MacGibbon and Kee, 1958); P. Cockburn, *The Years of the Week* (London: Comedia, 1968); Renton, *Red Shirts and Black*, pp. 45–6.
61. D. Hyde, *I Believed: the Autobiography of a Former British Communist* (Melbourne, London and Toronto: William Heinemann,1951), pp. 67–8; D. Goldfinger, unpublished memoir (1954), in the Communist Party archive (CP), in the National Museum of Labour History, Manchester, CP/IND/MISC/1/4; also D. N. Pritt, *Light on Moscow: Soviet Policy Analysed* (Harmondsworth: Penguin, 1939).
62. *Daily Worker* special issue, 'War! Communist Policy', copies at CP/IND/POL/3/6.

3 The Party at War: Its Finest Hour?

1. CP/IND/POLL/3/6.
2. Bernard McKenna, interview in *Socialist Review* No. 194 2/1996.
3. Bill Moore, interview by authors 11/1995.
4. Fred Westacott, interview by authors 11/1995.
5. Headline to *Daily Worker* editorial. DW, 9/10/39.
6. The terms Central Committee and Political Bureau were abolished within the party in 1943. The Central Committee became known as the Executive Committee and the Political Bureau was re-named the Political Committee.
7. For a detailed biography of Rajani Palme Dutt see J. Callaghan, *Rajani Palme Dutt: a study in British Stalinism* (London: Lawrence & Wishart, 1993).
8. K. Morgan, *Harry Pollitt*, (Manchester: MUP, 1993), pp. l06–9. In April 1979 the CPGB History Group organised a conference at Birkbeck College to investigate the controversy around the 1939 volteface. The conference proceedings were written up J Attfield and S. Williams (eds) *1939: the Communist Party of Great Britain and the War* (London: Lawrence & Wishart, 1984).
9. DW 13/1O/39.
10. DW 23/11/39.
11. CP/IND/POLL/2/8.
12. Letter from Rajani Palme Dutt to Harry Pollitt 2/11/39 CP/IND/POLL/3/7.
13. CP/IND/POLL/3/11.
14. DW, 13/10/39.

15. M. Johnstone, 'Introduction' in F. King and G. Matthews (eds) *About Turn: the Communist Party and the Outbreak of the Second World War* (London: Lawrence & Wishart, 1990), pp 41–2.
16. CP/IND/POL/3/13.
17. Charlie Darville, interview by author 11/95.
18. J. Beal, *Of the Rank and File*, unpublished autobiography N.D.
19. Thanks to Jim Johnson for this account of his father's experiences.
20. K. Morgan, *Against Fascism and War: Ruptures and Continuities in British Communist Politics 1935–41* (Manchester: Manchester University Press: 1989) pp. 311–13.
21. Bill Moore/Fred Westacott interviews. See also N. Branson *History of the Communist Party of Great Britain 1941–1951* (London: Lawrence & Wishart, 1997), pp. 50–61.
22. DW, 22/11/39.
23. D. Childs, 'The British Communist Party and the War 1939–41: Old Slogans Revived' *Journal of Contemporary History* Vol. 12, 1977, 245.
24. A. Calder *The People's War: Britain 1939–45* (London: Jonathon Cape, 1969) and A. Calder *Speak for Yourself: a Mass Observation Anthology* (London: Jonathon Cape, 1984) and C. Ponting, *1940: Myth and Realty* (Hamish Hamilton, 1990).
25. For an interesting and informative debate on early attitudes to WW1 see M. Trudell 'Prelude to Revolution: Class Consciousness and the First World War', *International Socialism Journal* 76, Autumn 1997 and I. Birchall 'The vice like grip of nationalism?' *International Socialism Journal* 78, spring 1998.
26. R. Challinor, *The Struggle for Hearts and Minds: Essays on the Second World War* (Whitley Bay: Bewick Press, 1995), p. 11.
27. Challinor, *The Struggle for Hearts and Minds*, p. 13.
28. Challinor, *The Struggle for Hearts and Minds*, pp. 11–13.
29. R. Croucher, *Engineers at War* (London: Merlin Press, 1982), p. 124.
30. N. Fishman, *The British Communist Party and the Trade Unions* (Aldershot, Scolar Press, 1995), pp. 289–91.
31. Fishman, *The British Communist Party and the Trade Unions*, pp. 255–61.
32. Croucher, *Engineers at War*, pp. 124–33.
33. Y. Sergeev, 'The Communist International and a "Trotskyite menace" to the British Communist movement on the eve of World War II' in T. Rees and A. Thorpe (eds) *International Communism and the Communist International 1919–43* (Manchester: Manchester University Press, 1998), pp. 87–94.
34. S. Bornstein and A. Richardson *War and the International: a History of the Trotskyist Movement Britain 1937–1949*, (Ilford: Socialist Platform, 1986), p. 27.
35. Callaghan, *Rajani Palme Dutt*, p. 131.
36. PRO/H045/25552/106.
37. CP/IND/POLL/2/7.
38. Morgan, *Harry Pollitt*, p. 177.
39. CP/1ND/POLL/3/11.
40. For a partisan account of the ability of the minuscule Trotskyist groups to gain a significant audience and influence, see S. Bornstein and

A. Richardson *War and the International: a History of the Trotskyist Movement in Britain 1937–49*. For a more critical comment which nevertheless confirms their influence see Croucher, *Engineers at War*, pp. 174–6. For a more sceptical view and an account of the rise and fall of the Commonwealth. Party see A. Calder, *The People's War: Britain 1939–45* (London: Jonathon Cape, 1969), pp. 631–5.
41. CP/IND/MONT/10/3.
42. I. Kershaw, *Hitler 1936–1945: Nemesis* (London: Allen Lane, 2000) pp. 369–81.
43. Callaghan, *Rajani Palme Dutt*, p. 197.
44. K. Morgan, *Harry Pollitt*, 117. Palme Dutt's magnum opus of the Third Period, 'Fascism and Social Revolution' was published just weeks before the official jettisoning of the Third Period and the embracing of the Popular front in 1934. See Callaghan. *Rajani Palme Dutt*, pp. 135–8.
45. Harry Pollitt, *Britain's Chance Has Come* (CPGB, 1941) cited Morgan, *Harry Pollitt*, p. 130.
46. Morgan, *Harry Pollitt*, p. 198.
47. Branson, *History of the Communist Party of Great Britain 1927–1941*, p. 33.
48. CP/CENT/EC/01/01.
49. Morgan, *Harry Pollitt*, p. 133.
50. Report to Ministry of Labour cited in Croucher, *Engineers at War*, p. 172.
51. S. Bornstein and A. Richardson, *Two Steps Back: the Communist Part of Great Britain and the working class from 1935–1945* (Ilford: Socialist Platform, 1982), p. 89.
52. Croucher, *Engineers at War*, p. 183.
53. N. Fishman *The British Communist Party and the Trade Unions 1933–1945*, pp. 277–8.
54. CP/CENT/EC/O1/01.
55. Bornstein and Richardson, *Two Steps Back*, p. 86.
56. Calder, *The People's War*, pp. 637–9.
57. CP/CENT/EC/01/02.
58. N. Branson, *History of the Communist Party of Great Britain 1927–1941*, p. 80.
59. Callaghan, *Rajani Palme Dutt*, p. 211. Browder was subsequently attacked in an article by the French Communist leader Jacques Duclos which is widely interpreted as having been authorised from Moscow. At the end of July 1945 the CPUSA was restored and Browder removed from its leadership. See M. Isserman, *The American Communist Party during the Second World War: Which Side Were You On?* (Chicago: University of Illinois, 1993), p. 187 passim.
60. *Communist Party Statement on National Unity* CP/CENT/EC/01/03.
61. *For the Information of the EC 13/3/1945* CP/CENT/EC/O1/Q3.
62. *Communist Parliamentary Candidates* Press Release 18 April 1945 CP/CENT/EC/01/03.
63. Callaghan, *Rajani Palme Dutt*, p. 212.
64. *For the Information of the EC 13/3/1945* CP/CENT/EC/01/03.
65. *Document E* CP/CENT/EC/01/03.
66. H. F. Srebnick, *London Jews and British Communism*, (Chelmsford: Valentine Mitchell, 1995), p. 1; P. Piratin, *Our Flag Stays Red* (London: Thames, 1948).

4 Past Its Peak: 1945–56

1. N. Branson, *History of the Communist Party of Great Britain 1941–1951* (London: Lawrence and Wishart, 1997), pp. 23, 96; S. Jeffreys, 'The Communist Party and the Rank and File', *International Socialism Journal* 10 (1980), pp. 1–23, 19, 21; for the *New Propeller*, D. McShane, *International Labour and the Origins of the Cold War* (Oxford: Oxford University Press, 1992), p. 169.
2. Branson, *History of the Communist Party*, pp. 35, 111; R. Emmett, 'Socialists in the Labour Movement', *Socialist Review*, mid-November 1958, reprinted in J. Higgins (ed.), *A Socialist Review* (London: International Socialism, 1965), pp. 157–63. The tensions following from the party's wartime support for increased production in engineering are discussed in R. Croucher, *Engineers at War 1939–1945* (London: Merlin, 1982).
3. I. Birchall, 'The British Communist Party 1945–964', *International Socialism* 50 (1972), pp. 24–34, 24; there is a similar analysis in Ernest Mandel's later book, *From Stalinism to Eurocommunism* (London: New Left Books, 1979), and in F. Claudia, *Eurocommunism and Socialism* (London: New Left Books, 1978).
4. Birchall, 'The British Communist Party', p. 26; R. Black, *Stalinism in Britain: a Trotskyist Analysis* (London: New Park Publications, 1970), p. 204.
5. H. F. Srebrnick, *London Jews and British Communism* (Chelmsford: Valentine Mitchell, 1995), p. 1; P. Piratin, *Our Flag Stays Red* (London: Thames, 1948).
6. Birchall, 'The British Communist Party', p. 26; the best account of strikes under the Labour government is in G. Ellen, 'Labour And Strikebreaking', *International Socialism Journal* 24 (1984), pp. 45–74; also Branson, *History of the Communist Party*, p. 116.
7. Black, *Stalinism in Britain*, p. 206.
8. Branson, *History of the Communist Party*, p. 138.
9. J. Hinton, *Shop-Floor Citizens: Engineering Democracy in 1940s Britain* (Aldershot: E. Elgar, 1994), p. 6; also J. Hinton, 'The Communist Party, Production and Britain's Post-war Settlement', in G. Andrews, N. Fishman and K. Morgan (eds), *Opening the Books: Essays on the Cultural History of the British Communist Party* (London: Pluto, 1995), pp. 160–75; and J. Hinton, 'Coventry Communism: a Study of Factory Politics in the Second World War', *History Workshop Journal* 10 (1980), pp. 91–188.
10. Communist Party, *Marxist Study Themes No. 1: the Communist Party, Unity and the Fight for Peace* (London: Communist Party of Great Britain, 1950), p. 17.
11. Branson, *History of the Communist Party*, pp. 177–90; Birchall, 'The British Communist Party', p. 27.
12. G. Allison, 'The Trade Unions and the Drive for more Production', *World News and Views*, 4 December 1948.
13. J. D. Bernal, *The Freedom of Necessity* (London: Routledge and Kegan Paul, 1949); A. McLeod, *The Death of Uncle Joe* (London: Merlin, 1997), p. 26; *Labour Monthly*, December 1949, quoted in Birchall, 'The British Communist Party', p. 27; Branson, *History of the Communist Party*, pp. 174–5, 197–8; for Zilliacus, J. Schneer, *Labour's Conscience: the Labour Left 1945–1951* (London and Winchester: Massachusetts, 1988).

14. P. Flewers, 'Hitting the Pits: The Communist Party of Great Britain and the National Union of Miners', *New Interventions* 7/1 (1996); Black, *Stalinism in Britain*, p. 211.
15. J. R. Campbell, *A Socialist Solution to the Crisis* (London: Communist Party, 1948), pp. 8–10; Communist Party of Great Britain, *The British Road to Socialism* (London: Communist Party, 1951 edn), p. 10; P. Goldring, 'The Menace of the Comic Strip', *World News and Views*, 14 April 1951; also D. N. Pritt, *The Star-Spangled Shadow* (London: Lawrence and Wishart, 1947). The politics of the anti-comic campaign are discussed in M. Barker, *A Haunt of Fears: the Strange History of the British Horror Comics Campaign* (London: Pluto, 1984).
16. The section which follows is based on the account in D. Renton, *Fascists and Anti-Fascists in Britain in the 1940s* (London: Macmillan, 1999), pp. 71–100.
17. The best source for information regarding the *Mosley Newsletter* is the transcript of the trial of three trade unionists who tried to 'black' its distribution, 'Mosley Publications Ltd vs. Morrison and Others', transcript of trial, March 1947, in the National Council of Civil Liberties (DCL) archive in the University of Hull, DCL/70/2. For the Mosley Book Clubs outside London, 'Report on Fascist Activities in Lancashire and Cheshire', 3 May 1948, in the Communist Party archive (CP), in the National Museum of Labour History, Manchester, CP/CENT/ORG/12/7. Also M. Beckman, *The Forty Three Group* (London: Centreprise, 1992), 89; Special Branch, 'Fortnightly Summary' 15 August 1947; Special Branch, 'Fortnightly Summary' 31 August 1947, both in the Home Office records (HO), in the Public Records Office, HO 45/24470/423; Stanley Marks, 'Fascist Meeting Places', 43 Group internal document, in 43 Group material at London Museum of Jewish Life (LMJL): LMJL/194-1990/9.
18. *Daily Express*, 1 August 1947; *Eastern Daily Press*, 4 August 1947; *News Chronicle*, 6 August 1947; *Jewish Chronicle*, 8 August 1947; D. Leitch, 'Explosion at the King David Hotel', in M. Sissons and P. French (eds), *Age of Austerity* (London: Hodder and Stoughton, 1963), pp. 55–79; B. Lapping, *The End of Empire* (London: Granada, 1989), p. 177; C. Holmes, 'The Vitality of Anti-Semitism: the British Experience since 1945', *Contemporary Affairs Briefing* 4/1 (1981), pp. 2–5; *Keesing's Contemporary Archives* A8782, 16–23 August 1947; E. Heffer, *Never a Yes Man: the Life and Politics of an Adopted Liverpudlian* (London: Verso, 1991), p. 46; *Jewish Chronicle*, 14 September 1979; J. Gross, 'The Lynskey Tribunal', in Sissons and French, *Age of Austerity*, pp 255–76; H. T. F. Rhodes, *The Lynskey Tribunal* (London: Thames Bank Publishing, 1949).
19. D. N. Pritt, *The Labour Government 1945–1951* (London: Lawrence and Wishart, 1963), pp. 307–9; Beckman, *The Forty Three Group*; A. Hartog, *Born To Sing* (London: Dobson, 1978), p. 75
20. C. Rauden, 'Parliamentary Elections and the British Communist Party', unpublished manuscript in Marx Memorial Library.
21. K. McLachlan, *One Great Vision: Memoirs of a Glasgow Worker* (Glasgow: Kenny McLachlan, 1995), p. 105; B. Behan, *With Breast Expanded* (London: Select Books, 1991 edn), p. 154; Branson, *History of the Communist Party*, p. 142; Heffer, *Never a Yes Man*; E. Heffer, 'Abandoning Marxism', *World*

News and Views; 1 February 1947; H. McShane and J. Smith, Harry McShane: *No Mean Fighter* (London: Pluto, 1978), pp. 241–4; R. Samuel, 'The Lost World of British Communism'; *New Left Review (NLR)* 154 (1985), pp. 3–53; *NLR* 155 (1985), pp. 119–24; *NLR* 156 (1986), pp. 63–113; and *NLR* 165 (1987), pp. 52–91; here *NLR* 155; D. A. Hyde, *Communism from the Inside* (London: Catholic Truth Society, 1948); B. (C. H.) Darke, *The Communist Technique in Britain* (London: Penguin, 1951); R. Osment, *Experiences of a Jewish Communist* (Bromley: CMCW, 1975), p. 10; L. Moss, *Live and Learn: a Life and Struggle for Progress* (Brighton: Queenspark, 1979), p. 71; C. Cockburn, *Crossing the Line* (London: MacGibbon and Kee, 1958), p. 176.
22. E. Upward, *The Rotten Elements* (London: Quartet, 1979 edn), pp. 36–7, 118.
23. A. Croft, 'Authors Take Sides: Writers and the Communist Party 1920–56', in Andrews, Fishman and Morgan, *Opening the Books*, pp. 83–101.
24. There is a useful discussion of the origins of E. P. Thompson's Marxism in T. Steele, *The Emergence of Cultural Studies: Adult Education, Cultural Politics and the 'English' Question* (London: Lawrence and Wishart, 1997), pp. 144–75.
25. D. Torr, *An Introduction to The Paris Commune* (London: Gollancz, 1936); M. Morris (ed.), *From Cobbett to the Chartists: Nineteenth Century Volume 1. 1815–48* (London: Lawrence and Wishart, 1948); E. J. Hobsbawm (ed.), *Labour's Turning Point: Nineteenth Century Volume III. 1880–1900* (London: Lawrence and Wishart, 1948); C. Hill and E. Dell (eds), *The Good Old Cause: the English Revolution of 1640: its Causes, Course and Consequences* (London: Lawrence and Wishart, 1949).
26. E. P. Thompson, *William Morris* (London: Lawrence and Wishart, 1955); G. Thomson, M. Dobb, C. Hill and J. Saville, 'Foreword', in J. Saville (ed.), *Democracy and the Labour Movement: Essays in Honour of Dona Torr* (London: Lawrence and Wishart, 1954), pp. 7–9; D. Torr, *Tom Mann and His Times* (London: Lawrence and Wishart, 1956).
27. For one example, T. Rothstein, *From Chartism to Labourism: Historical Sketches of the English Working Class Movement* (London: Lawrence and Wishart, 1983 edn).
28. The minutes of the historians group in 1956–57 are held at CP/CENT/CULT/5/12. For the New Left, M. Kenny, *The First New Left: British Intellectuals after Stalin* (London: Lawrence and Wishart, 1995), pp. 16, 63, 69–85; V. G. Kiernan, 'The Unrewarded End', *London Review of Books*, 17 September 1998; interview with Dorothy Thompson, 23 September 1998.
29. Branson, *History of the Communist Party*, pp. 118–28; N. Branson (ed.), *London Squatters* (London: Communist Party of Great Britain, 1989); J. Hinton, 'Self-Help and Socialism: The Squatters' Movement of 1946', *History Workshop Journal* 25 (1988), pp. 100–26.
30. J. Dash, *Good Morning Brothers!* (London, 1969), pp. 74–81.
31. McLachlan, *One Great Vision*, p. 98.
32. B. Moore, *Cold War in Sheffield: the Story of the Second World Peace Congress, November 1950* (Sheffield, 1991), p. 19.
33. 'The Communist Party and the Atom Bomb', *Socialist Review*, October 1954, in Higgins, *A Socialist Review*, pp. 181–3.

34. M. Ben Reuben, 'Gagarin and the Jewish Problem', *Socialist Review*, February 1962, in Higgins, *A Socialist Review*, pp. 249–53.
35. *World News and Views* 32, pp. 126–7.
36. For Percy Glading, see HO 45/25520; for Dave Springhall, R. Thurlow, *The Secret State* (Oxford: Blackwell, 1994), p. 117.
37. A. Rogers, *Secrecy and Power in the British State: a History of the Official Secrets Act* (London and Chicago: Pluto, 1997), p. 49; P. Wright, *Spycatcher* (New York: Dell, 1988 edn); N. West, *MI5 1945–1972: a Matter of Trust* (London: Coronet, 1983 edn); for the 1970s, T. Bunyan, *The History and Practice of the Political Police in Britain* (London: Quartet, 1977).
38. H. Adi, 'West Africans and the Communist Party in the 1950s', in Andrews, Fishman and Morgan, *Opening the Books*, pp. 176–94. 'Stop the War in Malaya', *World News and Views*, 28 August 1948. Ironically, the party's opposition to British imperialism was generally more coherent in the 1940s than it had been twenty years previously. For an example of the CP's earlier position, T. A. Jackson, *The British Empire* (London: Communist Party of Great Britain, 1922).
39. K. Laybourn and D. Murphy *Under the Red Flag: a History of Communism in Britain* (Sutton: Stroud, 1999), p. 138.
40. CPGB, *The British Road to Socialism*, p. 12; for a later 'theoretical' elaboration of the party's rejection of Leninism, A. Hunt (ed.), *Marxism and Democracy* (London: Lawrence and Wishart, 1990), pp. 13–18.
41. Birchall, 'The British Communist Party', p. 30; Kenny, *The First New Left*, p. 16.

5 The Monolith Cracks: 1956–68

1. *Labour Monthly* April 1953
2. K. Morgan *Harry Pollitt* (Manchester: Manchester University Press,1993), p. 171.
3. *Labour Monthly* May 1956:NOTM was a series of editorial comments on the key events of the preceding month which opened every edition of *Labour Monthly*.
4. CP/IND/DUTT/09/01
5. Morgan, *Harry Pollitt*, p. 171.
6. For an in-depth account of the left during this period is D. Widgery, *The Left In Britain 1956–1968* (London: Penguin, 1976).
7. CP/CENT/EC/04/03
8. *From Trotsky to Tito* by James Klugmann, which had been published in 1948 exposing the 'crimes' of Tito, was withdrawn by the EC after the 20th Party Congress.
9. Rudolf Slansky, the general secretary of the Czechoslovak party, was executed in 1952 as part of the far reaching purges which were carried out in East European parties after the break with Tito.
10. CP/IND/KETT/05/09
11. CP/IND/DUTT/32/07
12. CP/CENT/EC/05/08
13. Students in Britain. CP/CENT/EC/09/06

14. *Daily Worker*, 14/8/45
15. *Tribune* 12/9/58. Cited in Bulkley, Goodwin, Birchall, Binns and Sparks "If at first you don't succeed..." Fighting against the bomb in the 1950s' and 1960s' *International Socialism* 11 Winter 1981.
16. *Weekly Letter* Nos10and12 1960 CP/CENT/CIRC/06
17. *The British Road to Socialism* p. 24
18. C. Bambery *The Case for the Socialist Newspaper*, (London: Socialist Worker, 1984), p. 14.
19. For a Marxist analysis of trade unionism see A. Callinicos, 'The Rank and File Today', *International Socialism Journal* 17, Autumn 1982
20. *I'm All Right Jack*, 1959, British Lion. *The Angry Silence*,1960, British Lion.
21. In the case of the Engineering Industry the national negotiations took place between the Engineering Employers Federation (EEF), and the Confederation of Shipbuilding and Engineering Unions (CSEU), an umbrella body of the many unions involved in the industry dominated by the AEU.
22. *Pay and Conditions of Service of Engineering Workers* Price and Incomes Board Report No. 49 6/1968 p. 51
23. T. Cliff, *The Employers' Offensive: Productivity deals and how to fight them* (London: IS Books, 1970) p. 189
24. For a detailed exposition of this argument see D.Gluckstein *The Western Soviets* (London: Bookmarks, 1985)
25. Cliff, *The Employers' Offensive*: Productivity deals and how to fight them, p. 196
26. E. Wigham *The Power to Manage: a History of the Engineering Employers Federation* (London 1973) p. 203.
27. Industrial Research and Information Services (IRIS) News March 1959. IRIS News operated as the unofficial house journal of the right inside the AEU.
28. Industrial Research and Information Services (IRIS) News July 1963.
29. P. Undy, 'The Electoral Influence of the Opposition Party in the AUEW Engineering Section 1960–1975', *British Journal of Industrial Relations,* March 1979 p. 19.
30. John Tocher along with Bernard Panter, AUEW district secretary in the Manchester AUEW, were to resign the party in 1976. Interview with John Tocher 13/2/85–J. Eaden.
31. CP/CENT/DUTT/10/09
32. W. Thompson, *The Good Old Cause: British Communism 1920–1991* (London: Pluto,1992) p. 127.
33. J. Callaghan, *Rajani Palme Dutt: A Study in British Stalinism* (London: Lawrence and Wishart,1993) pp. 277–278.
34. *Report to EC* 14/9/63 CP/CENT/EC/09/07
35. Birch wrote an introduction to the 1966 publication *Incomes Policy, Legislation and Shop Stewards* written by two prominent International Socialists, Tony Cliff and Colin Barker.
36. For an in-depth glossary on left wing groups from 1956 to 1960 see D. Widgery, *The Left In Britain, 1956–1968* pp. 477–505.
37. *Weekly Letter* no. 27 11/8/61 CP/CENT/CIRC/66/02.

38. 'An Opportunity to Reverse the Trend', sales drive on the launch of the *Morning Star, Weekly Letter* No: 17 24/5/68 CP/CENT/CIRC/67/04.
39. CP/CENT/EC/11/01
40. *Letter to all Branches* 12/1/66 CP/CENT/EC/11/01.
41. CP/CENT/EC/11/02
42. Letter from Ida Hackett to John Gollan 13/3/1967 CP/CENT/SEC/11/02
43. CP/CENT/EC/09/10
44. *Report to EC* May 23/24 1964 CP/CENT/EC/10/01
45. *Morning Star*, 5/2/73.
46. *Weekly Letter* No: 18 1964 CP/CENT/CIRC/66/05.
47. *Weekly Letter* No: 19 1964 CP/CENT/CIRC/66/05.
48. CP/CENT/EC/09/04.
49. CP/CENT/IND/13/05.
50. *Electoral Reform,* Communist Party policy document 25 Feb. 1965. CP/CENT/EC/10/08

6 Not Fade Away: from 1968 to Dissolution

1. D. Bell, *The End of Ideology* (Illinois: IUP, 1960); Herbert Marcuse, *One Dimensional Man* (Boston: Beacon Press, 1964).
2. Butskellism, a hybrid term formed by the combination of the names of Rab Butler the then Tory Chancellor and Hugh Gaitskell the then leader of the Labour opposition was coined in the 1950s to illustrate the convergence of both major parties around a 'postwar consensus'.
3. C. Harman *The Fire Last Time: 1968 And After* (London, Bookmarks, 1988) p. 36.
4. Harman, *The Fire Last Time*, p. 94.
5. D. Widgery *The Left in Britain 1956–1968* (London, Penguin, 1976) p. 376.
6. J. Klugmann, *Rebellion, the Left and the Ultra Left.* Internal CPGB document presented to EC 12 May 1968. CP/CENT/EC/12/08
8. B. Reid, *Ultra Leftism in Britain* (London CPGB pamphlet, 1969).
9. 7 CP/CENT/EC/09/10
10. D. Widgery, *The Left in Britain,* p. 306.
11. Harman, *The Fire Last Time*, p. 40.
12. C. Harman, D. Clark, A. Sayers, R. Kuper, M. Shaw, *Education, Capitalism and the Student Revolt* (London: IS, 1968) pp. 68–69.
13. D. Cook, *Students* (London: CPGB, 1973) pp. 18–23.
14. T. Ali, *Street Fighting Years* (London: Collins, 1978)
15. Ali, *Street Fighting Years*, p. 227.
16. *Employment Gazette*, July 1984, special Feature 'Stoppages Caused by industrial Disputes in 1983'.
17. J. Foster and C. Woolf, *The Politics of the UCS Work In: Class Alliances and the Right to Work* (London Lawrence and Wishart, 1986) p. 416
18. A. Murray, *UCS–the Fight for the Right to Work* (London; CPGB, 1971), p. 11.
19. Engineering Employers Federation of South Lancs., Cheshire and North Wales, *Newer Forms of Industrial Action adopted by manual and staff workers in the North West*, Internal Memorandum, Jan. 1972

20. W. Thompson, *The Good Old Cause–British Communism 1920–1991* (London; Pluto, 19920, p. 239.
21. R. Darlington and D. Lyddon, *Glorious Summer: Class Struggle in Britain 1972* (London: Bookmarks, 2000), pp. 56–62.
22. V. Allen, *The Militancy of the Miners* (Shipley: Moor Press, 1981) pp. 63–4.
23. J. Thownsend 'The Communist Party in Decline 1964–1970', *International Socialism* 62, Nov. 1973, p. 20.
24. J. Charlton, 'The Miners Since Nationalisation'. *International Socialism* 56, March 1973, p. 11.
25. T. Cliff 'Patterns of Mass Strikes', *International Socialism Journal* 29. 1985, p. 42
26. A. Callinicos and M. Simons, *The Great Strike: the Miners' Strike of 1984–5 and Its Lessons*, (London: Socialist Worker Publication, 1985), pp. 21–26.
27. CP/CENT/SEC/04/11.
28. Thompson, *The Good Old Cause*, p. 81.
29. J. Mcillroy and A. Cambell, 'Organising the Militants: the Liaison Committee for Defence of Trade Unions, 1966–1979', *British Journal of Industrial Relations* 37:1, March 1999, p. 15.
30. Mcillroy and Cambell, *Organising*, p. 26.
31. F. Lindop, 'The Dockers and the 1971 Industrial Relations Act, Parts 1 and 2', *Historical Studies in Industrial Relations* 5/6 1988. Keele University Centre for Industrial Relations.
32. Lindop, *The Dockers*, p. 39.
33. McIlroy and campbell, *organising*, p. 19.
34. Lindop, *The Dockers*, p. 93.
35. Darlington and Lyddon, *Glorious Summer*, p. 162.
36. Darlington and Lyddon, *Glorious Summer*, pp. 199–201.
37. S. Bilds, 'How they Got There' *Socialist Review*, 1984, 71 p. 13.
38. R. Coates, *Teachers Unions and Interest Group Politics* (Cambridge: CUP, 1972) p. 61
39. E. Porter, 'The history of rank and file' *Rank and File* 24, Spring 1973. Eric Porter was one of the former Communist Party teachers who formed *Rank and File*.
40. R. Seiffert, *Teacher Militancy: a History of Teacher strikes 1896–1987* (Lewes: Falmer Press: 1987) p. 138
41. Darlington and Lyddon, *Glorious Summer*, p.199.
42. Thompson, *The Good Old Cause*, p. 218.
43. All figure taken from 'Factual Report to Yorkshire District Committee 18/11/72', Cited in C. Harman Communist Party in Decline', *International Socialism* 63, 1973, p. 27.
44. Letter to John Gollan 5/1/1974. CP/CENT/SEC/4/11
45. The right wing organisation Aims of Industry produced a booklet in 1978 naming 17 'fellow travelling Labour MPs: Ernie Roberts, Tony Benn, Stan Orme, Judith Hart, Frank Allaun, Eric Heffer, Neil Kinnock, Tom Litterick,Ian Mikardo, Joan Maynard,Audrey Wise, Stan Newens, Sid Bidwell, Robert Hughes, Renee Short, Sanley Thorne, Michael Foot: G. Mather *The CPGB-Freedom's Foremost Enemy* (London: AIMS, 1978)
46. F. Beckett *Enemy Within: the Rise and Fall of the British Communist Party* (London, Merlin, 1995) pp. 179–180.

47. For an analysis of these debates from a broadly pro Eurocommunist perspective see G. Andrews, 'Young Turks and Old Guard: Intellectuals and the CP Leadership in the 1970s' in G. Andrews, N. Fishman and K. Morgan eds. Opening the Books (London: Pluto, 1995); and G. Andrews *Gramscian Moments: The Communist Party and Social Movements in the 1970s*, Conference Paper, Alternative Futures and Popular Protest, Manchester, 1996.
48. B. Ramelson, *The Social Contract–Cure All or Con Trick?* (London: CPBG, 1974).
49. A. Spence 'The Decline and Rise of the Wages System' *Marxism Today* 14/8 p. 256
50. J. Bloomfield, *British Leyland – Save It* (London: CPBG, 1977) p. 6.
51. Bloomfield, *British Leyland*, p. 8.
52. T. Cliff, *A World to Win: Life of a Revolutionary* (London: Bookmarks, 2000), p. 127.
53. Cliff, *A world to Win*, p. 126.
54. I. Birchall, *The smallest Mass Party in the World: Building the Socialist Workers Party 1951–1979* (London: SWP, 1981), p. 15
55. The International Socialist (IS) had changed their ame to the Socialist Workers Party (SWP) in January 1977.
56. A. Callinicos and A. Hatchet, 'In Defence of Violence', *International Socialism* 101, September 1977, pp. 24–8.
57. *Morning Star*, 27/8/1977, Cited in C. Rosenburg, 'Labour and the Fight Against Fascism', *International Socialism Journal* 39, Summer 1988, p. 77.
58. For a participants eye view of Rock Against Racism and the Anti Nazi League see D. Widgery, *Beating Time: Riot 'n Race 'n Rock 'n Roll* (London: Chatto and Windus, 1986).
59. For a Marxist critique of the interpretation of Gramsci developed by Eurocommunists see C. Harman 'Gramsci or Eurocommunism?' *International Socialism* 98 and 99 May/June 1977.
60. M. Waite, 'Sex 'n Drugs 'n Rock 'n Roll (and Communism)' in Andrews et al., *Opening the Books*.
61. For a critical analysis of the politics of *Marxism Today* from a Marxist perspective see A. Callinicos 'The Politics of *Marxism Today*', *International Socialism Journal* 29, 1985, pp. 128–68; for a reply on behalf of *Marxism Today* see J. Bloomfield '*Marxism Today*–a reply to Alex Callinicos' *International Socialism Journal* 30 1985 pp. 107–115.
62. *Marxism Today*, Volume 13/4, 1969, p. 120.
63. A. Gramsci, *Selections from the Prison Notebooks*, Q. Hoare and G. Newell-Smith eds. (London: Lawrence and Wishart, 1971)
64. M. Jacques, 'Notes on the Concept of Intellectuals', *Marxism Today*, 1971 Vol. 15/10 p. 316
65. *Marxism Today*, Oct. 1974 p. 308
66. E. Hobsbawn, *The Forward March of Labour Halted?* first published in *Marxism Today*, Sept 1978.
67. For a review of the debate see M. Jacques and F. Mulhearn (eds) *The Forward March of Labour Halted?* (London: Verso, 1981). All references from this text.
68. Hobsbawm, Forward March, p. 18.
69. *Marxism Today* January 1985.

70. S. Hall and M. Jacques, *The Politics of Thatcherism* (London: Verso, 1983), p. 23.
71. *Marxism Today* April 1985 p. 12.
72. *Marxism Today* March 1984.
73. Callinicos, *The Politics of Marxism Today*, p. 139.
74. CP/CENT/IND/13/07
75. CP/CENT/IND/12/07
76. One group of 'tankies', supporters of the journal *Straight Left* were careful not to breach the rules of the party and were not expelled remaining a minor irritant to the party leadership until the formal dissolution of the party in 1991.
77. CP/CENT/IND/13/09.
78. *Seven Days*, 26/3/88.
79. Cliff, *A World to Win*, p. 221.
80. *Seven Days*, 24/2/90.
81. The *Historikerstreit* had conservative historians arguing that the rise of Nazism in Germany was essentially a 'reaction' to the Soviet regime. The left-wing German philosopher, Jurgen Habermas has criticised the writers involved a showing 'apologetic tendencies' towards nazism. For a brief discussion see A. Callinicos, *Theories and Narratives* (Cambridge: CUP, 1995) pp. 12–13.
82. K. McDermott 'The History of the Comintern in light of new documents' in T.Rees and A. Thorpe, *International Communism and the communist international 1919–1943* (Manchester: Manchester University Press, 1998) p. 33.
83. H. Wilford 'The Comintern and the American Communist Party' in Rees and Thorpe. p. 230.
84. M. Mosbacher, *How the Demise of the Soviet Union Affected The Communist Party and its Successor Organisations* (London: Libertarian Alliance, 1996) p. 17
85. One of the authors recalls on a visit to Moscow in 1986 that the *Morning Star* was the most easily available English language newspaper.
86. K. Morgan, *Harry Pollitt* (Manchester, Manchester University Press, 1993) p. 179
87. Morgan, *Harry Pollitt*, p. 165.
88. Letter 'To All EC Members and District Secretaries' from Betty Reid, Central Organisation Department 10 May 1956 CP/CENT/EC/03/24
89. Beckett, *The Enemy Within*, p. 207.
90. Thompson, *The Good Old Cause*, p. 207.
91. P. Wintour, 'Tony's got a brand new guru', *The Guardian*, 25/6/1999.
92. S. Hall 'The Great Moving Nowhere Show' *Marxism Today* Special Edition, October 1988
93. S. Munby 'Marxism Today. Wrong!?' *New Times* 17 www.democraticleft.org.uk/newtimes/articles/issue17/nt00171.html
94. *Morning Star* 6/10/2000
95. www.cpgb.org

7 Conclusion

1. At the Preston and Glasgow Anniesland by-elections in November 2000 the Socialist Alliance and the Scottish Socialist Party (SSP) scored 5.6 per cent and 7.2 per cent of the vote respectively. This followed the election of the

SSP's Tommy Sheridan to the Parliament in 1999 and other similar by-election results. Sheridan was the first successful openly far left parliamentary candidate to be elected in Britain since Willie Gallacher and Phil Piratin lost their seats in 1950. In the June 2001 General Election, results recorded by the Scottish Socialist Party, the Socialist Alliance and Arthur Scargill's Socialist Labour Party delivered the most significant vote for left of Labour candidates since the Communist Party's effort at the 1950 General Election.
2. J. O'Farrell, *Things Can Only Get Better: Eighteen Miserable Years in the Life of a Labour Supporter* (London: Black Swan, 1999), pp. 97–8.
3. Cited in D. Widgery, *The Left in Britain* (Harmondsworth: Penguin, 1976), p. 12.

Bibliography

Adler, A. (ed.), (1983). *Theses, Resolutions and Manifestos of the First Four Congresses of the Communist International*. London.
Ali, T. (1987). *Street Fighting Years*. London.
Allen, V. (1981). *The Militancy of British Miners*. Shipley.
Attfield, J. and Williams S. (1984). *1939: the Communist Party of Great Britain and the War*. London.
Barrow, L. and Bulloock, I. (1996). *Democratic Ideas and the British Labour Movement*. Cambridge.
Beckett, F. (1995). *The Enemy Within: the Rise and Fall of the British Communist Party*. London.
Beetham, D. (1983). *Marxists in the Face of Fascism*. Manchester.
Bell, T. (1937). *The British Communist Party: a Short History*. London.
Black, R. (1970). *Stalinism in Britain: a Trotskyist Analysis*. London.
Borkenau, F. (1962). *World Communism: a History of the Communist International*. Michigan.
Bornstein, S. and Richardson, A. (1982). *Two Steps Back: the Communist Party of Great Britain and the working class from 1939–1945*. Ilford.
Bornstein, S. and Richardson, A. (1986). *War and the International: a History of the Trotskyist Movement in Britain 1937–1949*. Ilford.
Branson, N. (1985). *The History of the Communist Party of Great Britain 1927–1941*. London.
Branson, N. (1997). *History of the Communist Party of Great Britain 1941–1951*.
Callaghan, J. (1993). *Rajani Palme Dutt: a Study in British Stalinism*. London.
Callinicos, A. and Simons, M. (1985). *The Great Strike: the Miners' Strike of 1984–5 and its Lesson*. London.
Challinor, R. (1977). *The Origins of British Bolshevism*. London.
Chappell, R. and Clinton, A. (eds). (1974). *Trotsky's Writings on Britain Volume 2*. London.
Claudin, F. (1978). *Eurocommunism and Socialism*. London.
Cliff, T. and Gluckstein, D. (1986). *Marxism & Trade Union Struggle: the General Strike of 1926*. London.
Cohen, P. (1997). *Children of the Revolution: Communist Childhood in Cold War Britain*. London.
Crick, M. (1994). *The History of the Social Democratic Federation*. Keele.
Croucher, R. (1982). *Engineers at War*. London.
Croucher, R. (1987). *We Refuse to Starve in Silence: a History of the National Unemployed Workers' Movement 1920–1946*. London.
Darlington, R. (1998). *The Political Trajectory of JT Murphy*. Liverpool.
Darlington, R. and Lyddon, D. (2000). *Glorious Summer: Class Struggle in Britain 1972*. London.
Dewar, H. (1976). *Communist Politics in Britain: the CPGB from its Origins to the Second World War*. London.

Fishman, N. (1995). *The British Communist Party and the Trade Unions 1933–1945*. London.
Fishman, N. and Morgan, K. (eds). (1995). *Opening the Books: Essays on the Cultural History of the Communist Party*. London.
Flett, K. and Renton, D. (eds). (2000). *The Twentieth Century: a Century of Wars and Revolutions*. London.
Foster, J. and Woolf, C. (1986). *The Politics of the UCS Work In: Class Alliances and the Right to Work*. London.
Francis, H. (1984). *Miners Against Fascism: Wales and the Spanish Civil War*. London.
Frow, E. and Frow, R. (1979). *The Communist Party in Manchester 1920–1926*. Manchester.
Gluckstein, D. (1985). *The Western Soviets: Workers Councils versus Parliament 1925–1920*. London.
Groves, R. (1974). *The Balham Group: How British Trotskyism Began*. London.
Hallas, D. (1985). *The Comintern*. London.
Harman, C. (1988). *The Fire Last Time: 1968 and After*. London.
Hinton, J. (1973). *The First Shoe Stewards Movement*. London.
Hinton and Hyman. (1975). *Trade Unions and Revolution: the Industrial Politics of the early British Communist Party*. London.
Hinton, J. (1983). *Labour and Socialism: a History of the British Labour Movement*. Brighton.
Hinton, J. (1994). *Shop-Floor Citizens: Engineering Democracy in 1940s Britain*. Aldershot.
Jacques, M. H. S. (1983). *The Politics of Thatcherism*. London.
Jacques, M. and Mulhearn, F. (eds). (1981). *The Forward March of Labour Halted?* London.
Kendall (1969). *The Revolutionary Movement in Britain 1900–1921: The Origins of British Communism*. London.
King, F. and Matthews, G. (eds). (1990). *About Turn: the Communist Party and the Outbreak of the Second World War*. London.
Klugmann, J. (1969). *History of the Communist Party of Great Britain Volume 1. Formation and Early Years 1919–1924*. London.
Klugmann, J. (1969). *History of the Communist Party of Great Britain Volume 2. The General Strike 1925–26*. London.
Laybourn, K. (1997). *The Rise of Socialism in Britain*. Stroud.
Laybourn, K. and Murphy, D. (1999). *Under the Red Flag: a History of Communism in Britain*. London.
Macfarlane, J. (1966). *The British Communist Party: its Origin and Development until 1929*. London.
Macintyre, S. (1980). *A Proletarian Science: Marxism in Britain 1917–1933*. London.
Macintyre, S. (1980). *Little Moscows: Communism and Working Class Militancy in Inter-War Britain*. London.
Mahon, J. (1976). *Harry Pollitt: a Biography*. London.
Mandel, E. (1979). *From Stalinism to Eurocommunism*. London.
Martin, R. (1969). *Communism and the British Trade Unions 1924–1933: a Study of the National Minority Movement*. Oxford.

Matthews, G. (1980). *All for the Cause: the Communist Party 1920–1980*. London.
McDermott, K. and Agnew, J. (1996). *The Comintern: a History of International Communism from Lenin to Stalin*. London.
Milton, N. (1973). *John Maclean*. London.
Morgan, K. (1989). *Against Fascism and War: Ruptures and Continuities in British Communist Politics*. Manchester.
Morgan, K. (1993). *Harry Pollitt*. Manchester.
Newton, F. (1969). *The Sociology of British Communism*. London.
Pearce, B. and Woodhouse, M. (1995). *A History of Communism in Britain*.
Rees, T. and Thorpe, A. (1998) *International Communism and the Communist International 1919–1943*. Manchester.
Renton, D. (1999). *Fascists. Anti-Fascists and Britain in the 1940s*. London.
Rosenberg, C. (1987). *1919: Britain on the Brink of Revolution*. London.
Rothstein, T. (1983). *From Chartism to Labourism: Historical Sketches in the English Working Class Movement*. London.
Samuel. R. (ed.) (1981). *People's History and Socialist Theory*. London.
Squires, M. (1990). *Saklatvala: a Political Biography*. London.
Srebrnick, H. (1995). *London Jews and British Communism*. Chelmsford.
Thompson, W. (1992). *The Good Old Cause: British Communism 1920–1991*. London.
Thorpe, A. (1989). *The Failure of Political Extremism in Inter-War Britain*. Exeter.
Thorpe, A. (1998). 'Comintern "Control" of the Communist Party of Great Britain', *English Historical Review*, 63 (452), 610–36.
Widgery, D. (1976). *The Left in Britain*. London.

Index

air raid, 78–80
aircraft industry, 48, 70, 87, 88
Alexander, Bill, 61
Ali,Tariq, 147, 150
Anglo-Russian Trade Union Committee, 22, 24, 25, 192n
Anglo-Russian Parliamentary Committee, 65
Anti-Nazi League (ANL), 158
Amalgamated Society of Engineers (ASE), Amalgamated Engineering Union (AEU), Amalgamated Union of Engineering Workers, (AUEW), 11, 78, 79, 88, 98, 99, 105, 127, 130, 131, 163, 166, 174
Amalgamated Society of Locomotive Engineers and Firemen (ASLEF), 98, 99
Aircraft Shop Stewards National Council (ASSNC), 87
armed forces, 22, 75
Arnot, Robin Page, 18, 31, 33, 65
Attlee, Clement, 53, 105, 115
Amalgamated Union of Engineering Workers Technical and Supervisory Section (AUEW TASS), 159
Amery, Leo, 96

BBC, 69, 85, 106, 140
Baldwin, Stanley, 50
Balham Group, 45
Barbarossa, Operation, 84, 85, 91, 92, 97
Behan, Brian, 109, 121
Bell, Tom, xix, xxi, 1, 7, 8, 18, 23, 29, 31, 32, 35, 44
Benn, Tony, 172–4
Bernal, J, D, 123
Bevan, Aneurin, 54, 113, 115, 125
Bevin, Ernest, 27, 88
Birch, Reg, 131, 132, 134, 135
Birchall, Ian, vii, xx, 5, 100, 117

Birmingham, 9, 49, 88, 96, 107, 152, 154, 160
Blair, Tony, Blairism, 172, 181, 182
Blunt, Anthony, 114, 115
Bolshevism, ix, x, 1, 2, 6, 9, 11, 15, 20, 44, 55, 65, 91, 145
Branson, Noreen, xv, xviii, xix, 36, 44, 52, 53, 62, 66, 93, 95, 101
Britain for the People, 93, 99
British Council for Peace in Vietnam (BCPV), 149
British Leyland, 158, 163, 164, 165
British Road to Socialism (*BRS*) 53, 106, 116, 127, 138, 141, 142, 144, 156, 159, 161, 172, 179, 182, 186
British Socialist Party (BSP), 5, 8
British Union of Fascists (BUF), 48, 49, 50, 58, 59, 107
Broad Left, 128, 131, 132, 138, 147, 148, 156, 158, 159, 161, 163, 164
Brockway, Fenner, 53, 92, 149
Browder, Earl, 94
building workers, 24, 48, 102, 109, 112, 121, 134, 157, 160
Bukharin, Nicholai, x, 20, 33, 65
Burgess, Guy, 114

Cable Street, Battle of, xix, 57–60, 65, 167
Callaghan, James, 172
Callaghan, John, 21
Cambridge University, 27, 114, 115, 181
Campaign for Nuclear Disarmament (CND) 123–7, 137–9, 142, 149, 172
Campbell, John, 23, 46, 71, 72, 82, 90, 102, 106, 114, 120,
Cannon, Les, 121, 132
Carter, Pete, 160
Castle, Barbara, 54
Central Committee (of CPGB), 37, 39, 48, 51, 56, 61, 69, 70, 71, 83

215

216 Index

Chamberlain, Neville, 66–9, 72, 75, 77, 80, 83, 96
Chapple, Frank, 121, 132
Chater, Tony, 175–6
Churchill, Winston, 23, 67, 75, 85–87, 94–6
Citrine, Walter 54
Clarion Movement, 4
Class against Class, 1, 31–6, 43–50, 54, 56, 194n
Cohen, Jack, 65
Cohen, Phil, xx
Cohen, Rose, xv,18
Cold War, xii, xviii, xx, 20, 40, 97, 104–6, 113–15, 124, 138, 145, 147
Communist Information Bureau (Cominform), 104
Communist International (Comintern), ix–xv, xix, 2, 7–35, 41–7, 51–3, 66, 70, 71, 78–83, 86, 94, 104, 135, 179, 180
Comment, 161
Communist Party Historians' Group, 121
Communist Party of Britain (CPB), 178, 179, 182
Communist Party of Great Britain (Marxist–Leninist), 132, 136
Communist Review, 23, 39, 44, 50
Communist University of London, 149
Connolly, James, ix
conscription, 6, 67, 84
Conservative Party, xi, 2, 23, 26, 43, 46, 55, 57, 67, 77, 80, 91–2, 94, 95, 101, 107, 115–16, 143, 147, 151, 155, 166
Cook, A. J., 15, 25, 26, 32
councils, town or parish, 13, 59, 117, 129, 137, 139, 140, 166
Councils of Action, 7, 27, 30
Coventry, 78, 88
Communist Party of the Soviet Union (CPSU), ix, xviii, 135, 136
Cripps, Sir Stafford, 46, 54, 104, 115
Czechoslovakia, 66, 79, 118, 144, 145, 169, 180

Daily Herald, 8, 17, 39, 58
Daily Worker, xix, 38–40, 44, 49, 52, 61, 62, 65, 67, 68, 71–5, 80–2, 90, 91, 98, 102, 106, 109, 113, 114, 119, 120, 124, 126, 128, 136, 137–41
Daly, Lawrence, 121, 153
Dash, Jack, 166
Democratic Left 179, 181, 182
Dimitrov, Georgi, 52, 57, 180
Discussion, 56, 65
docks, 3, 27, 44, 89, 102, 105, 107, 112, 113, 150, 156, 157
Dubcek, Edward, 144
Dutt, Salme, 17, 18

East Germany, GDR, 118, 169, 177, 179
education (political), 16, 33
Education, Today and Tomorrow, 159
elections, CP participation in General, by–, council, 34, 47, 53, 74, 77, 78, 80, 91, 92, 94–6, 101, 102, 119, 129, 139, 140–2, 182
elections, Trade Union, 15, 38, 55, 88, 129, 131, 132, 133, 153, 161
engineering industry, xii, 13, 15, 70, 77–80, 87–91, 98, 109, 127–31, 134, 136, 152, 156,
Electricians' Union (ETU) 98, 116, 121, 127, 130–3, 142, 153, 155
Eurocommunism, xv, 100, 138, 141, 148, 149, 165, 168–82, 186
Executive Committee (EC) of the CPGB, 85, 92, 99, 119, 120, 121, 123, 135, 141, 175
Executive Committee of Communist International (ECCI), 2, 12, 21, 29, 33, 45–7

Fabian Society, 18, 55, 82
fascism, and anti-fascism, xix, 31, 41, 49, 50, 51–3, 57, 59, 61, 63, 66–70, 80, 82, 86, 100, 107, 108, 112, 165–7, 186
Fire Brigades' Union (FBU), i, 98, 99, 116, 121, 125, 127
finance, party funding, 'Moscow Gold' 37, 39, 179–81
Finland, 68, 78, 82, 83
Foot, Michael, 172
For Soviet Britain, 93
France, xi, 32, 44, 52, 63, 100, 104, 143, 144, 145

Index 217

Franco, General Francisco, 60, 61, 63, 66, 82
French, Sid, 145, 171
Fryer, Peter, 106, 120, 121

Gaitskell, Hugh, 125
Gallacher, William, xxi, 1, 8, 9, 19, 20, 28, 31, 34, 35, 46, 53, 71, 96, 98, 102, 109
General Strike, xiii, 13, 22, 24–32, 41, 43, 45, 152
Germany 20, 21, 31, 44, 45, 50–5, 126
see also East Germany, Nazi Germany
Gill, Ken, 159, 170, 175
Glading, Percy, 115
Glasgow, 5, 6, 7, 9, 28, 41, 42, 43, 78, 89, 90
Gollan, John, 117, 121, 122, 136 140, 153
Gollancz, Victor, 63
Gorbachev, Mikhail, xv, 176, 177, 178
Gramsci, Antonio, 162, 163, 168–71, 183, 185
Groves, Reg, 45
Guardian, The, 137
Guevara, Che, 144

Haldane, J. B. S., 106
Hall, Stuart, 171, 182
Halpin, Kevin, 170
Hannington, Wal, 13, 28, 33, 40, 41, 42, 87, 99
Haston, Jock, 114
Haxell, Frank, 132, 133
Healey, Dennis, 174
Healy, Gerry 120, 122
Heath, Edward, 155, 156, 163, 171
Heffer, Eric, 109, 172
Henderson, Arthur, 50
Hicks, George 24,25,28
Hill, Christopher, 110, 123
Hitler, Adolf, xv, 31, 51, 52, 63, 66, 67, 658, 73, 74, 84, 85, 92, 96, 178
Hilter–Stalin Pact 67, 68, 79, 80, 82
Hobsbawm, Eric, x, 110, 121, 123, 170, 173, 174, 178
Horner, Arthur, ix, 33, 56, 99, 102, 106, 153

Horner, John, 99
Hungary, 74, 117–21, 123, 126, 127, 132, 133, 136, 142, 144, 145, 180
Hyde, Douglas, 168, 109

imperialism, and anti-imperialiam, xi, xx, 21, 39, 72, 96, 106, 115, 144, 186
Independent, The, 181
Independent on Sunday, The ,178
Independent Labour Party (ILP), 2, 3, 4, 8, 10, 41, 46, 49, 53, 55, 58, 79, 89, 92
India, 21, 39, 96
Industrial Relations Act, 155, 156, 161
Inkpin, Albert, 8, 16, 23, 31, 33
International Brigades, 61
International Marxist Group (IMG), 147, 148, 160
International Socialists (IS), later Socialist Workers Party (SWP), 144, 148, 152, 160, 166, 167
Invergordon Mutiny, 44
Italy, 7, 100, 143, 145, 148, 168, 169, 183

Jacks, Digby, 148
Jacques, Martin, 170, 171, 181
Jews, and anti-Semitism, xix, xx, 57–60, 68, 96, 107, 108, 114, 121
Johnstone, Monty, 73, 169
Joint Production Committees (JPCs), 87, 88
Jolly George, ix
Jones, Jack, 163

Klugmann, James, 106, 121
Korean War, 113, 117
Kruschev, Nikita, 111, 117, 118, 122, 135

Labour Co-ordinating Committee, 173
Labour Monthly, 25, 45, 53, 56, 65, 75, 85, 102, 105, 119, 132
Labour Party xi, xii, xvii, 1, 8, 9, 10, 15, 18, 22, 24, 31, 32, 35, 36, 50, 53, 54, 75, 91, 95, 98, 102, 106, 108, 111, 127, 128, 131, 139, 140, 172, 173, 186

218 Index

Labour Research Department, 18
Lansbury, George, 13
Lawrence & Wishart, 81, 169
Left Book Club, 63, 82
Left Review, 62
Lenin, Vladimir, ix, x, xiv, xviii, 6, 9, 15, 16, 18, 19–20, 35, 38, 40, 54, 72, 81, 91, 109, 169
Lenin School, 21
Liaison Committee for The Defence of Trade Unions (LCDTU), 134, 155, 156
Liberal Party, 2, 4, 9, 18, 23, 45, 55, 67, 79
'Little Moscows', 24, 96, 139
London, xix, xx, 23, 27, 31, 33, 41, 48, 58–9, 60, 75, 78, 80, 102, 111, 119, 132, 135, 139, 149, 156, 157, 166–7, 182
London School of Economics, 147
Luxemburg, Rosa, 16

MacDonald, Ramsay 10, 22, 23, 25, 27, 32, 43–6, 48
Maclean, John, 5, 9, 41, 53
McLennan, Gordon, 175
McManus, Arthur, 1, 8
McShane, Harry, 41, 109
Manchester, 8, 9, 38, 40, 43, 69, 73, 74, 76, 107, 132, 151
Manuilsky, Dimitri, 46, 81
Mao Tse Tung, 46, 81, 132, 135, 136, 144, 146
Marx, Karl, x, xx, 10, 16, 17, 37, 56, 64, 65, 100, 103, 109–11, 122, 132, 168, 177, 184
Marxism Today, xv, 101, 123, 148, 161, 163, 168–75, 178, 179, 181, 182
Matthews, George, 61,118
Maxton, James, 53
Members of Parliament, 3, 4, 5, 7, 18, 23, 31, 43, 45, 55, 64, 93, 98, 102, 109, 111, 117, 142, 161, 167, 186
MI5, 50
Militant Tendency, 175, 183
miners, Miners' Federation, National Union of Mineworkers (NUM), ix, xii, 4, 6, 9, 12, 13, 15, 24–8, 32, 33, 37–8, 54, 56, 64, 98, 99, 102, 106, 116, 121, 125, 127, 134, 148, 152–5, 175, 176
Miners' Next Step, The, 4
Morgan, Kevin, xii, xiii, 17, 74, 119
Moore, Bill, 44, 70, 71, 73, 79, 82
Morning Star, 101, 137, 138, 149, 153, 155, 157, 160, 161, 166, 167, 174, 175, 179, 180, 182
Morrison, Herbert, 54, 91, 92
Moscow Trials, xv, 65, 66
Mosley, Sir Oswald, xx, 48, 49, 50, 57, 58, 59, 74, 90, 92, 107, 108, 112
motor vehicle industry, 87, 143, 154, 121
Mulgan, Geoff, 181
Munich Crisis, 66, 67, 72, 79
Murphy, JT, ix, xvii, xix, 8, 12, 13, 16, 19, 20, 21, 22, 28, 35, 44, 45
Myant, Chris, 178–9

National Association of Teachers in Further and Higher Education (NATFHE), 159, 174
National Council for Civil Liberties (NCCL), 42, 108
National Government, 42–6, 53, 57, 67, 91, 92, 94,
National Left–Wing Movement, 22, 24, 26, 32,
National Minority Movement, 14, 15, 22, 23, 24, 28, 29, 34, 47
National Unemployed Workers' Movement (NUWM), xx, 13, 33, 40–2
National Union of Seamen (NUS), 134
Nazi Germany, 51, 66, 79, 80, 81, 85
New Left, vii, xiii, xx, 100, 122, 123
New Left Review, 123
New Propellor, 87
New Statesman, 62, 65
Newsletter, 120
New Times, 177, 182, 184, 186
Newbold, J.T. Walton, 18, 34
National Union of Teachers (NUT), xii, 158–60
Nicholson, Fergus, 124, 149

Index 219

Observer, The, 119
Orwell, George, 55, 63
Oxford, 27, 49, 67, 74, 87, 135

Palme Dutt, Rajani, ix, 16–18, 22, 23, 25, 32, 39, 45, 50, 67, 70–3, 80 83, 85, 94–6, 117, 119, 121, 132, 135, 145, 171
Pankhurst, Sylvia, 7–9
Papworth, Bert, 98, 105, 155
parliament, Communist attitudes to, 4, 5, 8, 19, 34, 52–3
parliamentary road to socialism, 93, 96, 99, 116, 138–42, 156
Peace Pledge Union, 76
Peoples' Convention, 85, 88
Philby, Kim, 114, 115, 181
Piratin, Phil, 58, 96, 98, 102, 109
Political Bureau (of the CPGB), 47, 53, 70, 81
Political Committee (of the CPGB), 133, 136
Pollitt, Harry, ix, xxi, 1, 8, 14, 16–18, 21, 23, 31, 32, 34, 39, 46–8, 50. 51, 53, 55, 66, 67, 69–73, 77, 78, 81, 82, 85, 86, 89–91, 94, 96, 97, 106, 116–19, 121, 180
Popular Front, xv, 36, 37, 41, 48, 52–67, 72, 74, 75, 79, 81, 82, 84, 87, 93, 96, 100, 116, 126, 144, 149, 169, 172, 176, 182, 185, 186
Powell, Enoch, 143, 166
Peoples Press Printing Society (PPPS), 175
Petrovsky, xv
POUM, 55, 60, 61, 62, 66

racism, and anti-racism, 59, 60, 147, 165–8, 171
Radek, Karl, x, 82
Ramelson, Bert, 134, 157, 163
Rank and File Teacher, 160
Reasoner, The (New), 111, 122, 123
Red Army, ix, 84, 86
Red International of Labour Unions (RILU), 10, 13, 34, 47
Reid, Betty, 114
Reid, Jimmy, 140, 151

Revolutionary Communist Party (RCP), 108, 114
Robinson, Derek, 164–5
Russian Revolution, ix, xix, 2, 6, 7, 19, 20, 35, 44, 185
Rust, Bill, 23, 61, 70–2, 83

Saklatvala, Shapurji, 10, 18, 31, 55
Saville, John, 110–11, 121–2
Scanlon, Hugh, 132, 163, 164
Scargill, Arthur, 152, 153, 154, 175, 176
Scottish Mine Workers' Union, 37, 38
Scottish Socialist Party (SSP), 183, 185
Second Front, 86, 95
Seven Days, 177, 178, 182
Sheffield, ix, 6, 9, 40, 42, 70, 73, 79, 82, 109, 113, 128, 131, 160
shop stewards, ix, 6, 8, 11, 13, 78, 87, 88, 90, 99, 105, 115, 128–31, 134, 138, 156, 157, 163, 165
Slansky, Rudolf, 121,
Social Contract, 162–5, 172
Social Democratic Federation (SDF), 3, 4, 5,
Socialism in One Country, x
Socialist Alliance, 182, 183, 185
Socialist Commentary, 115
Socialist International, Second International, 10, 19
Socialist Labour League (SLL), 120, 121
Socialist League, xvi, 46, 53, 54
Socialist Labour Party, 4, 8
Socialist Workers Party, see International Socialists
Soviet Union, ix–xii, xv, xviii, 47, 62, 72, 80, 82–4, 86, 97, 100, 136, 169, 176, 178, 181
Spain, 47, 50, 55, 58, 60–3, 66, 69, 79
Special Branch, 81
Spender, Stephen, 63, 64
spies, 115, 179, 181
Spinghall, David, 55, 71, 83
squatters, 111, 113
Stalin, Joseph, x, 29, 33, 51, 66–8, 74, 82, 83, 85, 94–6, 99, 105, 106, 111, 114, 116–20, 136, 178, 179, 185

Stalinism, xx, xxi, 2, 17, 21, 40, 45, 66, 100, 117, 135, 138, 144, 169, 177, 185, 186
Strachey, John, 50, 63, 66, 72
students, National Union of Students (NUS), 27, 38, 65, 67, 114, 115, 124, 143–9, 158, 169, 173, 181
Sunday Worker, 26, 32
syndicalism, 4, 10, 11, 14, 100

Tehran Conference, 94
Temple, Nina, 179
Transport and General Workers' Union (TGWU),13, 26, 27, 98, 99, 104, 155, 156, 158, 163
Thatcher, Margaret, 171
Third Period, 31–4, 40, 45, 46, 48, 49, 51, 80, 186
Thompson, Edward, 110, 111, 121, 122
Thompson, Willie, xvi, xvii, 17, 133, 152
Tito, Marshall, 74, 100, 105, 106, 121
Trades Councils, 14, 26, 28, 42, 108, 138
Trades Union Congress (TUC), 7, 11, 14, 22–30, 32, 34, 43, 54, 64, 98, 104, 105, 125, 130, 133, 157, 159, 160, 162, 175
TUC General Council, 14, 22–30, 64, 98, 104, 105, 159, 175

Tribune, 62, 63, 115, 125
Triple Alliance, 13
Trotsky, Leon, ix, x, 12, 16, 19, 20, 44, 45, 54, 62, 65, 106
Trotskyism, xii, xvi, xx, 21, 24, 30, 44, 45, 50, 61, 66, 79, 80, 84, 88–90, 92, 108, 120–3, 143, 146, 160, 183

United Front, x, 12, 15, 19, 36, 48, 54, 55, 63, 113, 186
Upper Clyde Shipbuilders (UCS), 150–2, 164

Vietnam War, anti-war campaigns, 121, 138, 143, 144, 146, 147, 149, 150, 165, 178

Webb, Sidney and Beatrice, 27, 55, 82
Weekly Letter, 136, 140
Westacott, Fred, 70, 71, 73, 83, 137
Wilson, Harold, 127, 134, 140
Workers' Socialist Federation (WSF), 8
Workers' Weekly, 17, 22, 23

Young Communist League (YCL), xx, 23, 61, 75, 79, 127, 137, 154, 169

Zilliacus, Koni, 105
Zinoviev, Gregory, x, 15, 17, 20, 22, 23, 29, 65